A
DRAGON'S
TALE

FROM THE RICE FIELDS OF VIETNAM TO A CELL ON
AMERICA'S SHORES, ONE WOMAN LOSES EVERYTHING
YET GAINS IT ALL

A DRAGON'S TALE

LONG LEE

TATE PUBLISHING & *Enterprises*

Published by Tate Publishing & Enterprises, LLC
127 E. Trade Center Terrace | Mustang, Oklahoma 73064 USA
1.888.361.9473 | www.tatepublishing.com

Tate Publishing is committed to excellence in the publishing industry. The company reflects the philosophy established by the founders, based on Psalm 68:11,
"The Lord gave the word and great was the company of those who published it."

Book design copyright © 2009 by Tate Publishing, LLC. All rights reserved.
Cover design by Kellie Southerland
Interior design by Nathan Harmony

Published in the United States of America

ISBN: 978-1-60696-892-5
1. Biography & Autobiography: Personal Memoirs
2. Regional & Ethnic: Vietnamese
09.05.05

This book is dedicated to my fellow travelers—
may you find bliss on this, our celebrated journey!

ACKNOWLEDGMENTS

Love and gratitude...

to my children: Van, Shen, Thuy, Trang, Tyler, and Zu; and my husband, Acey, for being with me on this journey.

Peace and love...

to my parents, for teaching me so well the lessons I needed to learn.

Pat Lee, who did his part in loving and guiding me.

Nana and PopPop, for standing by us in our darkest hours.

Joelle and Matt, who loved us regardless.

My spiritual sisters, Cathleen and Jodi, who joined me in the search for God.

Teresa Price, who made prison life easy.

Margaret Taylor, Deputy Sheriff of the Sacramento County Jail—one of those who did the best they could—for her humanity.

The U.S. Marshals in Sacramento, California, for their humanity.

The generous people of Alameda County who sent the bookmobile to Dublin Correctional Facilities to help us learn and otherwise pass the time. Special thanks to the bookmobile staff—Steve, Carmen, Don, Tom, Marta, Pete, and Vidia—who accorded us respect and dignity where no one else did.

Harry Reo, for this precious second chance.

All the dedicated people at Tate Publishing who believe, and Kylie and Kellie for turning this modest endeavor into a work of art.

To the U.S. Department of State and former colleagues: my gratitude—for the beginning and the wondrous years that followed; and my regrets—for the end...

Praise to God for all his creations.

PROLOGUE

IN THE NEWS: 2/1/95–VIETNAM AND THE US OPENED LIAISON OFFICE IN EACH OTHER'S CAPITAL FOR THE FIRST TIME SINCE THE WAR ENDED 20 YEARS AGO.

American Embassy
Hanoi, Vietnam, 1995

The American flag, the symbol admired, reviled, and detested, stood in splendor amidst the humidity and the decay miles away from the country of its birth. The billowing flag's solitary stand and obvious incongruity to its surroundings were somehow fitting—it conveyed an image of arrogance of the righteous, long associated with the United States by both friends and foes around the world. Now the entire neighborhood seemed to huddle in the shadow of this proud figure, just as the city must have hunkered out of the sights of the fire-breathing sky warriors at the height of the American bombing. This was Hanoi, Vietnam, in 1995, a different time, and therefore a different place.

In an office in the newly established U.S. Liaison Office, to be called the U.S. Embassy several years hence, I slowly withdrew my hand from the telephone on the desk, reluctant to disconnect the link with the shocking events half a world away. I heard the distant rumbles of thunder and turned to the window. Waves of dark, somber clouds were rolling in from the horizon; their progress decisive... as was the call for help from one of my daughters.

The disjointed words of Shen's boyfriend began to reverberate and play back in my mind, from a stilted conversation lasting little more than a minute. In a voice seemingly unmoved by the tragedy it imparted, he told me, "Shen tried to kill herself. She's still in the hospital but will be home later in the day. You can call her then."

How could this have happened? I thought of the life of this precious middle child, a life I had tried so hard to shield from hardships. I compared that life to mine, then to the harder life of my ma. I could not fathom her feelings of alienation—she had everything in the world to live for, a future that was to be brighter than I could have ever dreamed of. To think she had attempted to throw all this away... for love of a boy? Didn't she know, men come and go, and he was but one? I knew what Ma would say if she were to find out..."*Ignorant girl, has everything—food, clothing, good student. What else she want?*" I took a deep breath and pushed aside echoes of that practical sermon I had heard so many times in my life.

Was Shen's attempt to take her life my fault? To a certain extent, I knew it was so. I had been indulgent and protective, but I had also been careless with her heart and her mind, where it really mattered. Whatever the cause, how could my daughter, my mother's granddaughter, inheritor of our indomitable spirit, not be strong enough to face life? How hard could it be to live that comfortable life of a middle-class American girl?

Exhaustion, or perhaps resignation, settled over me. In that mind-lessness, that comfort of near surrender, old memories came hurtling back. In the space of a single breath, I could taste the fears, fears that had, in that earlier lifetime, not only taken over my conscious thoughts but also hovered at the edge of my soul and whispered darkly of hid-eous, frightful things.

I had buried them, buried them deep so they would never be exposed to light, to scrutiny. I had known them once, and once was more than enough. I shuddered now, thinking of the desperation that had held on to me as days passed to months and months gave way to years, and still, it clung. Why would I ever want to know it again? Yet, at this moment, it was clear. I needed to look at my life to find answers in hers.

At the touch of a wish for understanding, the tide of memory bore me home, mercifully not to that tangle of confusion, but to the tranquil orchard where hope and innocence awaited another visit by the prodi-gal child. I closed my eyes and, just for a fleeting moment, thought I could smell the air redolent of the sweet fragrance of citrus. I could almost feel the gentle caress of the breeze on my face and the smooth grass yielding underfoot.

While I immersed in the tranquility of the past, a storm of the future gathered under the darkened sky. The wind gusted and battered the pot-ted plum tree on the balcony, whose leaves were too insignificant to shield the delicate blooms from the brutal onslaught. Mother Tree shivered as the petals shook and fell on the cold concrete. The precious blooms had just opened that morning—pink, soft, and full of promise. One by one, then two by two, they were torn from her limbs. She convulsed in sor-row as the ferocious wind pummeled glass and stone heedless of her, an inconsequential presence on its path. She struggled on valiantly, having found strength and wisdom at last. Now she bent into the gust, huddling to protect her young; now she straightened up again in the lull, unfurling the precious petals to dance in the tail of the wind.

Hastened to find similar answers, I moved down the familiar road of childhood and home, wanting to search every rise and hollow from the dawn of hope to the twilight of despair. I needed to know how I had survived the trials of life and why Shen almost did not.

The war helped to be sure. That proximity to death made us want to cling to life. That we did, with a vengeance. I didn't want just to live. I wanted to feel alive. But the single, most formidable impetus that kept us forging ahead was unquestionably my mother. What, then, had I learned from her unflagging spirit? Or was I too busy spurning her to pay attention? With the impulsiveness of youth, I had once held her responsible for our lot as if it had been her fault. With the wisdom of age, she had understood. Rather than berating me for that irrational anger, she let love guide her. It told her of my fear—fear of hardship. She would remember this when I reached adolescence and try every trick she could think of to help me escape the barrenness she knew I despised.

As I revisited the scene of my angst and joy and the idyllic childhood I'd had in spite of the hostile forces at play, I thought of the self-sacrificing mother who had ensured I survive the odds. I wanted to know her again. I wanted to take a look at her selfless life with the sensibility of the woman I had become, a woman she would have been proud of—not that my maturity would have made her love me any more. She had loved me even when there was little endearing about me to love. I also wanted my children to know their grandmother better and to gain a sense of their heritage, which began here on this long-suffering land. Sorrowful still, it mourned even now for the wandering souls of millions of its native sons and daughters who had perished by the greed and righteousness of men, and for the foreigners who came, and died, so senselessly.

Perhaps knowing the challenges we had to cope with during those maddening days of the war and of poverty would help my children handle life's obstacles with a clearer perspective. I had told them little of what it was like, revealing but a few disparate snapshots of a life so different from their own. I wanted them to know how we had lived through the war and how I'd survived the fear.

However, wanting this for them did not make it so. The nobility of that intention notwithstanding, the task was left undone. Having skated along the periphery of feelings for so long, I found I did not have the intellectual depth or emotional courage to tread where I had never been. It was easier to opt for the road frequently taken and set aside the matter of my children's needs.

It was not until I arrived at judgment's gate that I found the wisdom and courage to look at all that I did and did not do. What would have been a poignant tale of a poor child who had risen above her humble lot to bring honor to her parents' door was not to be. Instead, the story of my life became a wrenching accounting of horrific trials.

Finally, my children would learn that their mother had not always been that self-assured woman who could handle every one of life's challenges with poise and confidence. They would see how I'd planned for smooth sailing over the calm waters of midlife, only to find that my path had diverged and the road taken so fraught with peril it almost consumed me. It would be sobering for Shen to see how, in the most turbulent journey of man's experiences, I learned enough about despair to understand at last that there could come a time in a person's life when it would be so tempting, so easy, to simply surrender.

I had been plagued with ignorance, even though I had craved and sought knowledge all my life. Ah, what it finally took for me to gain the wisdom of the ages so as to find peace in the most tumultuous of storms and happiness in the most unlikely of places.

That place was one of dreams and nightmares, a place that was at once magical and diabolical, resplendent and grotesque, where the price of admittance was frequently too high: all the mystical intangibles that made us human—the mind, the pride, the ego, in short, everything I was, save for my soul. In that minimalist existence, I felt my emotions also slipping away, leaving nothing but clouds of misery in their wake. So reduced, I collapsed into myself, sustained only by remembered wisps of joy from a time gone. Days passed into nights with little distinction except for the continual bleakness that rejoiced with the dawn and danced at the gathering of dusk.

It was there that Truth found me.

We then took a trip together, my Truth and I, down that narrow lane to the shore of time where gathered shifting sands of the past. I groped along, not knowing what I would find. I certainly didn't expect to see images of heartbreaks but feel none of the pain. I had no idea the once-menacing shadows had changed with time and space and the extraordinary perspective whence I stood. They had turned what would have been an ordinary canvas of a life into a masterpiece, with dark, torturous shadows encroaching on the unsuspecting landscape, lending depths and a touch of splendor.

My eyes drank in the brilliant colors on the path, while my soul wept at the momentous discovery. It had taken us many days to get here, days through which I grieved and mourned for all that might have been. Alas, not until we reached the end of the trip did wisdom dawn, and I saw with shocking clarity the nature of this exquisite journey that had taken me full circle in a single lifetime, gracing me with mind-blowing joy one moment and heartbreaking sorrow the next. Harboring no fears now, of either the past or the future, I realized it was time to trace the twists and turns of this turbulent life of mine, this epic chase after a dream. Only this walk will not be one of usual silent contemplation, but a journey of images and sounds, words and prose, which wax and wane with the rhythm of the heart.

I reached for the notepad on the table, picked up the pen, and began. *My dearest children …*

ONE

IN THE NEWS: 1/1/56–PRO-WESTERN NGO DINH DIEM WINS IN FIRST NATIONAL ASSEMBLY ELECTION.

The Orchard
Saigon, Vietnam, 1956

Without the ever-present dozen or so of extended family, our household would have been considered small by Vietnamese standards, with only Ba, Ma, Brother Bong, and I. As a family, I must say we looked more handsome than the poor, less than the rich, just about right for us, I suppose, for we were poor but lucky enough to be living in the city, amid a large field with plenty of space for me to roam. We did not own the land, mind you, or we would not have been poor. We were allowed tenancy due to my father's job as its caretaker and foreman.

Ba was tall for a Vietnamese man, about five foot four, whose impressive stature he passed on to both me and Bong so that we would have the height, if nothing else, over others. Bong looked more like Ma with his flat, typical Asian nose, while I took after my ba, with a much-prized feature among Asians—a relatively higher-bridged nose. However, we shared those physical characteristics common to the poor—reed thin and dark skin. My skin smelled perpetually of sunburn, which could easily be blamed on my never-ending forage of the land for food. Whenever Ma caught a whiff of that scent, she would berate me for risking sunstroke, for turning myself into a savage. Dark skin, tangled, matted hair, tattered shorts, no shirt, snot-crusted cheeks? Yes, definitely a savage.

For the first fifteen years or so of their marriage, my parents didn't have anyone to scold or fuss over, having lost the first four of their children to infant deaths. That childless state changed on January 24, 1949, the day Bong was born. He became the first to survive, barely, for his birth was a difficult one—Ma was in labor for more than twenty-four hours.

Between waves of flesh-rending pain, she prayed with all her might to the gods. She asked the Goddess of Mercy to protect the baby from evil spirits and offered to be a vegetarian for six months, which was rather a standard penance. The length and type of penance was usually proportionate to the favor requested—the gravity of the situation, you could say. And the situation was dire. So she included Ba in the offering. She said he would also be a vegetarian for six months, which made eminent sense to her. She would not have to cook a different meal for him, and Ma was nothing if not practical.

As the story went, any time Ba wandered to the birthing bed—her simple, wooden bed made into a birthing station by stripping it off the straw mat for easy cleaning—Ma would send him off with another command. The same command, made graver only by her quickening breathing and deepening grunts. "To the gong, you lazy lout," she heaved out the words. And off he went, climbing up the high, often-wobbly chair, to reach the altars mounted just off the unusable attic, below the rafters. The warm sound of the gong must have offered her immense comfort as it always would—an entreaty had been made with a higher being, hence she was able to "go with the flow," a term that would become the spiritual dictum of the day.

On that cool January day, the midwife was present but could do little but whisper words of encouragement and comfort. Meanwhile, Ba did everything he could: consulting with one "expert" after another, moving from one remedy to the next. Joss sticks were burned continuously to send incense to the heavens to remind God of a situation still unresolved. But the baby, while making all the right moves for separation, remained ensconced in Ma's womb. Following another expert's advice, Ba cut down a young banana plant and tapped it gently on her swollen abdomen. At last, a small, jaundiced baby with slow-moving eyes was born. My brother, Bong, would remain sickly for some time and was not thought to live past the first year.

Ba and Ma tried to keep this precious child alive. They named him "Bong," which meant flower, to deceive malevolent spirits into thinking the baby was a girl and therefore not a very desirable soul to snatch. Bong grew slowly and tenuously under the watchful eyes of Ma. Even as a baby, he was slow and peculiar.

"Something wrong with his head," Ma proclaimed before he even turned two. Because of his delicate health, Bong was coddled throughout his adolescent years and into adulthood. He was favored and exempt from household chores, a point that incited jealousy and made me question our parents' love for me. I did not understand that they loved me just as much. In their simple reasoning, I did not need any special dispensation, so it followed that I would get none.

Ba and Ma lavished their affection on Bong in hope and desperation. When I was born three years later, an easy birth at last, Ma thanked God for Bong, since it was he who broke the curse so my life could be spared. The first child to live after a long string of infant deaths by his siblings reportedly had to pay a high price, usually a malady of some sort. He carried that noble honor so I could be born normally.

As we grew to adolescence, and then adulthood, my parents would remind me of Bong's sacrifice and ask me to look after him after they were gone. Feeling magnanimous for my "soundness," and therefore "superiority," of mind, I readily obeyed. By their entreaty and my acceptance, my fate was determined—I became the designated caretaker for the next generation. This responsibility would define the course of my life.

A scrawny child with knobby knees and the telltale distended belly of malnutrition and worms, I spent most of my time alone, first due to the accident of not having any female cousins near my age, then by design—as I became used to the solitude, I happily discovered that there was incredible peace and satisfaction in weaving fantasy. A product of my environment, the introversion eventually made me more contemplative and calculated than other kids.

On the matter of hunger, I just could not accept that the growling sound in my stomach for want of food was meant to be, that such was what it meant to be poor. I constantly searched for ways to fill it. To get money for a bowl of soup in the morning or a rice cake at midday, I flitted from Ba to Ma, currying for coins.

One way to do this was to go to the racetrack with Ba, which was not always easy to accomplish. I remember once when I refused to heed his command for me not to come and chased after the motorized *cyclo* that was taking him away. What is a *cyclo* exactly? The Vietnamese version of a rickshaw certainly. A regular cyclo operated like a bicycle, with the driver pedaling from the back of a three-wheel contraption that had a passenger cab in the front. A motorized cyclo, on the other hand, functioned like a motor scooter with a similar frontal cab.

On that one particular afternoon, after a block or so of proceeding at a snail's pace, his hoodlum of a driver finally realized that Ba was not going to relent and allow me to board, so he cackled as if a madman then revved his engine to speed away. Under the canvas awning of the cab in front of the driver, Ba looked straight ahead, acting as if I were not hollering for him at the top of my lungs. At the last minute, I reached out for the driver's shirttail and gave it a vicious yank. Almost losing balance, he wiggled back onto the seat and slowed just enough to turn and curse at me. The pause gave Ba a chance to reconsider his decision. At the end, I got what I had more or less expected—first a soft whack across the side of my head and then a seat next to Ba. I wiped my tears away, the pain forgotten as my senses swam in a delicious expectation of food. Feeling victorious, I lifted my face to the wind as the cyclo *brroomed* its way toward the racetrack at Phu Tho.

I had anticipated the outing and changed into my favorite, or rather, only, "*di choi*," or "out and about" clothing, of a pair of faded pink shorts and a different shade of pink shirt that had seen better days, to which Ma had added multiple pockets on the inside at my urging—just so I could store money taken from Ba's winnings.

For me, the real reward came when I got home and emptied the pockets in front of Ma. We would huddle at a corner away from prying eyes to count my gains. The volume and frequency of Ma's gasps of delight rose correspondingly to the size of the booty—both of which told me how well I had done.

By Ba's side, I tried to discharge my duty faithfully and earn my keep, even though such was no guarantee that I would get to come the next time. I would hold the racing tickets, memorize betting combinations, and follow the races closely so I could yell out to him when his most heavily bet horse had just pulled out ahead or if it still maintained the lead at the last turn. From my vantage point atop his shoulders, I rattled off positions and movements of the horses like a seasoned racetrack announcer. My superior eyesight was especially helpful in the event of a photo finish.

After a few races, he would stuff a bill or two in my hand and tell me to go to the grandstand section where the food hawkers were, knowing full well the reason for which I had begged to come along. I would return with food treats for both of us—a couple of steamed pork dumplings or a baguette sandwich for us to share and two plastic pouches of freshly extracted sugarcane juice. A thorough planner, I calculated carefully the expenses so as to retain some of the money for a snack the next day.

While Ba was unwittingly grooming me for the seductive world of gambling, Ma began to teach her only daughter the art of making ends meet. I learned how to spot the fattest hen from the crowded coop without creating too much disturbance and jinxing the chicken-monger's lot, how to pick out the freshest fish and the crispiest greens. I was taught how to bargain skillfully—in the non-aggressive, sweet-as-pie style of Ma.

"Miss ... two *dong* here for this bunch of bitter pok choy? No? Oh yes, I know it fresh—so crisp and green. I have too many kids at home. No money. *Tsk ... tsk ...* How about two and a half dong? Please ... you give me for that price ... can't sell our crop of lettuce yet. My children hungry all the time ... Yes, yes, when I have money, I come back to buy from you. Thank you, thank you ... You are so kind."

Still, the real art was in getting second-quality products for the bottom prices of last-quality goods.

I would approach a fishmonger, gaze intently at a slow-moving fish in the shallow sweet water vat, then, with all innocence, alert the merchant that perhaps the fish was close to expiring. This had to be very carefully done. It must be followed with a complimentary remark on the fish's finer attributes—like how fat he was. If I thought she was offended and interpreted my comment as a jinx, I had to backtrack and suggest that perhaps the fish was simply fatigued from swimming too much or profusely praise the awesome freshness of something else at her stand. If that didn't work, I was to make haste and leave the vicinity of the stand quickly. On the other hand, if she showed concern for the targeted fish, I would mention that my ma might not mind having a fish for our afternoon meal if it could be had for a low price since we were rather poor and did not have much money.

Going to market was a chore I relished, for the din stirred my senses. It was always busy as an anthill. Scarcely older than I, little boys and girls rushed to and fro, fetching this and that for their patron stall vendors or carrying laden baskets to the shoppers' waiting cyclos or horse wagons.

Sound came from every corner of the market—costermongers raising bundles of fruits, calling out the freshness and low prices of their wares; horses snorting and neighing from the wagon stand; wooden wheels rumbling by; cyclo drivers pedaling alongside of shoppers begging for a fare; customers bargaining, yelling out their last offers, then last, last offers; boisterous vendors shouting their final best prices, then heaping a string of curses at the customer's back upon the latter's supposed audacious rejection.

However far and wide I would go from there, the sounds and smells of the place would forever haunt me with a reminder of the enchantment that was. A lifetime removed and thousands of miles thence, I would be wandering through the open-air market of Dakar, capital of the West African country of Senegal, and suddenly found those same beats of home. More than once, the longing would seize me, and for a few blurring moments, I would see not the Muslim garb of the Senegalese or the bright colors of choice in Africa, but the familiar black trousers and blouses of modest brown, beige, faded white, and black of my youth and imagine that the throbbing of life around me came from the heart of that insignificant little hamlet on the other side of the world.

As in my trips to the racetrack with Ba, the highlight of a market outing was the food treat that came at the end. Ma often managed to save some money for a bowl of soup or a ball of sweet glutinous rice for us to share. After my hunger had been temporarily allayed, I would be ready to go home, to the waiting orchard, where short, stubby trees provided nooks and hollows in which a child could hide forever. In season, it would be bursting with fruits of different shapes and sizes, weighing down on low-bowing branches to the perfect reach of a hungry child.

This was a wonderland where I indulged in the world of make-believe. I played pretend games with creatures like the colorful beetles whose hard shells made them look invincible, and yet, with a drop from the vine, their world turned comically upside down. I would follow crickets, which moved so stealthily through the grass that hardly a blade fluttered at their passing. I ferreted out their homes—little caves under rocks or dead branches or within hollows of rotting lumber—and sprinkled soft, young blades of grass to entice them into coming out. I watched butterflies and moths through their metamorphosis and chased after dragonflies cloaking as one of their own—making buzzing sounds and flinging my arms wide and weaving among the grass. Then there was the praying mantis, or "heavenly horse." I would bend my legs at the knees and put my palms together in like supplication, trying to look solemn like the strange-looking creature he was. Not until I read a murder mystery in adulthood that described the ways praying mantis devoured their victims did I stir at the savagery of nature, or "survival of the fittest." It was fortunate that I remained intellectually ignorant of Darwin's theory as it was being practiced within my paradise. My illusions thus stayed intact, and the orchard, with its paradoxical abundance of life and perfect isolation, became a place of refuge, the source of my inspirations.

龙

I started school in the year I turned four. I was such a stubborn and rebellious child that Ma had her doubts on whether the schoolmaster would accept me. Surely, words of my shenanigans would have reached the gossipmongers at the coffee shop and, from there, a short trip to the schoolhouse and the headmaster, Master Hunchback. I simply could not follow convention. There were no other girls as willful as I, no one else who preferred the dark bowels of tree limbs to the cheerful hubbub of the household, who would openly challenge their ma's authority and dare to run away when threatened with a cane.

How did I know of my parents' doubt about my suitability to enter school? Ma and Ba talked about everything in their morning *tête-à-tête*, a time they imagined to be their private time. Being inquisitive as I was, once I discovered the routine, I willed myself to wake at the sound of their hushed whispers from the divan next to my cot and silently learned about all manners of things, including private, secret things.

I took to school soon enough if only for the storytelling, the snacks, and the play times. There were about thirty of us in one big room, all sitting on wooden benches behind long, gently sloping tables with drawers for books and book bags and a shallow, little compartment on top where we stored chalks, pens, and inkwells. At different levels of learning, we studied under one teacher, the schoolmaster himself, Master Hunchback. He really had a hunchback, and yes, Hunchback was the name he went by.

He monitored our progress by walking around the room, stopping to help one student with penning letters of the alphabet on the little chalkboard, assigning work to another before wandering on to the next row. A thin, stooped figure in soft, white, flowing pajamas, he had a stern, cadaverous face that inspired fear and dread. Animated and entertaining as he could be at storytelling time, Master Hunchback was a strict teacher who demanded absolute obedience and reverence. Spanking by a thin, slick bamboo cane was dispensed rather liberally; having dirty fingernails, for example, was considered a caning infraction. Even too much attention on penmanship could mean a cane over the head if one failed to respond as he sauntered by and beckoned from the aisle. Talking during class, even whispering, was considered disruptive and would merit a caning. To Ma's and Ba's amazement, I stayed out of trouble. At the beginning, they would ask me at the evening meal how school was and if I got caned. I would grin proudly and reply in all innocence, "You silly, of course not!"

What I remember most fondly about this earliest education in my life was the storytelling hour, which took place every Friday afternoon. From the story of Bluebeard, with his dungeon and his many wives, to the poor fisherman and the princess of the sea, Master Hunchback could recount them all with such drama. We were enthralled by the tales as well as the delivery, made dramatic by the clever intonation of his words. I did not know what the kids thought as they listened to stories of princes and princesses and their palaces, of rags to riches, peasants to mandarins. For me, the credible legends did more than entertain; they fueled my daydreams. Perhaps it was fated. Between the fables and the perfect isolation of the orchard, I had the tools to make up fantastic images of the life I wanted to have.

TWO

IN THE NEWS: 6/28/98–CHINA–
ON AN OFFICIAL VISIT
TO CHINA, PRESIDENT
CLINTON CRITICIZES THE
COMMUNIST REGIME'S
HUMAN RIGHTS RECORD.

Beijing, China, 1998

The road opened wide to the fleet of Mercedes, which was winding and unfurling in perfect sync with the black van and stretch limousine at its head, just like the tail of a dragon. In this land of the dragon dances, the vehicles' precise movements were to be expected. In truth, they were, but for quite a different reason. This was, after all, the presidential motorcade, shepherding not just any president, but President Clinton, the President of the United States.

Anywhere, any time, the limo and its support fleet would cover the asphalt the same way—as if it could not get to wherever it was going fast enough, like the devil was at its heel, an analogy not altogether far-fetched.

The visit was over. The administrative staff at the U.S. Embassy in Beijing would have to tie up loose ends—settling hotel and rental car bills, sending off cables reporting on the president's last-day activities, results of his latest meetings, and, later, local reaction to the visit. For the TDY (temporary duty) support group, the job was done. Soon Air Force One would be airborne and the president's schedule someone else's responsibility. Our vehicle, the next to last one in the motorcade, brought up the rear. The motorcade would head toward the far corner of the tarmac, where Air Force One and its crew anxiously awaited their charge.

My husband, Acey, and I had checked out of the hotel early that morning, our luggage safely stowed in the trunk of the vehicle. Our driver had been well briefed to veer at the fork in the road to drop us off at commercial passenger check-in. The gleaming presidential limo followed the Secret Service lead to the left, the tail of the motorcade trailed behind while we broke right. The police-follow jeep sped forward to take up the space vacated by our vehicle. A flawless move, just as the visit had been.

This was Acey's and my first support duty for a presidential visit. We had handled visits by Vice President Al Gore and Secretary of State Albright previously, but a presidential visit experience was definitely not overrated. After more than two weeks of countdown meetings, briefings, and haggling with Chinese government officials over logistics, it was finally over. In this trip, Acey was assigned the position of motorcade officer for Secretary of State Albright (SecState), while I handled that function for other Cabinet secretaries. Though VIPs in their own right while in the United States, or even overseas when they traveled alone, these dignitaries became almost nonentities when traveling with the president.

SecState still managed to retain a measure of importance since foreign policy was her area of responsibility; she had her own limo flown in and a host of State staff coming along to provide support. Treasury

Secretary Rubin was also treated more specially than the others were, because the Secret Service (SS) happened to fall within his jurisdiction. As such, he had SS escort and support in his own right. The remaining dignitaries were crammed into a van, including U.S. Trade Representative Barschefsky (Trade Rep), who was an important figure on this trip since China had been known as the most grievous offender in the trademark and copyright arena, an area of grave concern to the United States. This van was my responsibility, negligible as it was, since my principals had no separate meetings, and so our van's only movements were with the presidential motorcade. My task was to make sure they got in the designated Cabinet van before the motorcade sprinted forward to its next destination and protective shelter.

American diplomats had gathered here for the past ten days to support this presidential visit, as they had for all other POTUS (President of the United States) visits all over the world. Cables from the State Department had gone out days before, soliciting volunteers to support the visit, drawing from neighboring U.S. embassies those diplomats with specific language or management expertise.

As with other extended TDY trips, we brought our two youngest adopted children, Zu and Tyler, along with their caregiver, Trang, who also happened to be Tyler's birth sister. Since this was exotic and forbidden China, my older children also wanted to come, with the exception of Thuy, the youngest of my birth children, who was so encumbered with her five dogs to take any trips anywhere any more these days, let alone one to the distant land of China. Van, the oldest, had arrived in China the week before. Shen, the middle child, arrived a day later, giddy after having met a couple of Diplomatic Service (DS) agents on the plane who were coming to China for the same purpose and who made her feel as if she were a part of the team, not as a straggler, as I had called her. She said they had talked and joked, all enjoying the *esprit de corps* of long-term teammates rather than strangers at a first-chance encounter.

After several days of nothing but disappointing meals, we gave up on trying to find good Chinese food in China. It was quite baffling really.

How could one not get good ethnic food in the country of its origin? Finally, from the advice of those resident experts at Embassy Beijing, we found a hole-in-the-wall eatery near the embassy that was supposed to give us what we had been searching—good Chinese food. The experience was enlightening, if not in terms of culinary excellence. It was the menu. Some of the listed items could have made David Letterman's Top Ten list of favorite dishes of American diplomats in Beijing—fried ox balls, or "rape" in oyster sauce (a misspelling for a green called rabe). I was glad the kids were sufficiently entertained and distracted by the names of the dishes to grumble too loudly on the quality of the food, which remained mediocre.

Intrepid citizens of the world as we were, we stayed undeterred in our quest for good food. Next on the tryout came the Peking Duck restaurant that claimed former President George Bush among many of its past notable patrons. It was popular among the locals and tourists alike and apparently knew it—it occupied a vast dining hall with seating capacity for hundreds.

The duck was tasty enough, its roasted skin crispy, but the meal was no more special than what was available in a good Chinese restaurant in Sydney, D.C., or San Francisco. As if he could sense the desperation, Chris Runckel, the administrative counselor and head of the large administrative unit at the embassy, organized a dinner for us one evening before P-day, the day of POTUS's arrival. We were to dine at a house at the bottom of an alley somewhere in residential Beijing. Our host and chef supposedly came from a long line of chefs, the earliest of whom actually served emperors of past dynasties.

We dined on dishes China's emperors once had. Admittedly, the food was better than what we had previously had in Beijing. What I found perplexing was that there was no rice offered with any of the dishes delectably garnished with colors and fragrance designed to stir the senses. According to Chris, I should simply ask for it. When the wife of the owner came out with the next course, I conjured a congenial, diplomatic smile. "May I have some rice please?" For that well-executed request, completed with the deferential tone and a smile, I earned an evil-eyed glare. She set the plates of food she had in her hand just a tad too forcefully and gave me another wicked glance before leaving the small, three-table dining area. I was stupefied but for a few seconds... *Hmm, she must have had the same lesson on etiquette in dining as I did during my orientation days in the Foreign Service—asking for anything not on the table or even using what was, except for the main dishes, was considered a faux pas. In the case of salt and pepper, it would be considered a putdown for the chef and host; it implied that the taste had fallen short of perfection.* Anyhow, my fellow diners enjoyed the fried noodles dish that was the chef's choice just fine.

Food aside, China had much to offer to even the most discriminating of tourists, a role we played to the hilt: visiting popular sites such as the Great Wall, the Forbidden City, and Tiananmen Square. The Great Wall was indeed a sight to behold, a grand testament to man's vision and his might. Looking out over miles upon miles of hand-hewn stone and earthen fortifications amid luxuriant jungles, I could see with my mind's eye throngs of poorly clothed, stooping figures working the wall. I thought I could hear the sound of their moaning from coldness and hunger as they were pushed to outer physical limits to build this majestic monument that could be seen from space. The wall's purpose of defending the country from invaders now obsolete, it stood against time as one of the most formidable man-made wonders of the world.

While Acey and I spent the days attending meetings and briefings, Van took the younger kids sightseeing, going so far as flying kites at Tiananmen Square, a popular native pastime. I could have made time to show them the finer points about flying kites but instead chose to devote myself to those tasks that, though menial, were thought to be part of that great wheel around which freedom of the free world revolved.

I could surely have shown them a thing or two about flying kites, inspiring my children with yet another story of how things used to be. While I didn't have those "walking to school without shoes in the snow uphill both ways" stories, I could have managed quite well with the tropical developing country's version of the lamentation. In my childhood days, we had to make our own kites. There were kites for sale, but they were a luxury only to be dreamed of. My first effort as a kite maker and flyer quite predictably ended in disaster, for I was never a thorough technician of any sort. I was of the flying-by-the-seat-of-my-pants breed, just like my ma. We never aimed for the exact; close enough was sufficient. Quite a visionary of the time, however, I set out to do things that had never been tried before, or so I thought. I made an incredibly long tail for the kite. Made of regular paper, the tail became too heavy for the kite to take off. To show the other kids they were wrong for ridiculing me, I ran faster and faster on the narrow path, tugging and releasing all the while like the professional kite flyer I was, until I ended up in the ditch. The kite did not fare well; it had lost most of its tail by the time Ba retrieved it from the cornfield. With my chin up, I sneered at the cackling crowd of boys, "My kite didn't need such a long tail anyway."

I didn't have time to share with my children those happy moments of my childhood. I was otherwise occupied, conferencing with White House, State, and embassy staff on a site visit for the Trade Rep. Someone misspoke and suggested Silk Road as China's model of capitalism. It was that, and certainly a little bit more. Indeed, it was China's answer to Bangkok's night markets at Patpong and Salom Road. A tourist-shopping mecca, it boasted name-brand knockoffs at rock-bottom prices. It was one of the reasons for the Trade Rep's visit—to solicit China's cooperation in enforcing copyright and patent laws. It was definitely not a place to take her unless we wanted her to see the proof and extent of the violations.

The Chinese could think big. From monuments to roads, they built them in gargantuan proportions, as if to impress upon the world their large role in it. They seemed compelled to spend millions of *yuan* to create monuments for the ages, while the peasants among them struggled from meal to meal, getting just enough strength to work the land for another growing season, much like my ma. The brave and the desperate or, perhaps more accurately, the dreamers among them, set out for foreign shores, bracing against increasingly tightening airport controls or risking their lives in stifling iron confines of smuggling ships in search of a different and supposed better life, much like I was.

I reflected on my own circumstances. Had it not been for the Vietnam War and the serendipitous evacuation that came in its wake, I would have found myself in the same situation as these marginal, faceless millions. I would have borne half a dozen children for some man, then sent them out to alleys far and near to peddle some good or other. The extent of my family's world would have been limited to those dusty streets; the issue of the day would have been how to keep everyone fed rather than pondering America's foreign policy. In their shoes, I too would have risked much to escape that barest of existence.

The pearl market was most assuredly a Chinese-size enterprise. There was stand after stand, each with buckets of freshwater pearls of different sizes and colors. Although neither my daughters nor I was pearl aficionados, I could not resist what I thought were extremely good buys. I bought dozens and dozens of strands, just to have them. The kids laughed and teased, saying they could envision me sitting on my rocker at old age, fingering my pearls while reflecting on these days of unexpected glory. I was too embarrassed to tell them the real reason. From a wistful corner of my heart, I thought the pearls might help me bring about that sophisticated look I had not been born with and could never seem to create. True enough, dazzling as they were, the pearls could not accomplish miracles.

I had gone far from my roots, but obviously not far enough. I thought often of this impossible journey that began with my first posting, which, as old Foreign Service hands put it, would always be special, much like one's first love. The experience was indeed that—the feeling that it was not quite real, the joy that threatened to burst free, and that constant humming of the heart.

It was an enchanting foray to a wonderland on top of the world. Reykjavik, Iceland, was a fairy city beyond my wildest dreams. Everything about it was foreign to my world, including the kaleidoscope colors of the rooftops that were unusual enough to earn a mention by Tom Brokaw at the prelude to the Reagan-Gorbachev summit.

In 1988, the American Embassy in Reykjavik was a small posting by Foreign Service (FS) standards—only a handful of officers and a dozen local national staff. As was the case elsewhere in Scandinavia, food prices were high in Icelandic supermarkets and shops. To make ends meet with my junior officer's salary, we relied on the U.S. Naval Base at Keflavik, which was about one hour away by car. After breakfast on any given Saturday, we could be found heading out to the base to shop at the lower-priced Post Exchange and Commissary.

There we paid low American prices for American and Icelandic foods, enjoyed a hotdog at the small eatery at the USO, picked a few romance novels for me and Van at the self-service lending library, then headed home to cook an American dinner of pot roast and potatoes, with plenty of carrots and onions, the way Pat, my husband, liked it.

The summer of our first arrival in Reykjavik was glorious. It did not matter that there were no towering trees bursting with colors and foliage and no heady fragrance of jasmine and gardenia to lift the air. The land had its own unique scent, a curious mixture of sea and sulfur. Throughout the year, in darkness and light, the wind whipped that scented air across hauntingly beautiful lava fields, seemingly determined to chase away all things not indigenous to the land. Indeed, the ferocious wind further hardened the climate, keeping out the weak of heart and fragile of limbs, leaving the land to the hardy descendants of Erik the Red, the famous Viking conqueror.

So I happened to be there by a quirk of fate and the grace of karma. This sudden elevation of social economic status impacted my life in explosive ways. The best and worst of them was the new lifestyle, which changed the dynamics of my family. It put me in the driver's seat, the seat of a principal breadwinner, and upended our status quo. From an operational standpoint, I took to the new role like a tadpole to the rain, for I had learned well the lessons in childhood and knew how to take the lead in caring for a family. Providing for them was a duty; devoting all I had to a job that enabled me to accomplish that was my responsibility.

The stature of the job, or rather my pride in it, became my downfall. Because it had not been a part of my past, it was not among the lessons I had learned. I got carried away by the tide of success and neglected the one shining quality that was in both of my parents and once was within me—humility.

Later, much later, I would learn how the more educated, the wise, balanced what they called priorities and how they maneuvered so as to have the best of both worlds. In the dawn of my success, there was no room for such cumbersome introspection. I had become too important, too quick, for my own good.

Iceland would be the only posting I would have in the industrialized world. The remainder of my FS career would be spent in the third world, in developing countries where the human conditions were dismal, where poverty and hardships were the facts of life, and where I could see on a daily basis the affirmation of how far I had come.

Strangely, in the Icelandic way of life I found again the simplicity of the peasantry of my homeland. Icelanders were good stewards of the land, conserving their resources carefully in manners passed down from ancestors who had to survive the ravaged, almost inhabitable land. Progress, which came in the form of container loads of food from faraway lands, did not alter this laudable way of life.

To my eyes, the land was like that mythical Shangri-la, a near utopia with its fine sense of social justice and equality, except for the absence of luxuriant forests and sparkling warm water cascading from jungle waterfalls, even though Gulfoss, Iceland's massive waterfall, could rival any of its tropical sisters around the world. Its resplendent, voluptuous curtain of water, when frozen in the winter, could bedazzle spectators with a sight no less stirring in its slumbering state—nature in the throes of its naked, magnificent power, resolutely captured at a moment in time.

The paradoxical enchantments were myriad across the desolation—glacier and cold air enshrouded lonely, impassioned terrain, while fumaroles, geysers, and hot springs exploded from their rocky surface with unchecked fury. We did get to one such spring at the edge of a glacier at Landmanalaugur and experience the surreal and delightful sensation of seeing both the heat and the cold at work in the same location at the same time.

The surrealism seemed to have been potently peculiar to Iceland, for it also got carried over to the job. Feeling totally out of my league there, I worked hard to find my footing. A diplomat! What did I know of being one? So I watched and learned, calling forth all my perception and intellect—those same faculties I had relied on to survive the barrenness in my youth. I spent weekends and after hours studying the Immigration and Nationality Act and regulatory State Department procedures in order to rise to the Department's expectations of its foreign service officers (FSO), who were touted, during our A-100 orientation class anyway, to be the best of the best. They did not have to know that I spent four hours composing my first two-paragraph cable to the State Department only to have it redlined to near oblivion by my supervisor, the deputy chief of mission.

I practiced giving *demarche*, the process of presenting the U.S. government position on certain issues to a foreign government, in front of a bathroom mirror, choosing my every word with care. It was easy to speak with conviction. With the mind-set of the righteous, I believed that whatever my country wanted to do, it was right, and the world should take heed. I didn't see how others could believe differently and resolved to win over the ambivalent as well as the most ardent detractors of U.S. policy. Besides the satisfaction of a job well done, a foreign government response that was favorable to our stance usually earned kudos for both the messenger and the post.

I focused on learning my chosen craft, absorbing all those unwritten subtleties from my colleagues within the embassy as well as from outside. Steve Parris, the British consul whose office at the British Embassy was only a block away from our embassy, was one such mentor. Having done visa work for most of his career and knowing well those tactics used by *mala fide* travelers to obtain visas to enter the United States or Great Britain, he took time to educate me on the traditional modus operandi of the tired, poor souls who would cheat, lie, and steal to make it to the land of plenty. The desperate and calculating came to isolated postings like Iceland, where there were not many visa cases and where the refusal rate was so low the consul's alertness to scams was thought to be blunted. Even more important, the consul in posts like Reykjavik would have more time to conduct a thorough interview, during which her empathy might be stirred. This was a far cry from those sixty-second snap judgments that usually led to denials at the so-called visa mills at large embassies in Manila or Mexico City.

The more I interacted with the suave diplomats, the more inadequate I felt. The insecurity that came with my humble beginning rose from the subconscious with a vengeance. *What would happen to me if they ever found out I didn't belong?* Unprovoked, the niggling doubt had lain dormant during my climb to the top. No sooner had I arrived at that pinnacle of success than it made its presence known, causing me to question how I had gotten to where I was and if I would ever be good enough to stay. *When would I be discovered and rejected as the fake I was?*

As it happened, the shadows of yesterday had never really left. They were simply rendered oblivious and insignificant in the dawn of my struggle, gaining shape again only under the brilliant rays of glory.

While I chased after recognition and found insecurity, Pat was left alone to battle his own demons. In spite of having lost his father early, who had walked away from his wife and two children during the Depression, Pat grew up with a firm idea of a woman's subservient role in the household. I had nothing against that, no fiery opinions, no latent thoughts since I had grown up with similar thinking and expectation, regardless that such were in discordance with reality, even in wartime Vietnam.

The women I knew were strong women, women who could, and did, single-handedly ensure the livelihood of their husbands and children by their own callused hands and thickened soles. Guided by the traditions of a patriarchal society, these strong, vital women were content to remain in the background to be the force that ensured the well-being of their charges. The society in Vietnam helped preserve the male dominance and his pride. It would have been well and good if we were living in Vietnam, where there were no chanced remarks like, "Oh, lucky you, I wish I could find a wife who has such a good job to support me." Side jabs like those made Pat question his worth and forced him to compromise his long-held values.

I should have seen this and helped him through it. Instead, every time I looked into his clear blue eyes, I no longer saw the humor and love of old, but only chilling reflections of jealousy and obsession. My judgmental eyes saw only a man embittered by his wife's accomplishments, a man who sometimes seemed half crazed with wanting his wife to be his alone, a totally dependent wife.

I was aware of his injured pride in having to step back and yield the spotlight to me but discarded it as sensitivity nonsense. I expected him to accept the new status quo for the good of the family.

As I demonstrated my newfound authority, rushing here and there for a meeting with other diplomats, the ambassador, or officials at the Foreign Ministry, Pat watched and listened. I never grasped the extent of the envy, jealousy, and confusion he swallowed sitting in his small office across the hall, occupying the dual positions of community liaison officer and mailroom clerk. Our marriage would not have survived even the first six months of my tour had it not been for that notable program of the Department of State to hire spouses of its FSO to staff certain clerical, technical, or managerial positions at embassies overseas. The program was designed to compete with domestic employers for the best and brightest by providing employment opportunities for their spouses. The new and interesting jobs did keep Pat occupied for a time.

While I gave to the job all I had—no task was too small or troublesome for me—I stayed late, willingly taking on the additional duties as treasurer of the Fulbright board, savoring every single minute and everything I did. My priorities seemed crystal clear. The job was the means to keep us in the social and financial position we all enjoyed. Anything that was good for the job, for me, was deemed good for our family.

My insensitivity fueled Pat's insecurities and aggravated the problem, which, in turn, brought out the worst in him. Not a mean person, he never became physically violent to me and our children but simply unleashed his frustration to things around us. Reminded of the crude, chauvinistic men of my youth, I turned away from him more each day, even if he loved me to distraction. His obsession would become more intense in the face of my increasing detachment. The more he pushed, not understanding the reason for the distance, the farther away I retreated. I wrapped myself in my children's love and devotion and the absolute rightness of my job as a provider. I found his angry outbursts increasingly distasteful and repulsive. Never for a minute did I think I might have been at fault.

I had nothing to do with his demons. He just had to regroup and toe the line so we could have a good life. I had done my part. The least he could do was help.

But he was obsessed with me and my love and our sexual life. He wanted the mind-blowing sexual and emotional closeness we had had while dating, while for me, intimacy was not possible on the heels of violent disagreements or verbal attacks on the children. I would leave during his outbursts, retreating to that dangerous world of daydream to resurrect castles of hopes and fantasies, alone.

In more sobering moments, I would retrieve the ghosts from the deepest part of my heart and let pain and regrets wreak havoc upon me. Pat's first wife was the perfect woman for him. Submissive and dependent, she relied on him for all things. But he and I met, and in me he found the excitement of new love, new passion, and ended up leaving the woman who had been tailor-made for him. Not particularly philosophical or truthful to myself, I didn't know at the time that what he thought was me was only a shell I showed to the world. When we met, I was lost and rudderless and became, if only for a time, the woman he had fantasized all Asian women to be—weak and submissive.

Now he floundered, not understanding why or how I had changed so drastically. As for him, he had always been true to himself and to me, never pretending to be any different from the person he always was.

There were days when we were held captive by the virulent, jealousy-induced emotional tempests within our household, which, in some way, curiously mirrored the violent life force that swept over the land. Blessedly, there were many more days of tranquility and contentment, during which we gave ourselves up to the delights of the extraordinary, such as those powerful windstorms that raged around us and the beautiful simplicity of Icelandic life.

Ah, the wind, that untamable force from the Arctic. Foreign born, it became a wildly powerful part of the land, as permanent as the mud pots and lava fields on its path. Mindful of the wind's destructive power, native moss stayed under cover in crevices on the lee-side of boulders and flourished in the relative warmth of summer. The wind swept through, blowing its cold breaths on A-frame stands on which rows of fish were hung out to dry. A source of amazement to me were the locations of those stands—in the middle of nowhere. I used to wonder, *To whom do the fish belong?* The crime rate there was negligible to be sure, but was there no such thing as simple human greed? A fish for dinner would not necessarily be an unpardonable crime in the eyes of some.

Our flat occupied the entire upper level of an imposing, square brick house on Aegisida Street, which commanded a sweeping view of the ocean thanks to a row of wide, oversized windows running the length of the adjoining dining and living rooms. There were two bedrooms on the main floor and two smaller bedrooms on the loft level for Van and Shen. Houses of similar build lined the road on one side, each with its small square of lawn and a hedgerow. I remember hearing the sound of a lawn mower at three a.m. on a Saturday morning during the first week we were there. After the initial shock at the incongruent sound, we realized no one had gone mad, that our industrious neighbor simply wanted to take advantage of the midnight sun to take care of one of his household chores. Rather than being vexed, we marveled at the uniqueness of the land and the charming way of life, chuckled, and went back to sleep.

Only a small roadway separated us from the mighty waters of the North Atlantic and supposedly nothing but water between us and Greenland. Our landlords, an Icelandic couple, lived on the ground-level floor with their small garden and a well-anchored, hardy hedge. In the winter, we would go to bed every night to the angry howling of the winds, whose determined assaults were rendered rather ineffectual against the sturdy Icelandic houses, constructed especially to withstand the harsh elements. Indoors, the cold was effectively neutralized by another of Iceland's natural wonders—the geothermal heat modern-day Icelanders captured and routed to warm their water and their homes.

For two splendorous summers, Pat and I gloried in those weekend mornings, when we enjoyed our coffee from the soft, comfortable bucket twin chairs, watching our children skip and play along the shoreline as they waited for the lone fisherman to come back to the small dock off the narrow, stone-strewn beach. From the double-pane windows, we observed the stillness of the fisherman in the distance as he waited for his catches. The sea was dove gray and so calm we could see the boat lift with each ripple that passed by on its way to the rugged shoreline to meet up with the weathered stones. If we should lose sight of his progress, we would still know of his returning by the shrieking of Van, Shen, and Thuy as they abandoned whatever was occupying their attention and rushed out to the dock. They fluttered about as he emptied his meager catch into a bucket, giving them whatever crabs were accidentally caught in the net.

The crabs were smaller and hardier than any crabs we had seen before. There was not much meat to them, nor was the meat tasty. It was no wonder the Icelanders did not know what to do with them. However, my heart lightened as I watched my children rush toward the house with the crabs dangling from blades of grass they had woven into strings. As their laughter sliced through the tranquility of morning, I thought of the pride and exhilaration I had felt once upon a time when I fetched food home to present to my ma.

Happiness was in watching my three daughters acting without a care in the world. Unfortunately, I didn't realize that while I stood and pondered, time continued to move forward, taking away those precious moments. It moved with each of my children's footsteps, matching my strides as I came to take the crabs from them, and raced away as I touched their cheeks to see if they had gotten too chilled from the Arctic air. It caught up with my children again as they ate their morning snacks. If I had stopped to think about the term "time waited for no one," or perhaps "life waited for none," I would have hugged my children more often, taken the time to treasure their fresh innocence, and to enjoy every moment with them as if it were all there would ever be.

It seemed that none of my previous education, including that hard-won experience on the fringes of the Vietnam War, had any application at all in this new life. They could have, I suppose, if I had not been corrupted by pride and ego. For the first time in my life, I knew what it was to have pride. Rather than taking better care of it, I let it take over and cause me to make every possible mistake one could when it came to relationships and family.

A few things worked out, if only by accident. Van, my oldest daughter, turned herself into a studious pupil as well as a helpful and obedient daughter. She took us through some of the proudest moments of our lives in Iceland. From my tireless coaching through high school essays, she eventually distinguished herself by outstanding achievements on her own. I watched in awe as she was selected to go to The Hague for the 1989 Model U.N. Conference, representing Iceland at that; to Heidelberg, Germany, to present a winning science project; to the University of Cambridge for a course in English literature. I thought I had already created an exceptional childhood for her by giving her an upper middle-class life, the enviable life of a child of a diplomat, from getting on the embassy bus to go out to the base to the prestigious DODDS (Department of Defense Dependents) school, to being invited to a classmate's house to study (which I had never been privileged enough to do), to learning Russian and French and becoming proficient in both. That was my dream, and she was wholeheartedly living it. What Van ended up accomplishing boggled my mind. My imagination simply had never reached such heights.

Nor, for that matter, had it ever been so blunted. Van would come to resent the way I favored her two sisters, just as I had resented Ma for favoring my brother and held that against her until her death. I did not fully understand her dilemma until it was my turn to be faulted for the same "transgression" and empathized with her only on receiving that same cool reception from my daughters on the matter of inequitable dispensation of a parent's love. I thought of the irony of karmic turnabout, or poetic justice, as I tried to explain to my daughters how, as a mother, I loved them all unconditionally and would always be there for each of them, but that I simply had to take special care of whomever in her moment of greatest needs.

Van stayed out of her stepfather's way, the only father she ever knew. Pat, in his own way of coping with depression, had turned against her. Shen suffered an identity crisis that would extend through her adulthood. A middle child, she watched her older sister being praised, her little sister coddled, and somehow lost her way.

I could have helped her. Once, Shen asked why I didn't scold her as often as I did Van, why I didn't spank her. Did I not love her as much? I could have verbally blasted the insecurity into oblivion, but I didn't. What was tragic was that the vision and sensitivity that distinguished my diplomatic career did not extend to my family. I was so certain I knew all there was to know about being a mother and wife, having watched the best model that was my ma.

If only I had learned better the lessons of my youth, learned from my mother's humility, as well as her selflessness. If only I had learned more about unconditional love and the peace of acceptance.

THREE

IN THE NEWS: 5/11/57–IKE AND SOUTH VIETNAM PRESIDENT NGO DINH DIEM MEET, PLEDGE RESISTANCE TO COMMUNISM.

The Orchard
Saigon, Vietnam, 1956

While I bent my hellion ways and submitted my undisciplined self to the regiments of school, the rainy season descended with dark, suffocating heat and roaring thunderstorms. There were only two seasons—rain and dry—so it was easy for me to know even if the seasons tended to bleed into each other, making the changeover noticeable only to farmers who had to make plans for their crops. Unlike other kids, I knew the precise time the change took place, even with the imperfect reasoning of a child's mind, by following the telltale signs in the orchard. Blooms turned into fruits. Butterflies escaped their cocoons, airing their wings, then flitting among the honeysuckles on the barbed wire fence and the hibiscus shrubbery; burying themselves too deeply in the hearts of flowers, they sometimes emerged with noses smeared of pollens.

When the rain arrived, I knew it would stay. I knew it was not a rain dragon losing his way, making rains where he was not supposed to be. Sure enough, the rain lingered and the night was silent no more. With darkness came the croaking of frogs and chirping of crickets—the welcome sounds of my childhood. Frogs promised pools of tadpoles for me to play with and, later, perhaps a delicious meal; crickets, a season of fun and games.

Rain swept through almost daily—afternoon downpours that drenched flowers and herbs and flooded vegetable beds, overflowing and obliterating little borders built to retain water. The erosion was fortunate actually, for the inch-high water would have damaged Ma's precious seedlings and delayed the harvest we so desperately needed.

The clay dirt path that connected the gravel village road and the school became a puddle-strewn road. Along one side of it was a crowded cemetery of mostly dirt graves; on the other side were stands of bamboo. Everyone knew that bamboo groves were one of two favorite haunting places for ghostly spirits. The other was pine—the kind of pine with drooping branches and dark, despondent leaves. Drifting in with the wind, the spirits' soulful whispers could sow terror in the staunchest of hearts. Thanks to a country of well-meaning believers like Ma, there was always a bamboo or pine grove near a cemetery to allow lonely spirits their place to congregate and moan.

There were no pines in this cemetery, however. Ma said it was too poor to have pines. The one in the city, where rich folks were buried, did. That was the way it was. Tall, proud pines graced the more affluent cemeteries, while the rustling sound of lowly bamboo was heard only by the graves of the poor. It seemed the divergence of class followed our passage not only through life but also to the afterlife.

This burden of tradition may have kept Ba from growing frangipani and bougainvillea at our home. They were a status symbol. We did not have the status, so we could not avail the use of its symbol. In my parents' opinions, to do so would have been pretentious. Neither did we have potted plants or flowering shrubs, except for one accidental hibiscus, a honeysuckle, and a few unscented vines with tiny white flowers growing wild along the fence. Jasmine or gardenia or orchids were flowers for gentlefolk of whom we were not. They represented a genteel, leisurely pursuit for which we had neither the time nor the right to indulge.

It did not take me long to get into trouble at school, though it was not quite the sort my parents had anticipated. The schoolhouse, like all other schools at that time, had a big yard. Two mango trees and a star fruit tree stood at its edge. A flame tree, a must for all schools, extended her majestic limbs over one entire front corner, shading the latch gate and a thatched hut at its side. Old Lady Tu and her husband, Old Man Tu, lived there and ran a food stand, selling snacks such as boiled cassava and sweet potatoes, dalo, and inexpensive fruits like guava and coc. There were also boiled and roasted peanuts and little sections of tender, golden sugarcane. In season, Old Lady Tu sold steamed corn on the cob.

It was a late summer day. As soon as the gong sounded for break time, I was out the door, heading for the stand. With a coin in hand, I thought of buying a boiled sweet potato to fill me until the evening meal. Running at full speed, I reached the stand just ahead of a gang of kids. The hut was soon filled with little bodies—arms waving, fingers touching and squeezing fruits and boiled roots and dropping them. Old Man Tu was absent today. I braced myself then determinedly stepped forward to help Old Lady Tu handle the boisterous customers, pushing busy hands away from tender fruits and yelling out prices I had memorized. From that day on, I was Old Lady Tu's little helper, pitching in at break times when sales were brisk, customers pushy, and tiny hands quick, sometimes too quick for the eyes.

At the end of the break, and my day's work, she would hand me my reward—a paper-twist of boiled or roasted peanuts or whatever was not selling well that day. This was more than a sufficient bonus, for I would have been happy with simply the prestige of being on the other side of the stand, the proprietor's side. Little did I know this feeling was a hint of that thirst for distinction that would deliver me to unimaginable affluence and still find me yearning.

Blissfully unaware of the negative corollary of wanting, I absorbed the joy of commerce with all the wonderment of a child. The sound of coins dropping in the tin can was like music to my ears, while the sight of fruits dwindling from heaping trays filled me with delight. The food was a boon, a proof of accomplishment I held close to my heart all the way home to show Ma.

Then came a pause in the season during which the sun took a rest— a foretelling of my folly if only I knew. A soft rain, a farmer's balm, drifted in and lingered from one dawn to the next. By the third day of the mist, business had slowed down to a trickle at Old Lady Tu's. As I walked across the yard to head for home, Old Lady Tu waved me over and told me to take some corncobs home to my ma at a big discount. To sweeten the offer, she added, "Tell your ma she no need to pay right away, just whenever have money."

I stared at her, speechless by the surprising offer. Looking down at the shifting shadows of leaves, I contemplated the unthinkable. *Could I buy on account without asking Ma? How could I not accept such a generous gesture?* While my good sense warred with good manners, Old Lady Tu walked back to the stand and lifted the corn out of the steaming pot one by one, yanking half the shuck back from each ear to tie them together in a bundle. Testing its weight and obviously deciding it was too heavy for me, she grabbed a bamboo stick from the corner and snaked one end of it through the bundle.

I was still indecisive. There Old Lady Tu stood, her moon-round visage perceptibly brightened with anticipation of salvaging a disastrous day. Behind her, I thought I could see Ma's worried, scowling face. Old Lady Tu looked pleadingly at me and extended the bundle. "Go on, take it. Your ma and ba love these. Look, they are very good corn." I looked at the succulent kernels; they indeed looked very appetizing.

Old Lady Tu's right. Ma would love them. And they not cost all that much.

I hooked my book satchel to the other end, set the cane on my shoulder the way Ma did her pole and baskets, and started for home. The sun peeked through the breaks in the clouds and sent long golden fingers down to brighten my path. I studiously ignored the stirring of leaves from deep within the bamboo grove; I was simply too happy to be bothered with fear of restless spirits on that day. The sweet smell of corn surrounded me. I smiled and quickened my strides to match the pulsing cadence of my heart. I felt like a grownup, like Ma, bringing food home for my family.

But my springy steps halted before the threshold beam. Absent was the delicious smell of food wafting from the kitchen. There were only the rising voice of Ma, which shrilled in the stillness, and Ba's subdued murmurs, which made a perfect foil for her shouts. I listened with dread. *So he lost his pay at the racetrack again... all of it. What is she going to use to pay the merchants whose accounts she has drawn on all month long?* I backed out into the yard and sat on the log under the palm tree to wait. In between the highs and lows of their voices stood the suspending silence; no dogs barking in the distance, no hens clucking. Even the wind was intimidated into staying away, for there was not even a whisper of a breeze.

Finally, the hysteria faded away, leaving only the soft sound of Ma's sobbing. At last came the welcoming clanging of pots and pans as she started the evening meal. Rather late, I thought, but it was unquestionably the most cheerful sound at the moment. The smell of corn exacerbated my hunger. Corn! Suddenly, I remember the bundle that was still hung on the cane across my folded knees. No money, she had said. A weight pressed down on my chest. In the mood Ma was in, she would likely give me a few whacks over the head for acting foolishly and getting her deeper into debt.

Our cat, *Meo Om*, or "Skinny Cat," as she was called, came over and sniffed on the corn. Deciding that the smell was not to her liking, she arched her back and sauntered away. I stared absently as she made a wide circle past Kiki the dog, who was lying in repose, seemingly at peace with himself and the world. Head tilted and eyes sly, steps slow and measured, she looked as if she was ready to play that old game of pounce and flee.

My errant thoughts wandered... then halted on the black spots on Kiki's back, which suddenly looked like a nine of clubs from Ba's card deck. Clubs stood for money, and the nine, why, it meant lucky beyond measure. An idea came. *Hmm, I could ask him for some money when he wins at a card game. I have seen him win often, both at card games and the racetrack. The winning just does not stay with him for long because his love is for the game, not the money. Luck is usually with him, if only for a time. So if I can catch him during one of these winning streaks, then I can get some snack money, which could be used to pay for the corn.*

Hope flared. I skipped into the house, out the back, and to the kitchen. I stood and waited for Ma to look up.

"Ma, look!" I grinned and lifted the corn high. "I worked hard today, so Old Lady Tu gave me these to bring home to you." Her eyes, red from crying, lit up, and a sad smile came across her face, softening the hard edge of misery that had been there just a moment before.

"Let me see," she said, in a voice still thick with tears. She took the bundle from me, held it up, and saw for herself the round kernels on perfectly even rows of corn. She put a hand on my cheek. "Umm, what a good girl you are. How delicious these look! We have them tonight for snack. Help Ma wash these beans for frying. I just got a piece of lard. You love these string beans fried, right?"

I beamed, took the tray of beans from her, and squatted down next to the smaller of the two water vats at the washstand. Feeling her eyes drifting to me, I focused on the task to show her that I could do this too. This too? I was so caught up in the lie that I actually believed I had earned the corn, fair and square. Imbued by a feeling of pride, even if it was born of falsehood, I concentrated on the beans. *Snap... snap...* I was glad the beans were fresh and easy to pinch, so Ma could see and hear how quick I was at de-stringing and snapping beans. Perhaps it was my imagination, but I thought the clanging of pots had gentled and her steps lightened as she searched the kitchen for a shallow tin bucket in which to place the corn.

In the days that followed, the weather turned increasingly treacherous, as if contriving with Fate to hasten my doom. The dreariness of a cloudy day had never made much of an impression on me, until the day of the corn. Now I approached the end of day with dread—more corn to take home. I could not say no to Old Lady Tu even if I suspected the ledger was getting longer. For his part, Ba had not been to any card game lately; he had not been able to borrow any money. Old Lady Tu reminded me again of the account overdue. Again, I pretended to take the reminder home to Ma, only to return the next day with another promise to pay, and soon.

In spite of my troubled heart, time crept relentlessly forward, and the air became lighter and fragrant with ripening fruits. But the promise of plenty failed to ameliorate the heaviness in my heart. I would sit forlornly under the gnarled old orange tree and watch armies of yellow ants marching up and down the tree, swarming over fruits punctured by hungry birds or cracked by the baking sun. Within the bosom of the old tree I found diversion by tracing a butterfly's flight path overhead through her flitting shadow on the sun-dappled scrubby grass below. Even the succulence of an orchard fruit failed to give solace as I waited for the shadows around me to lengthen into oblivion, when it was time to go in for the evening meal.

I had lost interest in school, out of dread of facing Old Lady Tu. It was altogether a very burdensome time in my life. Merely four, I knew I was too young to be hiding from a creditor, even if I was very experienced in avoiding adults, having done so often enough at home. But evading my ma was in the natural scheme of things, while having a creditor at four years of age was not, no matter that I was well versed in the matter of debts. It was not just debt; there was precious little I didn't know. For example, I knew the rich treated their precocious offspring differently, shielding them from crude and unpleasant matters until they were a little bit older, when they were ready to be trained to be the next mandarins. I also knew that such sensitivity did not matter in our class. No one seemed to care that I loitered near when adults were having their conversations to listen to sorts of talks—talks of facts and fiction, often an exaggerated mixture of both—all of life's barest emotions.

In all of my young life, there was never a time when we were not in debt; I even knew well the term for hiding from a creditor, "*Tron no.*" I remembered a particular incident when Ma tried to recover from an embarrassing moment. When questioned why we had to go home via a different route, "Tron no," she admitted gamely then drew up her shoulders and grinned. With hunched shoulders and eyes askance, she looked like a little girl, mischievous and gleeful. Only on turning away did she drop that carefree mask and assume again the pinched look of a woman burdened.

Each day found me more morose, ensnared in the worst sort of agony I had ever known. Mercifully, the river of life moved steadily forward so that its swift currents finally caught up with my trouble.

I had left the schoolroom on unsteady feet, having been jostled thoroughly by the throng of kids vying to be among the first to exit. Pausing by the side of the door, I was knuckling my eyes to adjust them to the brightness of the sun when, over the merry chatter, I heard a loud voice. "Hey, Long, your ma is here." I lifted blurring eyes to the waning rays and saw, to my horror, Ma and Old Lady Tu in deep conversation in front of the hut. A cold dread moved up my spine, and panic gripped my heart. I felt as if I could not breathe. My arms felt numb as they hung from my lifeless body like vines from a foolish tree. I stood rooted in place, cater-cornered from Ma, oblivious to the noisy din of kids leaving the yard.

There was Ma, grim faced as she listened intently to Old Lady Tu, nodding and smiling, but with an artifice of expressions I knew well. Her face seemed to have frozen into a mask so that each smile, each movement, became an effort. I saw her manage another faint smile before reaching into her pocket and taking out a thin wad of money that must have been her proceeds from selling vegetables in the market that day. She counted several bills onto the open palm of Old Lady Tu. As she re-pocketed the precious few remaining bills, she glanced up and caught sight of me. Setting down the baskets and carrying pole, she stooped, leaned slightly forward, and stretched out her arms. A smile split my face. I leapt and ran to her in exhilaration, feeling like a pardoned prisoner. She scooped me up in her arms and swept an errant strand of hair back behind my ear with her hand. "Let's go home," she said simply, in a sad, little voice. She bowed slightly to Old Lady Tu, sat me in one of the baskets, dropped my book bag in the other, then placed the yoke on the back of her shoulders after adjusting the cane noose of each basket to fit in the groove at each end of the pole. She squatted and braced like a weightlifter ready to hoist his load, then straightened and lifted.

The baskets swayed rhythmically as she quickened her steps down the road. I sat upright and held on to the rim. A flock of sparrows rose from the bamboo grove, rustling the leaves as they took to the air. I followed their flight and found a sky bursting with colors—blue and gold and orange, with large patches of white and gray clouds forming rows upon rows of what looked like fish scales. To ingratiate myself with Ma, I laughed and pointed. "Ma, Ma, *Ong Troi*, 'Mr. God,' is having fish with his rice today." She looked up and smiled but did not break her strides as we swept into the pull of the bend where a lone bougainvillea stood, then out onto the village street.

The wind of good fortune that had taken away my trouble stayed on to bestow more blessings, this time on our President Diem. Government troops had finally gotten rid of the Vietminh, remnants of those Communist fighters who had stayed behind, no doubt to cause trouble, rather than joining "Uncle" Ho and other comrades in the North following the signing of the Geneva Accords. The wizened men, the all-knowing elders in the neighborhood, debated the merits of President Diem, the excesses of his family, and the vagaries of war and politics from their seats on rickety stools in Old Man Nam's coffee shop opposite the cemetery. They grimly pondered what the refugees had said earlier on arriving in the south. "The Communists said they follow us to wherever we went, there was no place we could hide, and we suffer when they catch up with us."

However dire the threat, during that short time there was peace. There was no need to think about *chay giac*, or "running from the enemy" again, at least for a while.

Even so, there was no resting for the busy Fate. Tragedies had to be dispensed, even without the cover of war. Aunt Phan, Ma's youngest sister, passed on soon after her husband, leaving behind five children for surviving relatives. No relations could take on another five mouths to feed. Neither could we. But Ma, being the oldest sister, could not neglect her duty. She opened her heart and arms to the orphaned children and gained us five siblings. With five more kids to feed, she had to work even harder. She increased our herd of pigs by borrowing money to buy a half dozen more piglets and looked for another patch of land to grow more vegetables for our table and the market. By a stroke of good fortune, or, as she believed, "kindness begets kindness," the caretaker of a large property in the village offered Ma the use of part of her land, free of charge. The land was level with good shading in one corner under a stand of jackfruit trees.

Within the shade of those fruit-laden trees, I would learn about the tragedies of life in schoolroom format.

First, the tragedies were made worse, infinitely worse, by Ma's penchant for drama, to teach me how bad things could be. Then the tragic edges were smoothed away, as only she could, by her compassion and kindness, to teach me how to help others in their misfortune, thus sowing karmic seeds. Last, a reminder of the certainty of predestination and of karmic debts to be paid, to teach me how to accept life's calamity, particularly my own. It turned out I didn't need those afternoon sessions on mores, duty, or kindness, for I would have a lifetime of learning simply by watching her live her life by those unbending beliefs and convictions.

In the Mekong delta, the fighting had started again as the guerillas began their campaign to destabilize the government by killing province and hamlet chiefs and other notable citizens in the hamlet, even teachers. The wizened men now had something other than the ills of the Diem family to ponder and debate. When there was time and money, Ba would join them. For further enlightenment on the state of the country, he would bring the gossips home for Eighth Uncle and Mr. Little Foreman to add their commentaries. (Ba was the first foreman in the compound, so he was called Mr. Big Foreman; the other man came later; hence his name Mr. Little Foreman.)

I would get to come with him only if I learned of his intended destination soon enough—that meant before he had gone and returned. I had little interest in politics or other gossips but merely came along for the divine taste of shop-made coffee. Of course, I did not get a whole cup; there was never enough money to be that wasteful. My treat was some of Ba's. Sipping my share of the sweetened coffee from a cracked, stained saucer while perching on a stool at his side, I listened to the different opinions and edicts on the war, on the governing of the country, the misfortune of so-and-so, or the taking of a "small," or "second," wife by someone they knew and the trouble the man had incurred because of that proclivity.

The wizened men, often speaking over each other's voices, kept me entertained with their jabbering.

"Ah, why the Vietminh listen to their Hanoi bosses and kill southerners? Their northern bosses think nothing of them. They are just being used … Oh, too bad about Mr. Diem. He good. Not care for riches. That family of his, his brothers and the wicked sister-in-law, Madame Nhu. They Catholics from the central have no liking for southerners or Buddhists … Ah, what a greedy bunch. They sabotage his government yet."

Even as the ashes of peace began to float away and dormant embers flared anew under the cauldron of war, Ma's thoughts on these afternoons were not on the lying northerners or their equally conniving central brethrens, or those southern lives mercilessly cut down in the rice fields along the Mekong river, or "*Cuu Long*," the River of the Nine Dragons. Rather, they were on a more pressing problem—how to influence Fate to get a better life for me.

I was to study very, very hard, so I would not have to toil as she did, day in and day out under the sun. Her voice would break as she decried the travails of our lot. I looked at her weather-beaten face, the leathery skin on her hands, the thick calluses at the bottoms of her heels—evidence of that hard life she was describing—and knew her words to be true. To banish the stirring of fear, I would take a bite of the almost inedible young jackfruit and keep busy by weighing the bitter taste of it on my tongue. It was as unpalatable as the destiny that had encumbered our family for generations.

Ma's voice would drone on, spinning a melancholia that gathered and clung until there was no escape. I would expel my breaths in one, two long swooshes to relieve the weight on my chest and turn to Ma. "Ma, not worry, I will study and work. I'll have a lot of money to care for you and Ba when you get old. And Brother Bong too, when he becomes crazy, you know ... " My tone was vehement, as if by force of will I could bend the Fate to make my want come true.

Watching Ma wipe her tears off with the sleeve of her faded and tattered work blouse, I would feel a lump rise to my throat. I would not know much about the warmth of a parent's embrace, for we were not a demonstrative people, but neither would I know the emotional or psychological burden of having to do without that physical validation of my parents' affection.

Through moments like those, I knew I was loved. The deep, searing love that flowed through my mother's silent tears, tears of dread for my future, would be my comfort, the talisman that would carry me through the turbulent journey Fate had designed for me.

For the moment, at barely five years of age, I could tell that Ma needed more, so I tugged on her sleeve and added a reassurance. "Ma, Ma, not afraid. I won't be poor." She quieted down as we sat together in thought. Then diversion came, in whatever guise—the cawing of a crow from the bamboo thicket, the chirping of birds from their roosts on the mango trees. Often, the wind picked up, a jackfruit fell, and I skipped away to gather more fallen fruits.

Ma would follow and give me a bath by the side of the well. I would strip, toss my clothes carelessly on the tattered cone hat of the scare-crow, and prance around as she sluiced one pail of water after another over me. Once, as my laughter filled the air, a scrawny refugee kid who had been studying at the window of his ramshackle squatter hut that overlooked the land from the other side of the perimeter wall leaned out and, in a high-pitched voice and heavy Northern accent, hooted, "*Me oi, Me oi,* that girl is naked." Arms akimbo, I hollered back, "Shut up before I beat you to death, you black-teeth, lying northerner." I glow-ered and shook my fist at him, not caring that I stood there completely naked. He continued in a singsong voice, "Grown up already and still naked, heh heh heh..."

I picked up a handful of little jackfruits from the pile I had collected, took aim, then let loose of one, which flew like a bullet toward his face at the window. The fruit went wide, missing the target, but nevertheless landed in the house. Immediately, his ma came to the window, shaking her index finger and cursing at me. As I glared back in defiance, Ma pushed me to the side, put her palms together in supplication, and called out an apology. While I got dressed, the boy came back and flicked both of his index fingers down his cheeks, a "shame on you" gesture in our culture. Furious, I stared hard at this irritating target, measuring the distance and direction, aiming with my eyes without moving my arm so as not to alert him or my ma. The aim held. I slowly drew out a jackfruit from the pocket of my shorts and let it sail, smacking him on the face. He doubled over and hollered in pain. I yelled back at Ma, "Ma, not apologize, not my fault, he teased me," turned swiftly away, and took a high jump to avoid a pile of manure, then ran on home like the wind.

With more pigs to feed and clean and a bigger vegetable patch to hoe and weed, Ma no longer had time to monitor Ba's gambling. He spent more time at the racetrack and in all-night card games. Somehow his gambling had taken on a nobler objective, so he explained to Ma. He would win big someday to help provide for us. We could then buy more pigs, or even cows. Yes, one corner of the compound where we lived was still laying fallow with plenty of grass, quite enough for a few cows.

Neither the cows, nor the promised pigs, ever arrived. As it was, Ma worked still harder to make up for the pay that didn't make it home.

Out of Aunt Phan's children, only the oldest boy, *anh Luong*, or Big Brother Luong, who was fifteen, was helpful to Ma. I called him big brother in deference to his age since, in family ranking, he was junior to me, his mother having been Ma's younger sister, her junior. And so it would follow that his children would be of lower ranking to mine. Big Brother Luong was a serious-looking boy with a long, thin face, like my ma's and his ma's. He was very tall for his age. Ma said he took after his ma, who was very tall. Big Brother Luong became Ma's faithful workmate, following her to the vegetable patch to help weed, plant, and water the crops that would feed all of us, while his brothers and I hid from daily household chores, taking off running whenever we heard Ma calling for help.

With the clarity gained through the years, I could see she did not need much from us. It was simply whether we had taken dry clothes off the line—this was especially pressing if thunder was booming overhead. Physically exhausted from the laborious work at the patch, mentally and emotionally drained from the stress of trying to decide what food to put on the table, which merchant to beg for yet another purchase on account, she would rant and rave and shout for help with the chores. Unperturbed by her plea, I was either daydreaming, or out searching far and wide for smooth pebbles with which to play jacks, or sitting with a pile to rocks to select one of perfect weight and texture for the game of hopscotch.

My mother shouldered the mammoth task of eking out a living from almost nothing at all. Ten-odd pigs and the vegetable patch were all we had. As we waited for the harvest of either crop, we fed on the edible weeds that grew among the vegetables or in the field by the house. For something more substantial, we searched the slop buckets collected from the different food stands for salvageable pieces of meat, even if they were intended for the pigs.

Only with hindsight did I realize how hard she had to work to keep the privations from being hardships. Against the advice of well-meaning relatives and just plainly practical considerations, she kept all of us at home rather than hiring us out as servants at well-to-do households. We were not at all too young to be groomed as maids, gardeners, buffalo herders, or laborers in the rice fields. But she soldiered on—surrendering parts of her already miniscule portions of food to us until her stomach shrank so she would need less and less. Where I saw abject poverty and despair, she saw progress and hope. As she told it, her life was much better as an adult than it had been as a child, just as her parents, *Ong Ngoai* and *Ba Ngoai*, had had it worse than she did.

Her words were meant to encourage—that things did, and would, get better with each successive generation. But as I looked at our food tray, barren except for a plate of steamed wild greens and a few spoons of seasoning *nuoc mam*, I was not convinced that it was so.

While she thought to console us by talking of the harder times of the past, I sneered and sometimes snapped at her in a hot rush of childhood anger. "You are lying, Ma. It not worse than this." Depending on my tone, and her mood, she either laughed away the accusation or hit my chopsticks with hers, hard, to show she was not happy with my behavior. There was a reason I never got spanked at mealtimes, although I deserved it on many an occasion. It was considered sinful to beat children, or anyone for that matter, while that person was eating. The moment was considered sacred, even to the gods. In this land of taboos and legends, it was easy to sell a myth, any myth, to a child, especially one with a fanciful mind as I.

Until I was about ten, I believed that the thunder and lightning god roamed the earth only to strike down disobedient children. Fortunately for those children, and me, this god was not allowed to touch anyone who was eating, especially rice. Rather than reforming, which idea never came to mind, I decided to beat the gods at their game. So I would rush to the kitchen at the first booming of thunder to get a handful of rice. By the window I would sit in arrogance, eating one grain of rice at a time and smiling at my invincibility as thunder rolled and lightning sliced across the sky ... until the day when I forgot about the rice during a thunderstorm and nothing happened. I was afraid no longer and went about my merry, rebellious ways.

I did not know much about my grandparents except from Ma's occasional reminiscence and my own memories of *Ba Ngoai*, Ma's mother, who was the only grandparent alive at the time of my birth. But she too passed not long after Aunt Phan. Long afflicted with Alzheimer's, she'd stayed in the lean-to Ba had put up on one side of the house. There was a door of split bamboo canes, which was kept locked to prevent her from wandering away and getting lost. The pieces of cane were nailed together in a haphazard, crisscrossed pattern with wide gaps to allow a free flowing of air and light.

I used to sit on the swing under the old cotton tree, "*cay gon*," at the far edge of the yard and watch her through the gaps. Sometimes she would sit on the floor directly in front of the door and stare back at me. When our eyes met, I would come close and touch the bony, crooked fingers curling on the shiny cane planks. She smiled her toothless smile, like that of a baby, and put through more fingers for me to touch. Encouraged, I put my face against the door and whispered, "Ba Ngoai." She withdrew her hands from mine and placed them on my face, cupping my cheeks, skimming my mouth and eyes, slowly, curiously, like a blind person. I remember the feel of skin and bones, and her soft, little voice as she asked in wonder, "Who are you? Are you Thanh's daughter?" I answered, "Yes, Ba Ngoai, this is Long."

At our last time together, she and I sat under the same ancient cotton tree to watch Ba and Ma splashing buckets of water on her bed, the door, and the walls in her room, scrubbing off the feces that she had spread all over everything. Apparently, Ma had forgotten to take care of Ba Ngoai's needs before leaving for the market.

I held Ba Ngoai's hand as we watched the frenzied activity before us. Then, in the stillness of the afternoon, she began to sing. Her tremulous voice rose and fell in fits and starts as she lost her way in the labyrinth of rhythm and lyric. At last, the sound steadied and rang pure and clear in the gentling glow of the setting sun. I had heard the song before, a lullaby Ma used to sing to me—a courting ballad men and women used to send across the fields to one another at harvest time, when life was simpler. These farmers of old would work side by side late into the night, gathering and threshing rice stalks and stacking hay. Cloaked in the soft haze of the moon, they shed inhibitions and laughed and bantered until the air around them sizzled with glee.

Unlike the harvest days of her youth, there was no response to Ba Ngoai's beckon. On this afternoon, there was only a halting call of a bird, lonely and bereft. Ba Ngoai's voice cracked, and the notes trailed forlornly like a plea from her soul. Their echoes throbbed and lingered... as if waiting for the mate of yesterday.

Ma had come out of the room and was standing in the lengthening shadow of the *vu sua*, or "milky breast" tree to watch us. Her lips quivered as tears pooled and spilled down her cheeks. She looked at Ba Ngoai, while I looked at her. Other families would have generational photos of their women to show the bond that binds. We had only this moment in time, except that I was too young to grasp its poignancy. Much later, I would learn that for the whole of my life, I would have but fleeting moments. I was to use them well, not just for the evolution of my soul, but for the glow and warmth those memories would bring to the twilight of my journey.

FOUR

IN THE NEWS: 1/17/91–U.S. AND
ALLIES OPEN AIR WAR ON IRAQ.

American Embassy
Accra, Ghana
West of the African
Continent, 1990–1992

Ghana was one of the two postings we had
seriously considered for an assignment after
spending two years in Iceland. The other was
on the opposite coast of Africa, in Dar Es
Salaam, Tanzania. If there ever was a case for
proponents of predestination, this was it. Fate
guided my hand in choosing one over the other,
and that would make all the difference.

At the time of bidding, November 1989,
about sixteen months or so into my two-year
tenure in Iceland, I was still too new to the
Foreign Service to be able to select a post based

on the reputation of future supervisors or of incumbent ambassadors, the way the old hands could. Neither Pat nor I knew anything about Africa, so we could not say we would prefer one coast to another. There were no clear choices—no clouds foreshadowing darkness on one side, no sun heralding light on the other. I went to Ghana, unaware that was where the villa of my dreams awaited.

We were assigned to one of the bigger houses in the U.S. Mission housing pool, on account of our family size. The house was grander than I could ever have wished for, complete with a circular driveway, manicured lawn, and sculpted bushes. Sculpted was a kind word for them. They actually looked like they'd had their heads lopped off—products of an overzealous gardener who wanted to try his hand at sculpting but did not quite make it.

Pockets of palms, bananas, hibiscus, and birds of paradise grew along the high perimeter walls, creating a spectacular tropical backdrop for the sweeping green lawn. Roses bloomed on a narrow ledge along a verandah encircling the living room. Tall glass windows dominated the entire first-floor dining and living rooms, making it almost impossible to find a solid wall space of sufficient size to hang those seascape paintings we had purchased in Iceland—not that the house needed any artificial adornment, for the sights and sounds of the tropics flooded the entire first floor.

The tropical landscape soothed but stirred my heart with images of home. When birds pecked noisily from the fruit-laden boughs of the mango tree by the gate or when a lost songster among them crooned out a bewildered tune, I would see another mango tree from that other life.

The primitive condition of the country and the low cost of living helped validate our feelings of affluence. While we were not wealthy like the clever Lebanese businessmen who populated the African landscape, we were privileged in our own right, somehow taking on the power of the country we represented.

I used to boast that I would never forget where I came from. While the truth of those words continued to hold, my empathy and sensitivity for those of my roots seemed to dull over time. In the ivory tower of the diplomatic enclave in each capital we resided, I became detached from the wretched poverty outside the gate. My heart stirred at the sight, but the sensation passed as quickly as it came. As those long-ago tragedies of war, the horrors of poverty soon became commonplace. At times, I believed I came close to resembling those snobbish creatures of the class society I had so despised. By no means did I turn into a conceited and thoughtless ogre, shooing away kids who gathered outside our wall to read by the luminescence of the security lights that flooded the perimeter. No, I actually smiled at them ever so kindly, in the perfect manner of the *noblesse*. I gave generous tips to the boys who helped carry my purchases to the car at the sprawling, dusty ground of the Arts Council, where handicraft items such as the famous kente cloth and intricate woodcarvings were sold. I paid handsomely to the women who wandered the beach in their faded sarongs to peddle fresh catches of lobsters to diplomats and expatriates.

My kindness was neither universal nor consistent. The only consistency was my complacency about their lot. They, the poor, were so numerous. There was nothing we could do to change their fates, so went the wisdom of the haves, to which I was slowly becoming a faithful adherent.

Even so, more often than not, I would feel a weight on my heart at the sight of weather-roughened visages, faces that carried the appearance and texture of old leather, faces that reminded me of my ba and ma. The young and wily affected me the same way. They reminded me of the child I was at their age, living on my wits. While they begged or hustled to carry packages for the rich, I watched … and remembered.

Other times I sat, in a manner that must have seemed inordinately haughty and proud, behind the wheel of my shining new car driving to work or behind a uniformed driver in an embassy car, both of which would bear the prestigious CD (Corps Diplomatique) license plate. On reflection, I am sure I looked disdainful in the air-conditioned car with the windows rolled up to protect me from breathing the same dust as the poor, from suffering the same stifling heat that sapped their strength as they trudged to and fro for all the deprived days of their lives.

While I was a kind and sympathetic supervisor to the local national employees, I was not the soul of humanity. My humble beginning included seven years as a national worker in a foreign embassy similar to theirs, which experience supposedly conferred me with an insight to their perspective. Presumably, I understood how they think and therefore would be more effective than my peers in motivating my staff.

The motivation did happen, not as a result of my intuition or management skills, but rather from the accident of my background. Simply put, I was one of them. They were proud of me, knowing what I had to overcome to rise to the top, to achieve the reversal of role, from staff to boss, rags to riches. My accomplishment validated their worth in a way. Now they could believe that with opportunity, they too could attain similar heights and that the only distinction between them and their American bosses were opportunities.

I assimilated into my new station so well that I became an FSO first and a person second. I pushed my local Ghanaian staff to produce to American standards, making no allowance for their limitations—malaria, disease, poor nutrition, and the absence of that powerful motivation called hope. No matter that my personal life was falling apart, I drove myself hard at work and wondered why my staff did not have the same drive.

With my heart disengaged, I forgot that we FSOs were a fortunate breed—breezing into a post, exhilarating at the promise of a new country to explore, a new course to chart to show our brilliance. Then before the new became old, we would be on our way out to bigger challenges and another adventure.

While those I supervised stayed behind, happily devoting their all to a job that, if they were lucky, would take them to the end of their lives and the status quo was the most they could hope to accomplish. Their ambition was to retain the same job until retirement and their children had grown. And their hope? That there would be no armed hostilities between now and then, knowing full well how routine an uprising was and how indiscriminate and bloody it had been and could be.

Once, I spotted a little girl peering in from outside the wall as we took advantage of a breezy afternoon to dine al fresco on the verandah alongside the wildly fragrant and silken roses. I saw her little face, hopeful and begrimed, under an unruly mop of curly hair, and smiled at her in a manner that was gentle and sweet. I thought of having the servants take her some food but got busy and forgot. For that failure, I would remember her sad eyes, luminous for that moment of hope, for the rest of my life. A kind gesture could have made a difference. Somehow, somewhere, when she might see nothing but ugly and murderous intent from the world, instead of surrendering to hopelessness and despair, she would have remembered an act of kindness and been able to retain the faith that she might know it again.

How fortunate was I that humanity was not a factor in my performance evaluation. I was diligent and committed and got perfect reports at work. The price for that successful career was a faltering marriage, a crumbling family unit, and my weakening humanity.

For a time, we did enjoy our life. Pat and I made the circuit, socializing and dining out with other diplomats at the Shangri-la Hotel or the American Club. Weekend pastimes included trips to the beach for the day or to the Port of Tema to buy fresh fish for the week or following the coastal road east to the seaside city of Lome, capital of French-speaking Togo, for freshly made sausages and lunchmeats at the locally renowned German-owned delicatessen.

But it was too late for all of us. The more spectacular my professional success, the more diminished my family values became. I'd discarded the lessons Ma had tried so hard to teach me, the lessons she had learned from her own mother. Successful now, in the eyes of the world by any standards, I was proud, too proud for my roots. Whenever I thought of my youth and Ma's life, I pitied her for the humble options of her times. Forever ashamed of our poverty, I could not see beyond the comforts of the flesh to the richness of the soul. I had no idea how fulfilling her life was. I didn't know her wisdom—she would leave this life as she had entered it, with no material encumbrances, only the knowledge that she had been kind and thereby made better those lives she had touched.

My marriage became the first casualty of my transformation. I was too shallow to know that the sanctity of marriage was not based solely on love, or that love was simply an emotion subject to fading over time. I had never taken the time while growing up to absorb what had always been there in front of me. I was too busy rejecting our society for its prejudice and its backwardness, or else despising the rich for their arrogance and the poor for their pitiful lot. I was preoccupied with finding a way to escape.

While Ma had a word to describe the relationship between husband and wife—"*nghia*," a word that encapsulated love, duty, honor, and responsibility. In her simple ways, she had tried to explain to me whenever the subject of matrimony came up about that unbreakable bond that was not made of some fleeting emotion but of decision, commitment, and character.

My marriage fell apart because I did not know how precious it was. I could have tried harder to understand, to help guide my mate, but I did not. With an inflated sense of the self, I felt I had earned the right to judge. And the judgment, when it came, was harsh and irrevocable.

Pat accepted the separation and left for Colorado. Van was already there, attending the University of Denver. On his return, she moved off campus to live with him at our house, expecting to find the comfort of home and lower living expenses. She did not fare well. Confused and depressed with the disintegration of our marriage, Pat became even more verbally abusive. Shen came back to spend the summer with them only to suffer the same fate as Van. She returned to Ghana disillusioned, not knowing how or why she had lost the father she adored.

I could have devoted my time to help Shen and Thuy through an adolescence that was made unstable because of the loss of their father, but I was otherwise confused and listless. I harped on the importance of education and saved every penny I could to pay off the debts we had accumulated through Pat's wasteful ways. I didn't think anything else was necessary. After all, I was doing all of what Ma used to do.

Pat left a gaping hole in our lives when he went away. I missed his childlike pleasures in the different things we encountered in our travels.

A perfect Foreign Service spouse, his delights made everything worthwhile for me, indeed providing the feedback I needed to know I had done well for my family. I had learned the arts of giving from Ma. In fact, I had learned it so well that I knew pleasure only through and by what I could give those I loved.

Pat had been the life force of the family. He could make the house ring with laughter or throb with anger and tension. He planned our meals, weekday routines and weekend outings, what to do, as well as when and how to do it. With his departure, he took with him those traditions he had been trying to establish for our fledging family, leaving us without an anchor and more than a little lost. Worst of all, he took with him my cherished role as a nurturer to my children. I had to be both a disciplinarian and a consoler now and failed at both.

For all of my seeming sophistication and expert navigation through the strange waters of the Western world, I never really gained a solid social foothold to understand the culture well enough to know what to do with, and for, my children.

For years I had worked hard to get a good job and now was working harder to keep it so they could have a comfortable life. I had no idea what else was needed or that there was such a difference between the traditional world of my ma and my own modern one. I worked hard, sure, but there was no earth-shattering sacrifice, not compared to the days of my ma. I had a white-collar job. Some would say it was a cushy job, worlds removed from the backbreaking labor Ma did from dawn to dusk. Consequently, it did not have quite the same impact hers did.

Though equally committed to providing for my children's livelihood, my efforts, however, did not yield the same result, because survival was not an issue of the day like it was in the abysmal days of my youth. While I loved my children absolutely and unconditionally, as Ma did me, the circumstances were just not dire enough for that love to be tested. It was not the same in her time, when she gave up her wants and needs, her very nourishment, her life, so we could survive. I had no such dramatic means to show my love.

Imbedded in the blessings that helped me break out of poverty was a curse, for on the heels of my outstanding accomplishments came a large measure of pride and arrogance, enough arrogance for me to close my mind to the possibility that I might have been wrong in the matters of child rearing and marriage and in knowing how to love. Much later, in the darkest hours of my life, when I had nothing but time and could do nothing but reflect, I would know how I had failed those I loved. I had taken their love and their devotion for granted, not knowing that it was their love and faith in me that had given me strength.

I didn't know they were the secret of my success.

On a separate continent, Ma was going through a trial of her own. Later, I would often wonder if Fate had decreed our lives to be such and such, that regardless of how seemingly clever our schemes, things were going to happen more or less the way they had been predetermined. At least that would explain away my error in encouraging Ma and Brother Bong to leave Vietnam for the foreign shores of America.

America was not for everyone. But I was flying high on the promises of the land I had dreamed of for so long that I was not capable of viewing it from other perspectives. That was what happened.

In about 1979, I was finally able to find my family through an address they had sent to Van's father at the American Consulate in Hong Kong years before. I began encouraging them to make the trip to America, sending my meager savings home so they could start building a boat for the journey. The timing was ripe. They happened to be anxious to leave on seeing the iron yoke of Communist rule tightening and witnessing widespread suffering of so many impoverished southerners.

In 1983, their careful planning culminated in a boat trip launched from the river near where Ma made her home. The prospect of escaping by sea was daunting, but they had that pot of gold by my promise to lead them on. By the time of his escape, my brother had become a successful minor merchant—buying fishnets in one city to sell at another, taking fruits and dried fish from the countryside to the big city, bringing city goods back to the farmers. He gave up that relative affluence and independence for the extravagant promise of America. After many long months languishing in refugee camps in Thailand and the Philippines, he would arrive in the land of my dreams. When he discovered money did not grow on trees, that he had to toil long and hard in menial labor jobs just to survive, he would remember the comfort of his hard-won status and the familiarity of home. This cultural shock and disillusionment would disturb his mental condition and bring on the first signs of schizophrenia.

As for my ma, on arrival in a society so different whence she came, she became a dependent for the first time in her life. No one needed her resourcefulness or the wisdom she had earned through a lifetime of sweat and tears. Brother Bong's three children had to show her how to work the electric rice cooker and how to operate the TV set. She did not know why Bong's wife would have a fit if embers from burning joss sticks sprinkle on the carpet. It was so much easier with a packed dirt floor—no burn marks to worry about.

A life giver no more, she was now a burden. Her cooking skills and the fabulous food she used to conjure dramatically to my insatiable appetites were no longer adequate. They were not good enough for Binh, her daughter-in-law, who thought she herself could do better than Ma, cooking in the flourishing ways of the haves as opposed to the economical manners of the have-nots. Prior to their arrival in America, she and Brother Bong had been living with her parents, well-to-do Chinese merchants in the Mekong delta who could afford the best and freshest of foods. She did not like the way Ma cooked—too much salt. Only the poor had to do that to make their meat or fish last longer. It was enlightening for me to discover after all these years that the extra bit of salt could reveal our humble roots.

In the foreign land of America, Ma accepted her diminished value as she did her life, with grace and courage. I, by one single, thoughtless act, the dissolution of my marriage, threw my life and all other lives within my orbit into chaos, including that of Ma. I no longer had the stability and peace of mind to even help her.

The year was 1991. I was floundering in the similar tidal pull I had years before on leaving my parents' side for the first time. But the loss was worse now, because I didn't know I was lost. The high-power job gave me a false security that all was well. I was successful in terms of money and status, which, in my narrowed view, were the only things that mattered. I was too ignorant to know that I had been among the few, the fortunate, to have lacked only the most superficial, and that for all the hardship and the poverty I had always had the most important ingredient for happiness: love. My children did not only lose their father; they also lost their mother, who was too selfish and ignorant to decipher their simplest needs.

There we were, three generations suffering at a crossroad. Among them, I was the only one who could have changed all of our lives for the better.

As my depression deepened and words of my new romance with Acey, a marine guard at the embassy, spread through the incestuous little community, Shen and Thuy struggled to cope with the upheavals. Thuy found pleasure in horses, spending more time at the Polo Club to help players exercising and caring for their horses. Shen discovered boys, in particular, a boy from a third-generation Indian-Ghanaian family. A smooth talker, he knew exactly what to say to a parent and how to say it. The kids began spending most of their times out—at someone's house, at the Polo Club, hanging out at the Shangri-la Hotel, or carousing on Labadi Beach.

It had been a long, hard road to the villa with the frangipani. Behind the gates of affluence, estranged from my husband, I found my reputation smeared and my children incomprehensible. My neglect drove Shen deeper into the stormy influence of the boy who would destroy her fragile sense of self. Partners in a shared journey, I had the lead for her and my ma but failed miserably.

My romance with Acey became a long-distance relationship on the end of his assignment to Ghana and subsequent return to the States. We got married just after I finished my tour in Ghana, before beginning Portuguese language training in preparation for my next adventure, a tour of duty in Praia, Cape Verde.

How did Acey's path cross mine? After participating in the evacuation of the American Embassy in Monrovia, Acey too had been given a choice of either Dar Es Salaam or Accra. He chose Accra.

From Ghana, we went to the desolate isles of Cape Verde, an archipelago of ten islands located about 350 miles west of the West African country of Senegal. I was given a choice of either Port Louis, Mauritius, east of the continent, or Praia, Cape Verde, on the west. I chose Cape Verde, mostly because it was out of the way, unappealing, and not very sought after, which was consistent with my commitment to the Foreign Service. Acey and I had assumed, somewhat naively, that a tropical island was a tropical island with all the usual attributes—seafood, palm trees, tropical fruits, and sandy beaches. Regardless of what the respective post report read, how different could they be from one another except the ocean from which they sprung? Unfortunately, there was not much that was tropical about Cape Verde except for the heat. If one did not look too closely, it could have been passed for Iceland. Both played host to fierce winds, little vegetation, and extreme volcanic terrain.

Worse, the Island of Santiago, on which the capital, Praia, was situated, was not known for its sandy beaches. There was only one—the beach at Sao Francisco. Seafood was not readily available inasmuch as there was no continental shelf and no coral reef, thus requiring fishermen to venture far from shores for their catches. Fishing boats were of the most basic, rudimentary kind and few in numbers. The land was dusty, dry, and too windy to allow for vegetation.

I chose Cape Verde for another reason. The country did not have an English language high school. That meant the Department would grant me an education allowance sufficient to send Shen and Thuy to a boarding school, which they had said they wanted in order to join friends who were also heading in that direction. I was ecstatic that they wanted such an academic experience, which was like a trip to the moon in my days. What an exceptional chance to get a first-rate education, or so I thought.

It seemed like a lifetime between departing Ghana and arriving in Cape Verde. The year I spent in the States for Portuguese language training was nightmarish. By then, I had already made many mistakes in my life and with my children, but the worst by far was to bring Shen's boyfriend to the United States and allow him to stay in our household while he attended the same high school as Shen. It began her downward spiral to depression and subjected her to unhappiness and abuse before she was mature enough to know how to handle life's harsher lessons. It destabilized our household, and I closed my eyes to it all.

The name Cape Verde was not a misnomer, like Iceland and Greenland, where one was green and the other ice, the opposite of what their names suggested. Once upon a time, Cape Verde, meaning the Green Cape, had earned its name. Overgrazing of livestock from colonial times had reduced the country to a pile of rocks and kept the rain clouds from the ravaged terrains for decades.

Embassy Praia was smaller than Embassy Rekjavik, which reflected the country's size and its relative importance on the U.S. foreign policy agenda. If I had found Ghana lacking in comparison to Vietnam on its ability to coax the land into yielding enough food for its people, Cape Verde was a basket case through no fault of its current inhabitants. The year-round wind was not as cold as its Arctic cousin but equally relentless. Only in isolated, depressed pockets on the land did banana groves flourish and palms sway, lending the land a modest claim to being an island in the tropics.

Just like the land, my now spread-out family withered in isolation. Van moved to a small house we had bought just before leaving the States and served as the girls' in-country guardian. The responsibility of that position and my arbitrary behavior on parenting would be the catalyst that eventually altered Van's relationship with her sisters.

Unlike I, who failed because of a lack of understanding of the psychological quagmire that littered the modern landscape, Van failed because of me. She tried to discipline her sisters the only way she knew—what she had learned from me. I overturned her decisions, undermining her authority with her sisters and making them resent her. In the years between her adolescence and theirs, I had adopted a more liberal outlook in child rearing, become more Americanized, more permissive, quite a different mother from the one Van had known. The distance between Cape Verde and the United States compounded the change. It was easier for an absentee parent to be forgiving; infractions just didn't seem as serious or grievous with the distance of time and space. I also wanted to make up for the loss of their father. My behavior would spawn a sibling resentment that would last for years.

On the streets of Praia, themselves as few as the fruits that struggled to come up from the inhospitable land, I would come into my role as a diplomat. Praia was an easy post to learn Foreign Service work. Political and economic issues were few, and administrative snags were of the simple kind, mere delays in getting consumable and durable goods into the country. Almost invariably, the lags were not a result of government red tapes but simply reflected the practical commercial practice of not stocking infrequently ordered goods, especially those of the quality that would be required by a consumer as peculiar as a foreign embassy.

I quickly learned how the different offices in the Department worked and tapped into the different budgets to renovate the Chancery building, a modest three-story building. Our financial needs were minimal in comparison to those of Embassy Paris, for example, so it was not difficult to get what we wanted.

Like Ghana, these unfortunate isles also gave me a chance to exercise my humanity. It tested my compassion and found it wanting. While I had always had that softening of the heart, I was too one-dimensional to know that it was not enough merely to feel. I embraced that quality as a badge of honor, a gift from Ma and Ba and the Divine, but dispensed it only sparingly. I brought home scrawny, starving dogs and puppies, cats and kittens to shelter and to feed, but ignored equally scrawny and bedraggled bands of kids who stood outside our gate to beg for water.

Sweet water was precious here. Government trucks had to go deep inland, an arduous trek to be sure, to bring water back to the city. The minimal allocation was barely enough for each family's daily needs, so kids and women branched out, loitering near big, rich-looking houses with their bent, twisted, long-salvaged Evian bottles, hoping to get a drink of water.

Our embassy truck was generous enough to fulfill our liberal American needs. It was such that the large tank behind our house was never empty; we even had enough water for a small garden in the back.

I had been warned by my predecessor to temper misplaced compassion. "Before you know it," he said, "hordes of them will show, then what do you do?" The water, after all, was not my personal possession but was paid for by embassy funds. Once the house became known as a place where water could be gotten, more and more would come. Then what?

While the young and old waited, hoping to catch sight of one of the house's occupants, I stayed out of sight, immersing in yet another venture by Clive Cussler's *Dirk Pitt*. Like the waif in Ghana, images of bright-eyed boys and girls and tired, weary women with eyes red, filmy and resigned, would lurk at the edge of my consciousness for always to remind me of those times when, for whatever reason, I failed to respond to that stirring of the heart.

Continents away, Van handled her university education, worked, and tended to her sisters on long weekends. I was flying high on my job, being the administrative officer in charge.

Then the sky fell.

Four months short of her high school graduation, Shen dropped out of school and disappeared. All I could do was weep. What had happened to her? I could get nothing out of Thuy but sensed she knew where Shen was and that all was well. But fear for her future, which had suddenly become uncertain, consumed me. What was her plan? How could she do this to me, to herself? Then she called. She was in Daytona, Florida, with her boyfriend, who had gone there to join a rich uncle. No, she was not sure she would go back to school. She didn't know what she was going to do.

How could a mother let her child go? How could I not want her future, her welfare to be secured? But I had to. I had to stay calm, acting as if all were right again now that she had called. I remembered her younger years, when everything was so easy for me to fix, when all she wanted was me and my attention. I did not know what to do any more but loved her enough to know I had to keep the door open so she could return when she was ready.

For a while I pondered the horrible circumstances that had unfolded. I thought I had done well for my children, so well they had grown up able to take things like food, clothing, a nice house, and a good education for granted. They had gone to a prestigious boarding school and had plenty of friends with whom to enjoy their teenage years. They were supposed to have many such joyful years at college and then a fabulous career and a wonderful family of their own. Yet something had gone wrong.

One day Shen's future was as bright as the sun. The next it was enshrouded in a moonless gloom. I had a road map that I'd thought would easily take her to that glorious future. Now what? But it did not take me long to regroup. I was determined not to let her falter.

I didn't know then that I could not live her life for her.

Whatever else was going wrong, getting off the beaten path to the forgotten isles of Cape Verde allowed me to find my daughter Flavia. She was a six-month-old girl born out of wedlock to a Cape Verdean teenager and a French man. Her birth mother had gone to France to work as a maid for a Cape Verdean family. They promptly sent her back to her family after she had gotten herself pregnant. She ended up giving birth at home with only a teenage friend in attendance.

However barren, Cape Verde did produce this precious child, who was my gift from God, handed to us by her relieved mother on a windy night off the beach in Prainha. Her small face crunched in pain, the result of acute pneumonia, as well as multiple infections, she reached for Acey's hand as her mother handed her over. An ultrasound revealed a severe case of cerebral palsy; she might never be able to talk, walk, or do anything for herself. The chief neurologist at Praia's general hospital suggested that we deliver her to the local orphanage, where she could get decent care for however long her life lasted.

But I could not surrender her to that fate. As long as she lived, I wanted her to have love and to know what it was. Perhaps I could even influence the Fate to gain her mobility and a productive life, despite the dire medical predictions. I could not banish her to an orphanage in a developing country where handicapped children were often neglected and left to die. Praia's orphanage may prove to be different, but I could not take the chance with the baby I had already gotten to know and love.

Flavia got a new name when the adoption papers were drawn— Azura. "Zu" brought happiness back into my life, giving me the opportunity to shower my love and attention on another human being, a child who needed me so much. Shen and Thuy were gone from me; each was becoming more independent each day. It was difficult to let them go, to watch them experience the pain and frustration of growing up and meeting the wrong boys.

It was the hardest thing I had ever done. I let go and did what I thought progressive parents would do, trying to talk sense into my children when all I wanted to do was to lock them up to keep them from the heartbreaks I knew would come. Even as my expectations for them crumbled, I resolved that when they returned from these inconvenient detours, they would succeed, for I could not accept anything less—not for my daughters.

But far as they had strayed from the path, they did not leave me in emptiness and despair but kept me heartened with the knowledge they had grown up to be kind, to be as I had endlessly preached to them. Kindness and compassion was what I knew. Like my ma before me, I wanted to be sure that those lives around my children would be better for having known their touches.

Acey and I settled well in our marriage. There was no great adjustment to be made, as we were both fairly even tempered. We still had to pay off the debt that was left over from my marriage to Pat but managed well enough on what we had. Neither of us was a big spender, so there was no conflicting interest. With no strong opinions on any aspect of our daily routine, we had no ground for disagreement. Owing to his influence, I became more active—playing tennis, jogging on the beach, all of which was a refreshing change from my rather sedate, passive lifestyle with Pat.

Weakened by this lively social agenda, my self-imposed isolation crumbled further when I found Betsy, an island girl from Truk, Micronesia. I met her in my first week at post when we happened to stand next to each other at a reception in honor of the new Chinese ambassador at his residence. Her husband, Steve, was an AID development officer and my colleague at the Mission. Until Betsy, I had no friends and needed none. I had had neither the time nor the inclination to make and keep friends or to engage in the kind of pastimes that embassy women typically enjoyed—shopping, cooking, taking art lessons, sightseeing, participating in humanitarian outreach programs.

Betsy forced her way into my life. Had it not been for her doggedness, we would never have become friends. She would bring lunch to our house on hearing our car rounding the bend, sit, eat, and chat with us, when all I wanted to do was finish lunch quickly to return to some unfinished tasks at the office.

Before long, she got both our families involved in playing tennis and volleyball, camping, fishing, and having barbeque on the beach. Whatever she planned, it was always fun because she was affectionate and giving. Her sweet nature so colored the landscape that the barrenness was gray no longer—ancient lava fields shimmered with joy, playful waves off Sao Francisco jumped and danced and spurred our boogie boards onward to land on golden sands, all in seeming celebration of the zest and love that was Betsy's spirit. Every weekend was a joyous event and every day a blessed day spent in friendship and affection.

From her kitchen, I tasted my first breadfruit.

From her heart, I knew the sweet wonder of a sister's love.

She truly delighted in my company, reluctant and uninspiring as it was many a time, and loved me even when I was at my worst, when I was less than amiable, resisting her every step of the way so as to retreat to the comfortable world I knew, that of solitude.

She made the two years in Cape Verde more than bearable; she made it warm and fun. Her beautiful spirit is gone now, but the heartbreaking memories of the times I spent with her shall always remain. They were her gifts to me, to remind me of the beauty of love and the generosity of the human spirit. They would help warm me as I walked the rest of this journey without her.

When I received the news she had passed, I thought I could feel the atmosphere change. It was as if the world had become a lesser, colder place because she was no longer in it. I did not know what true friendship was until she gave it to me unconditionally. And so it was with her sisterly affection. Tragically, as in the case of my mother, I did not know how precious her love was until it was too late.

FIVE

IN THE NEWS:
10/22/57–SAIGON–THIRTEEN
U.S. SERVICEMEN, FIVE
CIVILIANS INJURED BY
UNCLAIMED BOMBS.

The Orchard, Saigon, Vietnam, 1957

Ba Ngoai died shortly after that afternoon. As was customary, we kept her coffin in the middle of the house for three days so family and friends could come to pay their respect. The one photo we had of her was enlarged and propped on the altar at the head of the casket. Ma would stare at the photo, moan, then sink to her knees and keen like a lost wind.

On the last day of the wake, a strange thing happened that threw everyone into a quandary and stirred the hushed monotony of the mourning scene.

On this day, among the dozens of joss sticks left burning on the altar, three had curled up as they burned, forming perfect spiral columns of ash, losing not one bit of themselves to the ceramic bowl in which they sat. As everyone gathered to witness this preternatural event, a fetid odor emanated from the coffin, sending the women away in fright. But the smell diminished as abruptly as it came. The womenfolk, after the initial shock, returned and gathered around the coffin, taking turns prostrating on the straw mat in front of the altar. The signs were clear. Ba Ngoai's spirit had returned, proven by the curling columns of ash out of the joss sticks. What was more, she was not pleased about something, or someone, judging by the offensive smell she sent forth from the coffin.

The men congregated and watched the women from afar. Some looked quite disturbed and prayed fervently in whispered tones. Among them was Ba, who followed Ma with his eyes as she kneeled and mumbled entreaties to Ba Ngoai. She begged Ba Ngoai to come to her in a dream to let her know what was wrong so she could fix it. Did Ba Ngoai make a promise to someone that she wanted Ma to carry out?

When Ma left to refresh the tea on the altar, Ba took her place on the mat. I stared at the solemn face of Ba Ngoai in the photo and *knew* her displeasure was with me. I went to Ba's side and prostrated next to him. Putting my palms together, I whispered my apology to Grandma. I asked her not to be angry with me for being mean to Aunt Phan's orphaned children and promised not to do it again.

But death did not make a lasting impression on me. All I remember of the funeral procession was a feeling of pride as I sat on a long hearse that was resplendently decked out in gold and silver and sporting along its length two dragons made of cardboard wrapped in gold paper. So that I could easily observe the goings on, I strove to get a seat next to one of the dragons' heads. Unlike the fancy hearse being used here, ours was actually a flatbed truck camouflaged and decorated like a parade float.

Eighth Uncle, being the only surviving son, was dressed in a robe and long trousers, both made of white gauze. He also had on a twine crown, a belt made of twine, and a bamboo cane in his hand. Ma and Seventh

Aunt were likewise garbed, minus the crown and cane. According to tradition, the plain clothing was to demonstrate the extent of our grief—
pride on appearance and status forsaken in the face of sorrow. Eighth
Uncle led the procession of family and friends behind the hearse with
his head hung low and his body bent over the cane in inconsolable grief.
Here and there villagers stood along the road to watch the procession,
talking and pointing at the hearse and the long line of family and friends.
I was sure they were saying how grand the hearse was and how kind my
parents or grandparents must have been to have so many mourners. To
show my face, I sat up straighter at my spot to be more visible to the
spectators. Bicycles, horse wagons, cyclos, and oxen carts moved aside to
let us pass. Ma and Seventh Aunt wailed loudly as they groped their ways
behind Eighth Uncle. Overcome with sorrow, Ma had to be lifted up
from time to time by Ba to stay upright for the procession.

I watched but did not know how painful her loss was to her until it
was my turn to lose my mother.

My ambivalence at Ba Ngoai's passing became even more shapeless
over time, even if Ma continued to mourn her mother. Tears would fill
her eyes every time she walked by the little room that was Ba Ngoai's.
Ba had taken down the door, laying bare the room with its wooden bed
and the little chair that used to hold Ba Ngoai's food tray, where she sat
to stare aimlessly at the world she no longer recognized.

Eventually, Ma moved into Ba Ngoai's room. At noon, when the
sun was hot and her work had been done at the vegetable patch, when
the pigpen had been cleaned and the pigs in slumber, Ma would take a
short rest on the bed that once held her mother's frail and diminished
figure. Her own frame was not all that more substantial as age and lack
of food and nutrition reduced her body to more or less a bag of bones.

While our family and most of the southern poor remained in that all-
familiar poverty, many Catholic northerners steadfastly moved toward
prosperity. "Just enough to eat" was our modest and oft-repeated man-
tra. The northern refugees had squatter rights, bestowed on them by a
grateful president, who had gained considerable prestige by their rejec-

tion of communism and exodus south. Their strong anti-communist stand was just what President Diem needed to fight Ho in the latter's ambition to subsume the south under the communist banner. Diem was the only president I knew, so I gave him the respect befitting his position, even if he was Catholic and my family Buddhist. I defended him against Eighth Uncle's loud criticisms when rumors began to spread about his family's excesses, especially those of his sister-in-law, Madame Nhu, who acted as if she were a queen.

These were the watershed events in our country, but they could have happened in another continent for all the attention my family accorded them. "We always the lowly peasants, the serfs. Who cares who mandarins are," Ma said with the wisdom learned through our long and turbulent history of wars and poverty. "Powermonger's fight, war is—but peasants suffer," the wizened men proclaimed, which was true enough. We lived to serve the rich at peacetime and died serving their causes in war.

As Ma worked hard to keep food on the table, I helped ease some of her burden, if only coincidentally, by keeping my own hunger assuaged in whichever way I could. An accomplished scavenger and hustler, I managed to keep my stomach filled most of the time by using coins earned from running errands for this or that cousin or workers in the field. To make up for the dismal food tray, Ma tried to come up with little treats at mid-day to tide us over until the evening meal.

A small bag of boiled peanuts or half a dozen fruits was all it took for us to whoop with glee and rush to her side. I remembered the tears I shed in one of those rare occasions when she came home without treats. Her face crumbled as she brushed past me to go in the house, while I bawled at her retreating back, "But I am hungry." She whipped her head around and hissed, "No money, you know, no money! What do I buy with—chicken feces?" Tears streaming down my face, I yelled from the top of my lungs, "I hate you, you are ugly, and…I ha-hate you." Even though blinded with tears and anger, I was still mindful enough to watch her so as to prepare my escape just in case a cane was coming, but not before I saw her sad, sad face, which I mistook for displeasure with me. Later, much too late for me and her, I would know that it was a look of pain for failing to provide for her children, to bring about the joy that she accepted as her responsibility.

Ma did not have enough money for our main meals, let alone snack foods. In order to come up with the snacks, she had to spend an inordinate amount of time ingratiating herself either with any relative who was well off and who was sure to have a plate of fruits or treats on an altar just waiting to be dispensed of or with her friends the street hawkers.

She would stop at a fruit stand, chat for a while, then offer to walk to a well in the neighborhood to draw a pail of water for the wash bucket, peel a papaya, or cut up a ripened jackfruit. For her good-natured solicitude and an hour or two of work, the vendor would give her a handful of whatever food was slow selling that day, for the kids. Those were the times I resented my cousins the most—when Ma came home with only a handful of treats and I had to share. As it was, grubby little hands shot out from different directions as Ma dug into her huge pockets for the goodies. Sometimes, two hands would extend from one body, well placed to disguise their common origin. It was up to the rest of us to detect the offender and push his extra hand out of the way. Bong was special; he always got the best piece.

SIX

IN THE NEWS: 5/2/57–SENATOR
JOSEPH MCCARTHY DIES
AT THE AGE OF 48.

The Orchard, 1957
The Refugees from the North

Just as having five extra children in the household altered the dynamics of our little family, so
did the influx of Catholic northerners change
the southern landscape. Churches sprung up,
and farmland gave way to dwellings—from
lean-tos to shiny tin-roofed, one-room structures, to square little stucco houses squeezing
to fit on lots smaller than they were. Indeed,
there were frequent altercations on boundary encroachment, which had previously been
unheard of in the sparsely populated south.

The change did come very close to home,
literally. That was how I knew. You see, there

was a dirt road that ran along one side of the barbed wire fence of the compound. I still remember the red color of the dirt. In the dry season, it would get kicked up by passing cattle onto the orange and white bougainvillea blooms, which overhung the road from the meteorological station just across the way. The lane was not very wide; we had not thought it could accommodate houses.

In one week, posts were planted, beams set, and roofs of every conceivable material went up—from thatch to scavenged bits of tin, which were flattened by hammers and nailed together in a haphazard, patchwork pattern, to a strange mixture of both. The menagerie of different materials gave off a rather strange and interesting look. To a child's eyes, it was as if the entire street had dressed up to play house. When it was over, a five-foot-wide path remained to serve as the frontage for the new row of homes.

The refugees' needs were boundless. Spotting the short stubs of sugarcane left standing on our harvested field, they asked for permission to scavenge. One nod was all it took. Hordes of them—men, women, and children—swarmed across the barbed wire fence and over the field, taking every bit of cane, including the discarded tips, which were considered useless by us in the south. As we watched, they shucked cane tops off wilted leaves, dropped the cane pieces into a burlap bag, then bundled the leaves together. "Very flammable. Good kindling." A woman with blackened teeth raised a handful of leaves to Ba. They hooted and laughed at Ba's astonished look and furrowed eyebrows.

Even the rubbish heap at the edge of the field did not escape ravishment. The scavengers collected pieces of worn rubber tire "to make shoes"; one of the older men smiled ruefully and pointed at his feet, a gesture one would make among a foreign audience to facilitate comprehension. They too must have felt that they were in foreign territory. That was all Ba had to see. How much they needed! He searched around the compound, ventured into the little warehouse, and even our house, for anything that could be of use to our new neighbors in setting up their households.

The boys and I watched in fascination. They were like an army of ants, these foreigners in our midst. To us, they did look foreign. Most peculiar were their blackened teeth and the lilting tone of their language, which sounded familiar, and yet was not readily comprehensible.

"The northern dialect," Eighth Uncle informed us after a week or so of interacting with the foreigners, "is not hard to understand. Only some words are different. In context, you make out what they say. Very easy." We listened avidly to his proclamation, for Eighth Uncle was wise and seemed to have unlimited time and patience in deciphering these strange events in our lives, even if he forever had difficulty in holding a job. Ma thought he was lazy. Ba was more forgiving. He decided Eighth Uncle was really bright. On account of his being too bright, he just got bored and listless in menial labor jobs, which were the only jobs for which he was qualified to do having had only a third-grade education. He was a brilliant car mechanic, however. Ba supposed even that routine bored Eighth Uncle.

Although I could not immediately comprehend the northerners' manner of speech, I knew how much they had suffered. For it was during the height of their "invasion" of the south that the government began showing films—propaganda films, Eighth Uncle called them—at churches and schoolyards around the city. On a wide screen in the middle of the dusty ground at what would be my elementary school, we gathered nightly for days to watch the horrors that drove these people south. The films were grainy and the sounds crackled, but the images did not need much clarity. They conveyed the indisputable horror that had befallen our new neighbors, whose crimes were no more than ownership of land. Film after film, the almost identical images flashed on the screen. Land-owning peasants at different villages were being buried up to their necks in open fields and then decapitated by tractors. The victims' faces showed utter terror— eyes widened with fright, mouths opened to silent screams—while their children stood in rags and clutched on to one another at a distance, faces stricken with grief and fear.

We watched the scenes in horror. The women clucked their tongues and shook their heads, while the men gathered to discuss the communist menace. A few, like Eighth Uncle, were skeptical and voiced aloud their suspicion that the films had been fabricated by the Diem government to turn popular sentiments against the Communists. I did not have any doubt. I was sure that the Communists, whoever, whatever they were, did just as the films showed. After all, it had to be bad, or why would the northerners leave their homes to come south with barely the clothes on their backs?

Ma was forever feeling sorry for them. "*Toi nghiep qua,*" or very pitiful or poor souls, was a sentiment pervasive throughout our society. It explained our propensity to go for the underdogs. Eighth Uncle, in one of his less anti-establishment moments, said that such was one of the reasons those Communist bosses in the north found sympathy among southern peasants who could not have cared less about ideology but were only stirred by what seemed to them a lopsided fight—one standing tall and powerful in the light of day; the other, weak and hungry, furrowing in tunnels and swamps to emerge only at night to scavenge for food.

We knew why the northerners had fled south. What we did not readily discern was how different they were from us. How industrious and full of guile! Only much later did I learn how this might have come to be. Vietnam, like any other land, influenced its inhabitants' way of life and molded their values, even temperaments, in a natural flow of evolution. The land north just happened to be so unforgiving that it required more of man's skills and faculties—his best. He would become industrious and resourceful, as well as ingeniously cunning. He needed his best to conquer the elements, to extract every grain of rice and every morsel of fruit from the harsh land. He would be lauded for his ingenuity and hard work. But when pitted against a different adversary—his fellow man—his best would become his worst, for those ruthless survival skills left un-tempered would render him sly and amoral.

By the stroke of a pen, the Geneva Accords came to be, sending these cunning children of the north, that hardy, capable breed, to the balmy, hospitable, gentle land south of the 17th parallel, where the natives were modest in ambitions and guileless on life.

It was another case of evolution gone haywire. Fortunately, humans being adjustable creatures as they were, the ecological catastrophe was not realized—the entire southern species was not destroyed by those ruthless northern invaders. At the end, the southerners did not become unduly impoverished, even if they did lose the best land and the more lucrative economic opportunities to their northern and central brethrens. But it did take another twist of fate to avoid the disaster. The deepening of the north-south conflict, or, rather, the American aid dollars, arrived just in time. The economy heated up; the madness took hold and galloped into the future.

But prosperity would remain elusive for the southern poor. Generations of poverty had diminished our imagination and impaired ambition. To plan for the unattainable meant to generate discontent, so we didn't. Southern inertia and the Buddhist teaching of moderation then set in to keep us at our lowly class.

SEVEN

IN THE NEWS: 6/58–U.S.
SUPREME COURT BANNED
PASSPORT DENIAL TO
SUSPECTED COMMUNISTS.

The Orchard, 1958

The fires of battle erupted across the delta. The wizened men debated what was to be done about Madame Nhu, President Diem's notorious sister-in-law. "Diem had to get rid of her. Imagine, bathing in camel milk, and we have no food to eat. What a greedy, arrogant creature."

But the nation's political problems soon retreated to the periphery of our thoughts. For the war had reached inside our gate and delivered a casualty at the doorstep of Elderly Ninth Master, an old scholar who lived in a thatched hut just beyond the pigpen. He and his two sons had earned the right for abode in the compound in the same way we had—his older son had been working there for a long time.

Big Brother An, his younger son, had been affable and helpful to everyone and sometimes more of a brother to me than Bong was. His death on a battlefield somewhere in the deep Mekong delta devastated his father and shocked many in the hamlet. Ma tried to explain the reason for the good to die young. "They paid off karmic debts meant for this life; now they reincarnate to a better one."

That did not stop us from mourning his death. He had just finished basic military training. Eighth Uncle lambasted the government and the military school. "What they teach him in training that he not even survive a month in battle?" We took Uncle's words grimly. Ma looked apprehensively at the young faces of my cousins and Bong, possibly seeing the doomed destinies of the future conscripts, and the light went out of her eyes.

A gloom hung over the house of Elderly Ninth Master. A small photo of Big Brother An sat on the mantel, eyes bright and full of laughter. His death turned the house into a tomb, and its occupants, shadows of wraith. He would be the first of many young men in the hamlet to die in the war. Most of them were extraordinarily kind. Their swift deaths became a validation of the myth that only the good die young. I found certain assurance in the myth; I thought I would live long then because I was so contrary.

The rain eased, but before the clouds gave way to the hard blue sky of the dry season, a remnant of storms remained to spawn another tragedy, this time right in our household. Big Brother Luong disappeared from home one day. Questions on his whereabouts were met with angry retorts. "Children so nosy, such busy body, go play." Hushed conversations followed between Ma and Ba, Ma and Eighth Uncle, Ma and Seventh Aunt. Then Ma grabbed her cone hat and set out for destinations unknown. She would return but only to sit with Ba and sob. Work at the patch seemed forgotten. Only the pigs' loud protests could return her to the mundane task of caring for them. In the early-morning hour of the third day, she woke me up early and told me to change. We were taking Big Brother Luong to Cu Chi.

She had changed to her traveling clothes—a pair of newer black pants, dark brown blouse, and a dark scarf for her head. Ba fed the pigs; then the three of us sat down and ate a meal of rice and dried, salted fish. "*An dang bung*," or eat to settle our stomachs, meant eat just enough for the trip. At last, I learned that I was to come along so the police would not be suspicious of her and Big Brother Luong. I was scared at the mention of police, even though I did not know why they would be interested in us or why we were heading to Cu Chi.

Ma and I moved briskly through the deserted streets. My every sense was alert. I felt it was my duty to stay on guard since I was brought along to help detect and deflect suspicion. From deep in the thicket of huts and lean-tos, a wistful cock crowed as if to rush the dawn. There was not another soul on the road.

From the distance came the *click … clack … click … clack … kecha … k echa … kecha* sounds of pedals turning and wheels whirring, just as we made the turn down Cowshed Alley. Fortunately, the sounds did not follow but became more distant as we moved deeper into the alley. Ma kept glancing furtively behind us while lengthening her strides toward the largest cow corral in the hamlet. Several cows shifted; one lowed softly at our approach. Out of the shadowy depths of the corral, Big Brother Luong emerged, dressed in a pair of black cotton pajamas in perfect blend with the night.

We walked to the crossroads at Lang Cha Ca, where a multitude of horse wagons awaited their first passengers. The horses snorted and neighed while wagon masters exchanged the latest gossips atop rickety stools at a roadside coffee stand—wizened men in training. We climbed on one wagon and waited for it to be filled. One by one the passengers arrived. Five more got on before we pulled away from the stand.

The air turned cool as the wagon moved out of the city and into the farm country. We kept warm enough with shared body heat, sitting close to one another on the straw mat with knees drawn up to our chins. The wagon took us northwesterly to Cu Chi, where, at a small market on the side of a dirt road, we got off.

Into the deepening dawn we made our way on foot. Nature was stirring, but there was still no one about. For a while, there was no sound but the echoes of our steps. I heard a cricket sing lustily and wondered how big and ferocious he was; he definitely sounded like a good fighter. I almost forgot the mission at hand, so busy I was in scanning the weeds for a dot of color and a sign of puffed-up wings.

A pair of mangy dogs trotted toward us with tails wagging—no doubt on their way to the market for scraps. I noticed the yellow one, skeletal except for the size of her teats, which almost touched the ground. I tugged on Ma's hand and whispered, "Ma, look at her teats. She has babies and so skinny."

"That's right, poor thing, *toi nghiep qua*. You want to give her your dumpling?" I reached into my pocket for the dumpling Ma had bought for me at the market, broke it in two, and tossed both pieces to the dogs.

The sight of an approaching oxen cart startled Ma. She whispered to Big Brother Luong, "Quick, quick, look the other way." The cart drew closer. I smiled at the driver and called out my hello, "*Chao Bac*," while Ma and Big Brother Luong made themselves all the more conspicuous by turning their heads to look at the field, pretending they had not heard the only sound on the road, that of the clacking wooden wheels. I pointed this out to Ma later, only to earn a withering look. It was clear she was not in the mood to be corrected. Worse, she was in a correcting mood. She thought I was drawing undue attention to us by being solicitous to the wagon driver.

When at last we reached a coconut grove, Ma pointed to a rotted palm stump and told me to sit and wait while she and Big Brother Luong followed the meandering path deep into the grove to disappear behind a stand of bushes. Alone, I walked to the nearby "*trang*" flower bush, picked a flower head, and settled down to wait. As the sun gilded the swaying coconut fronds with flashes of gold and the wind feathered my face with soft whispers, I plucked free the hollow, needle-like petals of the flower and sucked greedily on their nectar.

I watched peasants in their black pajamas and cone hats working the distant fields and tall bamboo poles going up and down rhythmically at the wells as water was being drawn for the crops. Growing tired of following the poles with my eyes, then my head as I mimicked the up-and-down motions, I wandered off to the patch opposite to investigate the green growth. My heart hummed at the familiar sight of peanut plants. I squatted down and yanked up a thick clump. The roots broke free from the fluffy soil, even encumbered as they were with thick, mature peanuts along their lengths. I settled back down on the stump to enjoy the raw taste of the nuts and later staving off my thirst with tiny, wild fruits from a nearby vine.

The sun was riding high on the sky by the time Ma came back, alone. She dropped down on an adjacent palm stump and, in tearful mumbles, told me she had just delivered Big Brother Luong to the other side, the guerillas. Fear consumed me, for I knew what that meant.

On the way home, when her continuous sobbing caught the inquiring glances of fellow passengers on the wagon, I knew the nature of my assignment so immediately undertook to deflect suspicion. I tugged at a corner of Ma's scarf and wiped her tears with it while patting her face and consoling, "Ma, Ma, not cry. He is gone. We can't bring him back." To the curious faces around us, I confided desolately with a convincing little pout. "My brother died fighting the enemy."

I thought I had handled that rather well, letting potential police informers know we were loyal to the government. But Ma told me later I should not have said what I had. "There could have been a Communist guerilla on the wagon. No need to let him know which side we are on."

We got home just before nightfall, and the night, when it came, was eerily still and watchful. We gathered around the oil lamp and waited for Ma to compose herself. The wick slowly burned down and the light dimmed, blurring the tears on her face. In a subdued voice, she told us of the big secret about Big Brother Luong. He had gotten involved with a scoundrel named Hon, who was caught stealing some steel from a construction site the week before. Under "questioning" by police, he told them that Big Brother Luong was an accomplice, even though Big Brother Luong was not and, in fact, was nowhere near the site at the time of the theft.

After having been informed of this by an acquaintance at the police station, she immediately sent Big Brother Luong into hiding while figuring out what do to, for she could not let him face the brutal police. A friend of a relative suggested sending him upcountry to the guerillas until things settled. It was either that or getting him enlisted in the military. Ma thought the guerillas would be safer. After all, didn't we just lose Big Brother An after only one month in battle? She said she had told Big Brother Luong specifically to stay low, to hide, not to fight. "Just hide in the bush for a while then find your way home," were her parting words to him.

We were not to reveal this to anyone. If it got to the wrong ear, Ba and Ma could get arrested and tortured. Ma already regretted sending Big Brother Luong away. She had thought to save him by doing this. Now, instead of a common criminal, he had become an enemy of the state, and we, his accomplices. The brutal "*cong an*," or secret police, would have no mercy. To make sure we knew of the potential danger, she retold the story of Old Lady Nam, an acquaintance and a vegetable farmer. Because of a rumor that she was sending money to her son, who supposedly had joined the guerillas, she was kept at the police station and tortured for days. They finally let her go home, but not before she had been destroyed by the physical assaults. They had attached electrodes to her genitals and nipples, laughing and taunting all the while as she screamed and begged. She returned home a shell of a human being, bedridden as she lost the use of her legs. Her laughter was gone; her speech barely audible.

We never saw Big Brother Luong again. The news of his fate came two years later. He died about a year after we had dropped him off behind that coconut grove. The same woman who had advised Ma to send him away was the one who brought the news. Ma screamed at her, "Go, go, what else you want from me? Why I listen to you? Why I send my son away to die?" As the woman sidled hesitantly out the door, Ma dropped onto the floor, wailing and beating her head on the ground. I swallowed that last mouthful of rice with difficulty, for my throat had clogged up. Mai, the youngest girl in the brood of children Aunt Phan had left behind for Ma, cried and babbled, "Ma, Ma, *Anh Luong chet ha Ma?* Did Big Brother Luong die?"

Ba closed his eyes and held his head in his hands, while Ma mumbled mindlessly, "Give them, give them what they want. We are so poor. What else they want from us. Big Rat, Little Rat, Ngau, Bong, they all have to fight the enemy... they all are going to die."

Whenever I thought of that afternoon, I realized she cared not who had to surrender what; she just wanted us to be left alone, to live our modest lives in peace. Her wish was always humble; she did not want to risk offending God by being greedy. She should not have worried. At its most flagrant, her wish would have been capped at having enough food on the tray with a little extra for special offering days like Tet and death anniversaries.

We did not even have his body for burial.

Perhaps it was better that way. How were we to explain his death? But it was difficult for Ma. A sentimental and open person who wore her heart on her sleeve, her suffering was made worse because she could not openly mourn his death. What pained her more still was that without a funeral and the traditional rites, she believed his soul was still wandering where he had died, not knowing how to find the way home, then to the other side and reincarnation. He would be one of those lost souls, drifting, always drifting at twilight with no one to make offerings and no one to guide him home.

EIGHT

IN THE NEWS:
11/5/60–VIETNAM–U.S.
OFFICIALS AMBUSHED
BY GUERILLAS.

The Orchard, 1960

Just as the land took, it gave. After annihilation came creation. To make up for death, it gave life. A bumper crop burst forth from the orchard and the old mango tree. I would steal away to the site of the old orange tree with a couple of green mangoes. Ensconced in the warm hollow, I chewed on the crisp, crunchy young fruits and feasted my eyes on still more bounty around me. Fruits hung heavily on every branch in sight. I knew how much Ma mourned Big Brother Luong, so I kept searching for that elusive fruit that would be perfect for his altar. Ma had asked Elderly Ninth Master to write a small banner in

Chinese calligraphy, stating Big Brother Luong's name and age, which she then glued onto a bamboo stick with a pinch of cooked rice. Big Brother Luong didn't read Chinese, and neither did we. Nevertheless, the old language remained one used for worshipping the departed.

The tablet stood lonely in a slightly chipped water glass. It was all we had left of Big Brother Luong. Quite simply, he did not live long enough to know the luxury of having his photo taken.

The riches of the land finally extended to our kitchen table. There were basketfuls of wild, edible greens to steam or mix with dried shrimps for a delicious salad or tasty soup. A few eggs from the hen's basket, two spoons of lard, a few sprigs of green onion, and we had a main entrée to complete the meal. At dusk, especially after a rain, there was a musty scent of richness that the soil and vegetation sent forth in praise of the temperance of the season. Frogs and toads croaked loudly, lending voice to the pervasive contentment that enshrouded our home and my orchard.

As night deepened and fireflies looped and danced wildly in the inky darkness of the orchard, we would settle around the old oil lamp of the flickering flame. Once, I had suspected that such was the doing of ghosts, but Ba said it was the wind. I kept on wondering how a wind could touch the flame through the glass chimney until one night. I had heard about experiments, so thought I would conduct my own.

I gulped in a mouthful of air, making myself look like a half toad, then blew hard on the side of the glass chimney. The flame remained solid. With that possibility eliminated, there was only one thing left to try. I flicked my hand forcefully over the opening, mimicking a passing gust of wind. Sure enough, the flame danced. Still, I had to make certain. So I took in another pocket of air, hovered over the chimney, then blew as hard as I could. The flame sputtered and died, causing the kids to scream in excitement and fright and Ma to shout for Ba to relight. For my brilliant success, I was scolded and banished to the thick edge of the shadow, where I soon found another lively diversion, such as using my naked legs as bait to lure mosquitoes, then swatting and taking their bloody, squished carcasses to put on the knees of Ma's pants to show her I still had some redeeming qualities.

To do homework, we would assume the favored spots nearest to the flame. In the outer edge of the circle, Ma tended to her mending while Ba sat in the half shadow, listening to a program of classical opera on the radio. He would get up once or twice during the course of one evening to get his smoking pipe. The sound from the radio would be drowned out for a few moments by the gurgling noises of water and his indrawn breaths... *puff...puff...* at which time Ma would turn around and glare at him in disgust. She thought smoking, especially smoking that potent, foul stuff brought south by the northerners, would be the death of him yet.

His racking coughs, during and after smoking, would start her nagging. She said for sure he had tuberculosis, that it was only a matter of time before he would start coughing up blood and die of the disease like Aunt Phan and her husband. He laughed and dismissed her warning with a wave of his hand.

"Sooner or later, we all have to die. Why afraid?"

She would snap, half in jest, "You only worry about yourself. Uh huh... I know you are ready to go. You go, you free. Go, go, let me raise the kids alone. You lazy bum."

Ba smiled sheepishly and dropped the issue, wisely conceding defeat lest she loosen a fresh volley of biting words at him.

We learned to study amid the noises. In between Ba's blowing bubbles into the smoking pot and Ma's nagging, there were sounds of hands slapping on naked legs, arms, and faces, as mosquitoes swarmed all around and buzzed near our ears. Even Kiki did not escape this fate. Now and again, he would wipe one of his front legs against his face or wag his tail to shoo away the merciless feeders. Only wind provided a measure of relief. The breeze would come through the front door and the windows, dispersing some of the greedy bloodsuckers and sending the flame on a wild dance. Sometimes the rain would follow, drumming on the tin roof like bullets from a machine gun. The wind would pick up, and huge droplets of water would blow in and splatter, causing us to jump and shriek with exaggerated glee.

After I finished with homework, I would play with my shadow on the wall, using fingers and fists to create different animal figures. Ma would look up from her mending and scold, "Not play with your shadow, it come and haunt you in sleep tonight."

Her warning usually stopped me on my track. It was bad enough to worry about being haunted by wandering spirits; I certainly did not want to be harassed by my own shadow. But I did not want to lose face by stopping what I was doing right then and there just on her saying so. I would mumble something like, "That's not true," before flashing another image on the wall in a show of bravado. But I was nothing if not clever; I made sure that this last showing was done so quick that not even my shadow knew I was playing with it.

Forced to abandon the shadow game, I would turn my attention to something else, like pretending to swat a mosquito on my brother's face or the back of his neck when he was not paying attention. *Whack*... I would deliver the slap with force and accuracy, then sail over chairs, bodies, whatever it took to get to Ba's or Ma's side for protection, screaming all the while, "Mosquito! Ma, Ba, Bong's going to hit me. There was really a mosquito."

I loved the nights of the full moon. Following the fruit offerings to God, Buddha, and other deities, it was storytelling time. Ghost stories mostly. After the evening meal, Ba would drag his canvas cot to the middle of the yard around which we would gather. By the time night descended and darkness framed the round, yellow moon, the macabre tale had already been spun.

No one told ghost stories better than Ma. Her tendency to exaggerate added a certain dramatic flair to the tales. The Vietnamese had this way of accentuating the dramatics. "Work someone to death" or even "sick to death" are popular western metaphors. The Vietnamese take it a little further. In the language, one could do almost anything to death. Any state of being can be done to death—"sad to death, laugh to death, tired to death, funny to death," and so on. Among the dramatists par excellence, Ma was the reigning queen.

One story was her favorite, I supposed because it involved another person in the audience—me. Even though I could not remember the incident in question, since I was only two years old when it happened, I played into it for the attention. There were not that many ghost stories; the tales just got better and more bone chilling with each retelling, especially by a storyteller as gifted as Ma. The one that involved me had been told countless times, but ghost stories never really got stale, you see, so there it was again, on one night of the full moon. By her opening words, all could tell what was to come. A few pair of eyes shifted from her to me in heightened anticipation. From behind Ba, I sat up a little straighter. Ma began.

"It was dusk when I come home from Old Lady Hai's. I knew I stay long, so asked Ba not to wait for me, but to cook rice for Bong and him to eat with the leftover stewed catfish ... "

This part was not necessary to the story, except that it explained why she was not at home by dusk, for everyone knew her routine. This little detail also helped establish Ba as another one of her accomplices, lending further credence to the tale.

She paused and looked at Ba. "You remember? That day when I not come home until very late?" Ba nodded and murmured something, or perhaps he was moaning in exasperation. "Anyway, *con-Long-ne* was with me." The storyteller paused for maximum effect. It worked. All eyes fell on me.

"It was getting dark, so I walked fast." This, I was sure, was hard for anyone to imagine, for Ma was always rushing about as if in a race. Forever perceptive, she could tell what everyone was thinking, so she snorted loudly. "Well, I was carrying Long on my back. We reached the barbed wire fence ... " She gestured in the general direction of the fence, about a quarter mile from the mango tree. Eyes followed her hand, a few dangling feet drawn up to the respective bearer's chest on the cot. "I stooped and snaked through the fence, almost step on the wire, you know the one."

A few murmurs acknowledged the very wire she was referring to—the third one down, closest to the ground, so bent from frequent trespassing it almost got buried under the dirt. "I bent low so con-Long's head not touch the overhung branches. You know how she scared of caterpillars. I not want any to get on her head...heh heh heh."

She giggled at this comment, as if my fear was something to be laughed about. I glowered at her. All eyes shifted back on me. I could almost feel the tiny legs of caterpillars on the nape of my neck. The storyteller continued. "A boy, no shirt, with only a pair of black shorts—a poor boy for sure—suddenly appeared on the path and started to follow us...*phinh phic, phinh phic*...I hear his footsteps...I was scared to death. I began to pray...*Brrrr*..." She shivered dramatically.

I turned my head ever so slowly and peered into the gray shadows of the orchard to see if the boy spirit was lurking there. Under the silvery moonlight, the trees looked more ghostly than had they been covered in total darkness. Black on gray, the hazy scene looked like it came from another world. A wind came through, rattling leaves and branches. I pressed closer, pushing against Ba's back. I could imagine myself on Ma's back with the child ghost following us. Why, he could have pulled me off Ma's back, hidden me in the bush, and stuffed clay in my mouth to stop me from calling out for help. In case you wonder about this bit with the clay, it was well known that ghosts would use clay if it was available. Otherwise, clumps of plain old dirt would do, just so the victims could not cry out for help. This kind of antics never got anyone killed though, just scared mindless for a while—up to a day I was told.

Eighth Uncle burped. The kids screamed and shifted. On this night, the cot creaked and sagged. Ba yelled for us to get off, but it was too late. A loud tear and we were dislodged onto the ground.

Somewhere in the dark, a lost bird called, and the rustlings picked up as if there were ghosts at play. The kids screamed in fright and ran into the house, toward the pool of light around the oil lamp. I scrambled to Ma and huddled at her side while Ba examined the tear on the cot. He clucked his tongue and shook his head at the damage. Not wanting to let go of the mood, even if most of the audience was gone, Ma continued. "Hmm, I was so scared." She shuddered violently like a medium experiencing a soul entering her body and made the *brrrr* sound for special effect. "*Long's-dad-ne*, we have to remember to make offerings to him." Ba folded up the cot and mumbled something like, "All right, but no one seen him but you."

Ma stood up, brushed the seat of her pants indignantly, and snapped, "You just not know anything." Ba chuckled softly as she sauntered off inside. Up the high chair she climbed and brought down a plate of fruits from the altars to divide among us.

NINE

The Orchard, 1961

A product of the time, our life was remarkably simple. In the distant future, I would know of the angst of modern living—the stress and pressure that came with wealth and progress. But there was none of that in the threadbare existence of wartime Vietnam. It was life at its most elemental. There was not much anxiety about privations, thanks to the age-old wisdom of managing expectations.

The daily chores kept us occupied and centered. There was comfort in the certainty that if we did what we were supposed to, the payoff would come, and food would be there. It was part of my chores to tend to the ducks every morning, just as it was Ma's to cater to the pigs and the vegetable patch, and Ba's to sweep the yard, clean the coops, and feed the chickens. Before dawn even emerged, Ma had already had her coffee with Ba, fed the pigs, and gotten off to the patch and the search for food. On her rushing out, Ba would settle down on the divan for a bout of puffing at his smoking pot. As soft light bathed the orchard and dew-laden leaves stretched to greet the oncoming dawn, he would wander out into the yard, grab the bucket of feed from the henhouse, and head to one corner of the verandah. With one hand holding on to the bucket, he used the other to lift the different coops to release all the mother hens, each with her brood of baby chicks. Like their human family, the fowls also knew their daily routine well, and so they stuck close to Ba until the moment when he clucked his tongue and food came showering down. Roosters, hens, and baby chicks gathered within the arc of his toss, gobbling up the un-husked rice so quickly that they made me dizzy just by watching. While they fed, I grabbed the small spade Ba had fashioned for me and led the ducklings through the orchard to those moist patches of earth with telltale signs of worm. There I dig up colonies of worms for them to feed.

For each crop of ducks I helped raise, I earned enough from the sale to buy a few ducklings, baby chicks, or feed for my own crop of fowl. My long-term goal was to save enough to buy a calf—the one that Ba'd always talked about. The patch of grass at the far end of the compound was still rich and green, apparently awaiting that calf Ba had promised us years ago. That was to be our ticket to more food, better food, perhaps even wealth. But that grand plan remained just that—a plan, first for Ba, then me. It seemed destined not to be, for every time I had money in my pocket, either Ba or Ma would need a loan. The repayment sometimes took months to come, but I didn't mind. The pride and joy of being the catalyst that changed the color of my parents' day was worth any money I had to relinquish.

My sometimes-lending career went on until one afternoon when Ma arrived home to find me sitting on the hammock, staring longingly at the soup peddler who lingered at the edge of the yard, obviously hoping for a sale. Ma asked where my money was, that I should still have the money from the sale of two hens from merely days before. I told her Ba had borrowed it.

I had been only a little sad. She made it worse by looking at me with so much sympathy. In response, my heart throbbed with self-pity. Soon the throbbing gave way to tears that flowed like little rivers down my face. My stomach chose to protest loudly at the same time. When her curses had died down, Ma came up with an idea—that of locking my money in gold to keep it safe. The next time I had money, I was to buy gold jewelry—a pair of earrings, a bracelet, or a necklace. The price of gold always increased, which was certainly an added bonus.

She didn't count on Ba using it as collateral for a loan at the jewelry-*cum*-pawn shop. She cursed him out well and good when she didn't see my necklace at mealtime. At the next pig sale, she bought my necklace back from the shop and warned Ba in no uncertain terms not to con me out of it again, that he should be embarrassed for hocking his daughter's only piece of jewelry. Even as she lectured and warned, she knew saying no to him was almost impossible. I was as tenderhearted as she. A soft word from Ba, a sagging of the shoulders, and we would have surrendered whatever we had.

My fowl-raising enterprise was profitable, but only at the pleasure of the god of fortune. By the speed of a passing wind, the flu of the season could sweep through and take all our hope with it. The virulent flu did strike hard one year. When it was over, only two hens and a rooster remained of over two dozen fowls. All of mine perished. It was not a total loss since we managed to sell some of the carcasses, though cheaply, to the ice-cream peddler and the scrap heap dealer and had delicious meals for over two weeks, but it was devastating because, as always, so much hope was riding on it.

This time, I needed a new school outfit. The one we had bought at the beginning of the year would have lasted until the following *Tet*, the Vietnamese or lunar new year, if I had not taken a dare and executed a high jump over the hedgerow at school and gotten caught in the protruding nails on the barbed wire fence. Ma mended the pants, but I could not wear them to school for much longer. It was a matter of face. No one could miss that huge patch on the seat of my pants. How was she going to keep her head up among her acquaintances?

After agonizing for a time, she thought of Little Second Older Sister, a generous and kind first cousin who was enjoying a taste of prosperity through a brothel she operated that was doing well with the influx of American servicemen. Rumor had it that the business was growing so fast she had to recruit five more girls from Tra Vinh and also rented the house next door to expand her enterprise.

I hopped on the bike for the ride to her house. I was told not to enter the house since Ma didn't want to risk her friends seeing me at the supposed place of depravity. So I sat at the coffee stand on the sidewalk opposite and waited for one of the house's occupants to emerge to send words to my cousin. In the space of an hour, I watched several American soldiers leaving and entering; their uniforms looked dirty and unkempt, as if they had just come in from the field. They looked out of place among the plain tin-roof homes. There were no restaurants or shops nearby, no reason at all for them to be there, save one.

Then a girl came out. She looked young and pretty in her gossamer white, sleeveless pajamas. So transparent, they showed her pink panties and matching bra. She was clearly country bred, with coarse features—big nose, dark skin, and hair bleached slightly red by the sun. As I watched her approach, I knew her skin probably had that acrid smell of sunburn. Ma said that was the smell of the coolie, the poor, who had to labor long and hard in the sun.

I had to smile at the way she walked. She waddled in that peculiar way Eighth Uncle always made fun of, bowlegged like. He said that was how one could tell a prostitute from other women, even from a distance. It was the way they walked. "Too much sex, that's all. They spread their legs too often, for far too long, they can't close them back up." I didn't know whether I could really believe Eighth Uncle since Ma had shushed him, telling him to be quiet, that he was talking nonsense. However, the girl looked comfortable enough, in spite of her strange gait.

I waited until she had finished placing her order before asking her to let Little Second Older Sister know I was there. All at once, her eyes lit up as if I were *her* long-lost relative and proceeded to treat me as such, ordering an iced white coffee for me to drink while I waited.

I got the money I needed for the clothing, plus some for school supplies and a little extra. Little Second Older Sister gave me a lot more than I had asked for, quite enough to cover a couple of days of market for Ma, and also to have my hair cut for school.

I did not get as much supplies as I had hoped—fewer pieces of chalk, one less notebook, and a stinging lecture when Ma found out that I had lost some of the money playing "kick the feathered pad" against my cousin Hoang.

The game was similar to "hacky-sack." Instead of using a bag full of beans, we used a multi-layer plastic disc the size of a silver dollar, which clang together with each kick, generating a rather melodic sound. Out of the middle of this stack of round disc jutted a tall feather that was anchored to the bottom disc. The point of the game was to keep the feathered pad up in the air by kicking it with the inner side of the sole of the foot. The kicks were counted out; whoever kept the pad up the longest would win.

No sooner did the rain stop than the air became cooler, and Tet came. It was everyone's most favorite time of the year, a time of hope and renewal. A Tet of abundance showed a year well spent and prefaced a better one ahead. A modest Tet celebration simply strengthened one's resolve to do better after entreaties had been made to Buddha and God.

It was not a time to misstep, because anything that happened during Tet was likely to be replicated throughout the year. For me, I thought it would be wise to avoid being spanked. Ba laughed when I told him that I was going to be good for Tet so I would not get spanked so much any more. I had thought it would impress on him my contrition, my willingness to conform. But he said it was possible the taboo did not apply to me, about the spanking, since regardless of what I did, I was getting spanked throughout the year anyway. I was simply too stubborn, too disobedient. He chuckled, as if the image of my getting so punished was funny.

We relied on Ma's vegetable and flower harvests, timed to sell in the week of Tet, to fill our larder and the cooking pots. That meant we had to get the best prices for our crops. Whenever the broker's offer was not good enough, we would sell our goods in the market hoping to increase our take by eliminating the middleman's cut.

I would always remember that first occasion. On the day before the Eve of Tet, we arrived at Ma's vegetable patch late in the afternoon, a perfect time for harvesting. As we stood between the rows, the sun sprayed its last bursts of radiance on the west-facing swaths of bamboo, into which went my ba armed with a machete to gather young bamboo stalks to make twines.

As he snaked through the mature branches to get to the heart of the clump, I turned to help Ma and the boys, who had already begun pulling up white lilies and marigolds. Side by side we worked, sidling down the narrow aisle between the rows. Resolutely I bent, pulled, set the stalks aside, straightened up to ease the crick forming at my back, bent, and pulled again, steadily and quickly. I had a reason to be energized and lighthearted. Of all the kids, I was the one chosen to go with Ba and Ma to the market.

Eventually, the sun became as tired as I and slipped below the horizon for a rest. As the last row of flowers was picked clean, a breeze came through, stroking the grove for a familiar tune. Leaves rustled, bamboo creaked, and I rushed to where Ba was sitting, making twines under a jackfruit tree. There I plunked squarely down in front of him so no spirits could possibly snatch me without his seeing and putting up a fight, while Ma and the boys gathered the flowers and carried them to a spot near the water barrel by the well.

The flowers were then stripped of dead petals and leaves and given a good dunking. We wrapped them in burlap for the ride to the market—not the famous flower market on Nguyen Hue Street, which was for more substantial merchants, but the lesser, smaller market at An Dong. I got to sit on the cushioned front seat of the motorized cyclo among the flowers with Ma, while Ba sat on the tiny, hard metal seat behind the driver.

While my parents unloaded the flowers and prepared the site, I stood and watched the bustling scene. Other helpers of my age and older were running alongside cars, motor scooters, and cyclos, waving bundles of flowers and calling out to passersby. I listened to their beckoned chant and resolved to do better than they so my parents would be proud of me.

We could not find a good spot, since the choicest locations had already been taken by vendors who had set up days before. From the street, our little space was a negligible speck in the vast sprawl of flowers and humanity. Having no access to the street and buyers, I knew I had to chase after them, just like other sellers. Ba sat down to divide the flowers into bundles—twelve to a bunch—and wrapped a piece of banana leaf around each before twist-tying them with a piece of bamboo twine. With an armful of flowers, I took off running toward the mouth of the road to find a spot that was not so saturated with sellers. "Fresh flowers, only ten dong—plenty of buds left for Tet. Fresh, fresh flowers, buy for me. Uncle, uncle, here, please help me, or we not have any money to celebrate Tet. No money to make offerings to my *Ong Ngoai* and *Ba Ngoai*. Please, please … buy for me … "

To stir sympathy, I assumed a sad, sad face, which was not hard to do. I just had to think of having to "*an Tet*," celebrate Tet without the regular fare—succulent pork, roasted watermelon seeds, and candied fruits—to come up with a look of utter devastation. It was easier looking sad when hungry, so I put off eating my share of the roasted corncobs Ma had bought for our dinner. I took pleasure in correcting Ma when she pressed me to eat, telling her she should have known I could not very well assume a look of famine with lips coated with lard.

By nine o'clock that evening, Ma's pocket was full of bills, and the pile of flowers had dwindled. Ba opened up the remaining bundles and started adding more stems to each. We were now selling, for the same price, eighteen stems instead of twelve. With that timely discount, we quickly sold off the entire lot.

Ma had paid off her debts at the earlier pig sale; now we had the entire proceeds from the flowers to prepare for Tet. Even if I had not been eavesdropping on my parents' conversations, I would still have known that we were having a good year. There were four rather than the usual two watermelons on the ancestral shrine—big dark green melons of the first quality, and rich assortments of fruits on every altar in the house, including a few of the hoity-toity persimmons normally considered too rich for the likes of us.

The household bubbled with sounds of merriment. I helped Ma cut up radishes for fermenting in fish sauce, a delicious accompaniment to the bland-tasting rice cakes, and used tiny aluminum molds borrowed from Third Older Sister's kitchen to make flower and animal shapes of carrots and radishes for the pickling jug.

On the Eve of Tet, Third Older Sister, Older Sister Phuong, and Eighth Aunt-in-law, wife of Eighth Uncle, gathered to help Ma make the all-essential rice cakes. They started early in the day so as to finish before dusk, making dozens and dozens of cylinder-shaped (southern style) rice cakes, enough for the entire extended family. When the wrapping was done, the entire lot was turned over to Ba. With a bamboo cane, he hoisted the cakes already tied into pairs with twines and dropped them into the boiling water in an old oil drum.

The fire had to be kept going all night so the cakes could be done before dawn, when they would be hung to dry on the rafters in the kitchen and then later distributed to the extended family. Ma would keep only enough for us to eat in the three days of Tet, plus a few extra in case a needy family came to visit.

I stayed with Ba that night, curling up next to him on the divan so I could follow him out to tend to the fire through the night. At midnight, he would have me wake up the kids for the lighting of the firecrackers. As the firecrackers hissed and tore through the darkness, we laughed, clapped, and chased each other around the popping sound. When the noises died away, we rushed back to bed with the same exuberance on Ba's warning that there might not be any of those Tet envelopes of cash remaining for whoever failed to wake early.

We woke on the first day of Tet to the yard festively strewn with red confetti, remnants of the ritual at midnight, and to the anticipation of days of good food ahead.

I was my mother's daughter, so naturally believing in taboos, if not those traditions that sought to bind me to certain behavior. Clever and superstitious, I wanted to do everything possible to reap all the luck I could at Tet, the season of luck dispensation. I made sure my new clothes were washed and pressed for the occasion. Hmm, pressing clothes? Now that was special, especially in a poor household like ours. It was indeed a wonder we even owned an iron.

I begged Ma to spare a few coins from her market funds to buy a handful of charcoal and then personally saw to the burning of charcoal pieces and their placement inside the iron, for I knew how easy it was for little embers to fall out of the side-vents and onto the clothing. Of course, there was never any talk about having better luck with well-ironed clothes. I had simply figured that out on my own. If new clothes brought luck, I so reasoned, then *crisply pressed* new clothes should bring even better luck.

By the time the sky lightened on the first day of the new year, everyone had long been up and ready. On the divan, the kids sat waiting while Ma and Ba moved back and forth, bringing heaping trays of steaming hot bowls of meat, rice, and rice cakes from the kitchen to the ancestral altar.

As the joss sticks slowly burned down, Ma and Ba, having finished their chores, would enter the upper house together, to the divan where we had quickly gotten off to leave room for them to sit. Ba would make a show of patting his shirt pocket to make sure those little envelopes of good luck were still there.

We lined up before them, arms folding reverently across our chests and heads bobbing in respect. We sounded out a chorus of "*Chuc Mung Nam Moi*," as Ba returned our new year good wishes by handing out red envelopes containing newly minted bills. The quantity and denomination varied from year to year depending on how well the old year had gone or, rather, whether the games had favored Ba of late.

Afterwards, the kids ran outside to spin tops or roll marbles, while Ngau and I followed Ma to help her carry bowls of food from the altar back to the kitchen to be reheated for our morning meal, the first of the year. Before sitting down for the feast, Ma refreshed the tea on the altar of the kitchen god whom we had just welcomed home. He had been sent to the heavens days before to report on our conduct, to let God know if the winds of fortune had touched our household and if we needed help.

We wolfed down the fatty pork and browned hard-boiled eggs rolled in rice paper with lettuce, coriander, pickled bean sprouts, carrots, and radishes, and dipped in meat broth. The rice cake was sliced the proper way, with a piece of twine rather than a knife, and served with fermented strips of radish. A melon would be brought down from the altar for dessert. The melon would be red and sweet, another indication of good luck for the coming year. The redness of the melon was not altogether accidental. My ma rarely made mistakes in choosing her melons, except for one year. Ba and I would talk about that pale melon from time to time in subsequent years just to get a rise out of her.

Generally, visitors were not expected on the first day of Tet. Only the closest of family, and even then, only those who, by proof of their past Tet performances, had established that they would bring good fortune, dared to venture to another's home on this special day on which hinged all hope for the new year. No visitors meant no good-luck money. So most of the kids flounced off to see a movie, usually one made in India with good battling evil to save noble princes and princesses, complete with snakes and their charmers and flying carpets. When we got a little older and wiser about making money, Ngau and I would set off for the cemetery after breakfast to work the graves.

No game or chore could take us far from the house on the second and third days, lest we missed that rich, long-lost relative we didn't know existed but who still might come and find us. This actually happened twice during my childhood. Fourth Aunt somebody, a distant cousin whom I had sometimes heard about, decided to descend upon us.

As suddenly as the visits came, they stopped without warning. As we later reminisced on those two surprised occasions, Ma ventured to guess that perhaps in those years our visitor's luck was declining and the call on us was her way of reversing the wind of fortune. There was no way to tell which family could bring luck, so she had likely tried visiting all of her poor relations. Whatever the reason, on those two consecutive Tets, she came, and each time gave each of us two envelopes rather than one. Inside each was a bill of fifty dong, the largest gift we had ever received before or since.

Even if she never did return, I waited for the sight of her at every Tet, hope against hope that she would come again. On later reflection, I learned that it was simply enough to have hope. Faint as that glimmer of hope was, it was powerful enough to lift my spirit to unimaginable heights for the three days of Tet. By the time the fourth day came and Tet was officially over, I had forgotten about long-lost, rich relatives. I was otherwise preoccupied with finding ways to get a large share of those fruits still remaining on the altars.

Gambling was almost *de rigueur* in Vietnamese homes during Tet. It was something in the Asian blood, though I did not know this until my Foreign Service travels took me to the Asian-dominated casinos in Sydney and Auckland. In my childhood, gambling was a delightful pastime. At Tet, it was even more so. It became part of the warmth and happiness of the occasion. The congenial flow of chatter and periodic caterwauls enlivened the already festive air with whorls of general hilarity.

The scene changed little throughout Tet—just eating and having a merry time, no talk of debt or any other unpleasant topic. All worries vanished as if they had never been. Like other kids, I played cards or games like marbles or hopscotch while waiting for well-heeled visitors. Unlike them, I found the second day of Tet, or at least its dawn, somewhat disquieting. I had never told anyone about that heaviness I had upon my chest at waking, for even Ba would have found that silly had he known.

Traditionally, no sweeping was allowed on the first day of Tet, for such meant sweeping all future prosperity out the door. On the second day then, to make sure our home was ready for visitors, Ma would rise early to clear the ground of every piece of litter. By the time I woke, the yard had been emptied of the remains of the fireworks at New Year's

Eve and the house of discarded shells of watermelon seeds, both of which bore the red color of good luck and good fortune.

To me, the crimson remains were not simple rubbish to be swept away. Their presence signified the coming of Tet with all its joy and abundance, and their disappearance meant that soon there would be no more.

Quite predictably, my ever-changing heart didn't remain heavy for long. It lightened at almost anything—the sight of food, red envelopes of money, winning at cards, you name it. There was only one thing, however, that could turn my heart to jitters and make my skin tingle. It was the sound of drums announcing the presence of the lion dancers somewhere in the neighborhood. Yes, the object of my delight—the lion dance troupes.

Before the war got too close, the dancers used to come by unfailingly at every Tet, winding their way through village streets, rendering special dances in front of selected shops to bring prosperity and longevity to shop owners in exchange for tips.

To the insistent beats of drums and cymbals, the lion would hop, twirl, and dance through the streets. The lead dancer had the pivotal role as he jumped and rolled around on the ground, all the while holding on to the oversized lion head and moving it up and down in sync with the beats. One minute his face could be seen through the gaping mouth of the lion; the next minute it was gone. Other dancers under the tail followed his lead perfectly, leaping and rolling in the dirt.

Strings of firecrackers in front of shops would pop and explode as the lion picked up the tempo and gyrated frenetically. The dance became more frenzied as the lead braced the explosion and jerked the bonus money free from the root of the firecracker's string. Meanwhile, another troupe member, garbed in the costume of the Jade Buddha, including a painted wooden mask showing the deity's jolly features, fluttered his fan and sauntered around the lion, miming and setting the crowd off in rolling laughter in the lull of the dance.

Even if it has been years since I've last seen a lion dance, I still remember the joy that threatened to burst free from my heart. How fortunate was I that such joy was part of a tradition that came year after year; how extraordinary was this ritual of Tet so as to give us that much-needed respite from life's burdens. Every year, as sure as night followed day, Tet returned, as treasured by the poor as it was embraced by the rich. For all, it was an opportunity to take measure of past progress and to plan on the deliverance of the new year's promise—happiness, joy, reversal of misfortune—in short, whatever we lacked.

Inherent in the season was a hope so vibrant it eclipsed past sorrows and lightened weary spirits. Even the taboos, that part and parcel of the tradition, were essential to the process. The new clothing, the satisfaction of debts, the proper conduct, all helped solidify hopes to expectations, to beliefs, then faith. With faith in our hearts, we embarked on the year handling the pressures of everyday living with confidence, resolving to sow karmic seeds—doing good unto others, believing that if we only did what was expected of us, what we wished would come.

When the year-end ushered in another eve of Tet, we again reexamined. If it hadn't gone as well as expected, oh well, there was no need to be disgruntled. For one, Tet was definitely not the time to do that, since a negative sentiment could replicate itself for the rest of the year. For another, we accepted that the unchanging dismal situation or suffering was part of the karma we had incurred in this or other lifetimes. The answer became obvious—do more good to pay off the debt, with extra karmic seeds thrown in for future blessings.

My parents always closed the year well. Even when the larder was low, they found comfort in knowing they had done well where it mattered as they reminisced on the little things they had done to help others. And so it was that we welcomed Tet back again and again, and with it, the opportunity to take stock of our lives and to renew faith in the future. Somehow, in some miraculous way, all this wisdom was integrated into the myths and rituals of Tet. Such was the beauty and simplicity of my childhood.

TEN

The Orchard, 1961

Wandering Souls Day came on a midsummer's day in lunar July, a day of the full moon. On its eve, sleep eluded me, as I was consumed with thoughts of food—food of all sorts that would magically arrive at our house tomorrow. Whether it was a death anniversary or the day of worshipping Buddha and deities, offerings had to be made. And Ma always managed to find money to conduct a proper ceremony.

The anxiety kept me from dropping off to a deep sleep, fortunately, for the disturbance came in the early morning. I thought I had heard the clock in the upper house strike twice before I woke.

I felt someone getting on my little wooden bed, which was right next to Ma's canvas cot in the same lean-to where Ba Ngoai used to sleep. Then rough hands pushed my legs apart, and a hard knee pressed down to keep one of my legs in place. I became instantly awake and puzzled but not scared. The thing was, except for ghosts, I was scared of no one.

I opened my eyes in slits and saw a stubby body leaning over me. The moonlight gave me a good visual of the intruder. It was the drifter Ma and Ba allowed to stay with us while he did odd jobs in the hamlet to make enough money to buy gifts for his family and a bus fare home, to the same province my ba was from. He was a short, stocky youth of about seventeen, hard working and helpful.

I had figured out his intent in the few moments it took him to try to keep both of my legs open. Pretending to come out of a dream, I jerked my legs free and kicked viciously at his groin, a move Ma had taught me. I flung out my arms wildly, punching and flailing this way and that, mumbling all the while as if in mortal combat with a monster from another realm then watched as he crept painfully out of the mosquito net and off the bed.

Ma stirred and told me to go back to sleep, that it was only a dream. When we woke up the next morning, he was long gone, taking with him Brother Bong's new, shiny motor scooter, which was parked in the middle of the upper house, right next to the wooden divan where Ba slept. Ba got an earful from Ma for sleeping through that. " … So old and still sleep too much. He cut your penis off and you not wake for that."

Ba sent words to the province for relatives to be on the lookout for the boy. Sure enough, the thief was apprehended and the scooter returned to us some four weeks later.

I didn't tell Ma about the boy's other misadventure. She might have been tempted to go after him herself and try to cut his thing off. She had told us often enough of the story of an overly amorous admirer in her youth. She and her sister, my aunt Phan, with sharp sickles in hand, had been clearing weeds to put down a vegetable garden near their home. They were working through the little patch when a peasant came and sought to capture her attention by exposing himself. With a debilitating shout that would have made a martial artist proud, she had then given chase and threatened to cut his penis off if she should catch up with him. He was never seen anywhere near her again.

Ma was ranting still on the no-good thief even as we got busy preparing for the day's activities. This was one of the few days in the year when our ancestors were allowed to come home and visit from wherever—heaven or hell—so offerings such as fruits and flowers and their favorite dishes had to be made. The day of remembrance was especially meaningful for the homeless souls who did not have any family remaining to make offerings. Thought to be cold and hungry and prone to doing evil things to any human on their paths, these souls would be well tended on this day. Appeasement was necessary so both humans and ghosts could have peace.

The fare did not have to be sumptuous—simple little rice cakes, boiled peanuts, fruits, and sugarcanes would do. The food would be accompanied by gold paper to be used as gold pieces in hell, clothing, and a few big paper houses. The day was especially profitable for children, thanks to a metaphor that likened them to malevolent spirits, children being the living devils so to speak. After offerings, the food would be tossed to the children, completing the ritual.

I washed the raw peanuts and put them in a pot to boil, while Ma chopped long golden sugarcanes into shorter sections. We arranged the peanuts, the canes, and little rice cakes filled with sweetened coconuts, bananas, or black beans on two large, one-meter-diameter trays made of bamboo slats. Ngau, my cousin who was closest to me in age and Ma's next best helper after Big Brother Luong, washed guavas and *coc,* a green, usually sour fruit, and placed them on the trays. The boys, dirty and unkempt, sat under the stunted oil palm playing marbles or spinning wooden tops as they kept watch on the trays. Mai followed Ma and me around and babbled simple words and phrases.

"Coc, Ma? Sugarcane, ha-Long?" Mai was not whole, Ma had said, because she had been "damaged" by her mother's illness—Aunt Phan was dying of tuberculosis when Mai was born. Ma would be proven right. Mai's intellectual development would be arrested at about five years of age. In adulthood, she would become mentally sufficient to take care of her basic bodily functions but no more. Ngau, one of her brothers, would later assume the role of caring for her.

This year, Ma again assigned to me the task of leading the wandering spirits to our yard and the food. With a bundle of joss sticks in hand, I made haste to the hamlet's deadliest intersection. The "killer" intersection, it was called, because there had been many fatal accidents at the site. Whether it was a collision involving a truck, motor scooter, or bicycle, it frequently resulted in a fatality—the site was that haunted. To comfort the violently departed, Old Lady Hai, who owned the coffee shop there, set up an altar at the opposite corner where she offered fruits and joss sticks daily.

At my destination, I jabbed two joss sticks into the earth at each of the four corners, rushing from one side of the road to the other, making sure the roadway was clear of all forms of conveyance each time I did so. My feet were planted firmly on the ground, so there would be no chance of a spirit pushing me onto a path of a galloping horse or under the rolling wheel of an oxen cart.

On the way home, I had to stop at every five yards or so to insert another joss stick into the soft earth on the shoulder of the road. Feet hardly touched the ground, eyes darting in all directions, I quickened my pace ever more with every joss stick down. The feeling that there was a ragtag group of mean spirits following closely on my heels made the hair on my neck stand and cause my heart to constrict. I scarcely heard the traffic noise; the only sound audible was that of my thumping heart.

I arrived home without any incident, which I attributed to my cleverness. But Ma showed no concern on hearing how scary it had been for me, how I'd almost gotten pushed in front of a truck, or how capable I was to have resisted it. She patted my head but gave me no extra food for my bravery, save for that single rice cake she had promised as payment for the task.

As I pouted and blubbered, she simply turned to the trays and started whispering prayers to the lost and hungry spirits. May they enjoy our offerings, be at peace, and go on to the next incarnation.

Meanwhile, the kids, the devil reincarnates, waited on the sideline. The rush promised to be brutal; there seemed to be more and more cousins in each succeeding year. Their parents, being poor, escaped the task of making direct offerings by "going in" with Ma. She would include their names in her chant to the spirits as one of the benefactors.

There were at least six or seven kids around. One must be quick of eye and quicker of feet to get one's share in the stampede. The joss sticks burned down. Any pretense of a game vanished. All eyes were ready as we braced ourselves for the charge, like football players at the scrimmage line.

Ma picked up a tray and hurled the contents upward. Like a first-rate assault team, we rushed the site, grabbing as many of the falling foods as possible, stretching our shirt hems to hold the loot. All of us got a little of what we wanted, having followed a plan of sort—each knew precisely what he wanted on the tray, so followed those items' erratic ascents and anticipated their landings with surprising accuracy. Another tray hurled skyward. I got jostled and pushed, fell forward, and hit my face on the ground. As stars burst through my dazed eyes, I spilled a sharp cry of pain. I wailed loudly for Ma's intervention while crawling forward determinedly. I may have been hurt, but I was far from immobile. I managed to grab a few more peanuts and another section of sugarcane. Even with knees scraped, face smudged with dirt, and lips bloody from the melee, my share was substantial. That was all that mattered.

Wiping the tears and dirt off my face with the back of my hand, I cursed loudly at the boys then ran off to the old tree to count my treasures. I sat on the ground beside the bounty of foods, counting and wiping clean the peanuts and the sugarcane with my shirt. Tucking the hard-won rice cakes carefully into the waistband of my shorts, I next tackled a section of cane, tearing the hard, yellow skin off with my teeth, biting into the sweet, soft fiber. Gnawing voraciously, I gulped down the sweet nectar in between sniffles that would not quell, even though I had long stopped crying. All was well. I would have enough for at least another day of good eating.

Eleven

The Orchard, 1961

It was late in the rainy season, but afternoon showers still came down with enough regularity to keep our fun and games alive with cricket and fish fights. I was barely tolerated in either game, on account that I was neither a humble winner nor a gracious loser. The boys were much the same; hence there was always trouble when we got together. All too often, when the winning side got a bit carried away, I would trip on the fish jar and spill the victorious fighter on the ground to gasp his last breath or "accidentally" knock down the brick wall of the makeshift fighting arena to allow the winning cricket to escape a life of captivity.

Still, I was included in many cricket fights, partly because I usually had a good fighter that everyone and his cricket wanted to beat, but mostly because of my long hair, which was often necessary to the game. It worked like this. Sometimes, a cricket did not want to fight. If so, he had to be properly motivated. Whoever the owner was would pick a hair out of my head, loop it around the cricket's thigh joint, and give the reluctant fighter a few fast twirls. On getting to the ground again, even the most confirmed pacifist was enraged enough to do battle.

When the boys were not desirous of my company, but wise enough to resort to flattery or bribery, I would go away quietly rather than noisily, which could provoke Ba into banishing the game altogether.

While the games went on, I would carry my fish jar and a little paper box with my prize cricket in it to my hideaway, that little recess in the wall where Ba had built a shelf to store our bedding during the day. Atop this four-foot high cushion of pillows and blankets, I immersed in poems of love and tragedy or novels on Chinese martial artists of the genre similar to the famed *Crouching Tiger, Hidden Dragon* movie I would later see as an adult.

Renting books was a luxury I had to have. Though my mind wasn't yet sufficiently formed for me to recognize or articulate the need to satisfy my passion for words and fantastical tales, I instinctively sought to find that which provided nourishment for my mind with the same fervor I had in searching for food to sustain my body.

While the books fueled my hopes and dreams, they also unleashed a discontent that kept me from knowing the bliss of accepting the "what is." But I didn't know anything about the negativity of craving for what I didn't possess, having resolutely ignored Ma's "outdated" wisdom. At nine years of age, I reveled in the pleasure of dreams and the satisfaction of my modest wants.

It didn't take long for this want of reading materials to be modest no more but instead an expensive hobby. I read much too fast. I could certainly have done so in moderation but for one fatal flaw: my insatiable curiosity. I so badly wanted to get to the end of the story before Ma found me out and ordered me off to some household chore.

Book rental was a brilliant idea in our dirt-poor country. Its entrepreneurial brilliance told a tale all its own—it had to have been a brainchild of a Chinese or a northerner. A few years from now, the burgeoning war economy would help the southerners attain the kind of mental acuity required to compete effectively with their northern and central brethren. In the days of my youth, the market belonged to the fitter race—the non-southerner, just as books belonged only to the rich and middle class. There was only a handful of bookshops and no public libraries. Reading materials available to the poor were newspapers and magazines, but even they were not always affordable. On many a rickety stool, one would find a cyclo driver, one of the lucky ones who knew how to read, engrossed in an outdated magazine that had been resold as scrap to street vendors as food-packaging materials.

I was grateful for the invention. I would save a few coins from here and there, even foregoing a snack at school, so I could rent the sequel to "The Ninth Hero - The Revenge," or something equally absorbing. Of the list of school subjects I did not master, reading was not one of them.

I was an exceptionally good reader for a child of nine. I read anything and everything I could get my hands on, completely ignorant of the notion that something might not be appropriate for a young child to read. In all likelihood, the concept did not apply to rural Vietnam in the 1960s. Truly, I was not a child for very long, not in the Western middle-class idea of the word anyway. I watched husbands beating up their wives to find money for a bout of drinking with their buddies. They did not seem to care how their wives came by the funds, turning a blind eye to a wife's borrowing or possibly trading favors to other men. When the urge hit, all they wanted was some money for a jar of rice wine and a small dish of what you would call "beer food." Meanwhile, I immersed in tales of star-crossed lovers killing themselves so as to be with each other in the afterlife, of young girls "selling" themselves as second or third "wives" to rich, old men to provide for their families, forsaking their own happiness for duty.

The book rental shop sat on what used to be a ditch, which ran along the front perimeter of the compound, where a line of beautiful cherry trees once stood. I remember how the trees swelled with buds just before Tet, sporting green nubs on every branch, including the trunks. The nubs would turn into bright, thick clumps of pink and white blossoms. The delicate fragrance wafting down from that floating piece of heaven would make my senses swim with joy. I would climb up a tree when it was bursting with blossoms, and there, on a sturdy limb, sat and watched pedestrians and traffic on the main roadway, calling out to an acquaintance of Ma or Ba to attract the attention of other passersby, who, I was sure, would think I looked dazzling among the blooms.

I got to know the shop so well, the owner eventually offered me a job helping with customers and stacking books back on the shelves. I believed he was tired of me coming in to sneak a read and wisely decided to make me barter for the privilege. There would be no money, he said, but I could read for free. It did not take me long to decide on the generous offer. I would get to read to my heart's content without paying? Whoever had heard of such a fantastic arrangement?

Neither Ba nor Ma was home on my arrival with the news of my employment, and I had to tell someone. I executed a high jump over the pig-refuse ditch rather than using the log sitting across its mouth and made it to Elderly Ninth Master's house. I huffed and puffed and rattled on while he listened and looked at me thoughtfully over his spectacles. Lifting a hand to stroke his long grey beard in contemplation, he nodded.

"Very good, Long. Now you read a lot and learn more. You must read other books, you know; something besides Chinese martial artists and their powers. Magic mushrooms! Quite fantastic... I must say!" His eyes twinkled at this, and his head shook slightly from side to side.

His warm reception lightened my heart. I knew right then that reading was good for me! Suddenly remembering the reading treasures in his house, I asked, "Elderly Ninth Master, could I borrow some magazines?" Glancing at the pile of magazines on the small table at the corner, he gestured with a wide sweep of the arm. "Yes, take as many as you want. Remember to bring them back. I am not sure if Big Brother Suong (his eldest son) read them yet."

"Yes, Elderly Ninth Master. I bring them back tomorrow." I bowed slowly, taking my time to do it properly, even though I was breath-less with anticipation and could not wait to riffle through the pile. He smiled encouragingly. "Umm, you read fast, huh?"

I gathered the magazines to my chest and bowed again. I was so elated that I practically flew over the threshold beam then sailed high across the ditch. The stack of magazines felt warm against my thump-ing heart. There would be stories of this movie star and that opera star and the serial love stories. I wondered how long it had been since I had last visited Elderly Ninth Master and resolved to do it more often, partly to show my respect but mainly to catch up on my reading.

I told Ma and Ba about the job during the evening meal. Ba thought it was clever of me. Ma reminded me not to spend too much time there but to stay at home to help her with housework. I started rolling my eyes but instantly caught Ba's warning look. I made a quick turnabout and assured Ma. "Ma, I not go there so often, only sometimes, after I finish with the housework." Ma narrowed her eyes and looked skeptical but said nothing.

The boys looked puzzled rather than envious. "How you get a job like that? Why you want to? No pay?" I thought to myself, *Of course they can-not understand; they don't even like to read.* They shook their heads as they chewed, creating enough noise to disturb the atmosphere and make fun of my accomplishment. Big Rat looked contemplative. I beamed, believ-ing that he understood. He was the smartest one among us after all.

Ma picked up her bowl, flooded the rice with spoonfuls of broth from the steamed swamp cabbage, lifted the bowl to her mouth, and took a big, loud slurp. I fidgeted under the familiar, penetrating look from dark, shining eyes that directed at me over the rim of the bowl.

There was something about those eyes. My ba had them too. No docile, slow-moving eyes there. Rather, they were all-knowing eyes that seemed to be able to read my deepest thoughts. Intimidated, I responded in my typical manner. I stuck my tongue out at her back as she turned to pick up the pot of broth to refill the serving bowl.

I could tell she did not think too much of this job. *Reading... bah,* I could hear her thinking. *More reading, filling her head with nonsense.* She knew if I was of little help before, I would be totally useless once I started this nonsense of working without pay. Ba simply smiled into his bowl. The matter lingered in the air for another few moments. The noisy slurping of soup and smacking of lips intruded. The boys broke the silence by talking about crickets and fish fights, and Ma started on the price of lettuce.

Just as well, for my thoughts had shifted to a more pressing matter. Noticing that the boys' bowls were empty of the two pieces of chicken we had each been allotted, I surreptitiously dug up the remaining piece of salty-sweet chicken I had buried under the rice. I licked the favored meat, biting into it gently, getting just enough of a taste to help me swallow a mouthful of rice. I covered the chicken back up as I chewed, keeping the bowl tilted so no one could see what I had, lest I was made to share.

龙

In the shadow of war, prosperity grew. More food stands appeared by the side of the roads, more vendors of all sorts of goods in the market. Most visible of all were the multi-story concrete townhouses, previously squatters' huts. Now the squatters turned successful entrepreneurs lived on the upper levels, while their electronics or scooter shops or restaurants occupied the ground floors. Their buildings stood tall and fancy next to the modest, run-down southern homes and derelict shops.

Another family moved into the compound—a widower with two young children, a boy and a girl. The man had left his rice field in the Mekong delta after the death of his wife and young child in a mortar attack. She was the last one to leave their hut for the outdoor shelter, having delayed to pick up her child. A mortar came, decapitating her and the child she was carrying on her hip. Through a friend at the local agricultural office, this man got a job in the city as my ba's assistant and, with it, the right to lodge in the compound. Ba gathered thatch, cut down bamboo canes, and recruited the labor needed to put up a house for them on the other side of the path.

The girl was younger than I but already charged with a big job of looking after her father and brother. Her father did the cooking, while she kept the house and their clothes clean. The kids' names told of their simple country roots—hers was "Cai, or "female"; his was Duc, or "male."

Both had the sturdy build of well-fed, well-labored kids from the countryside. I remembered looking at the girl and thinking that she looked a little fat, like a rich kid, except for her dark complexion, which revealed her peasant background. I wondered if she would enjoy playing in the orchard and if she knew the same games we did. She did, but we did not get to enjoy each other's companionship for very long. It took only a few short weeks after their arrival for her father to decide that I was too saucy, too wild, quite the opposite of how he wanted his daughter to turn out, so he promptly broke up our budding friendship.

There was no worry about Duc being influenced by our undisciplined ways, for he managed to be mean quite on his own. He called us chicken-hearted city kids and dared us to fight him. He would be proven right, for we were weaker, if not cowardly. Surely, he was much stronger than any of the boys in our group, with a muscular, square body of a kid used to hard labor. However, it was not his strength alone that won fights. Rather, what made him unbeatable was the savage way he fought. One by one, my cousins got knocked out. Then it was my turn. Being a girl didn't exempt me from the elimination round. Watching the boys fall scared me, but I could not back out of the fight—too much face was at stake. He took me down with one rush, the same way he demolished others, by backing away for about five yards or so, then charging full-speed ahead, using his hard head as a ramming device. He aimed for my stomach and hit it head-on. My insides hurt for several days.

With the winner firmly established, one would have thought there was no longer a reason to fight. But there was not much else to occupy our time, so the fights continued, this time in teams. It would be my misfortune to be on his opposing team almost every time. I got knocked down so often that I sometimes felt the pain and dropped to the ground before the impact.

Gradually, he became part of our extended family, flitting in whenever, sharing a meal sometimes. Now and again, he helped us catch the water overflow from the newly erected compound behind our house. What had been a grazing pasture and my extended playing field turned into a compound of exclusive, sheltered villas for high-level executives of the National Bank, courtesy of some sort of foreign aid. The compound had its own water tower, which overflowed once or twice a week, lasting an hour or so each time before the caretaker would turn it off. For a long time, I thought that was the way of water towers—always overflowing. Each time the water spilled over, it invoked a rush similar to what one would nowadays refer to as a Chinese fire drill.

It usually happened during the evening meal. The thundering roar of water served as our call to "general quarters." At the sound, we rushed to our respective stations. Ba with the tin trough, Big Rat with our novel contraption of two bamboo canes tied together and then pried apart into a lopsided X. Ba would sit on the rooftop, holding on to the trough, one end of which set at the cross of the X. He would use all his strength to hold on. I knew this because I used to watch the play of veins on his neck, his hands, and along his arms. Big Rat also had a tough job. First, he had to get over the barbed wire fence on top of the wall. Then, under the pounding water, he stood and held onto the stand. The water would hit the trough, run along its length onto the roof, and down the spout into the large water vat. From there, like worker ants, the rest of us hustled to make the transfer to other vats and barrels and tin buckets, filling every available container so the water would last for a couple of days, saving us a trip to the well.

Duc, the bane of my childhood, would grow up to be strong and tough, just as he was as a child. He would return in time to the rice field where his mother had died, preferring life on the farm to languishing in the city, apprenticing for one trade or another. He had planned to hide out in the farm rather than responding to the draft.

I heard of his tragedy a few years after that. He did join the military, only to have that career cut short merely months later when he stepped on a mine during patrol and lost both his legs all the way to the groin. I did not see him until much time had passed, when he came up for a visit. His powerful upper body was all that was left. He sat on a wheel-chair, pushed by his wife, a country girl he had married on returning home with half his limbs. Ma had told me of the practical arrangement about his wife: he needed someone to look after him; she was of marriageable age with few prospects. I looked at him and saw a glimmer of the strange, invincible boy he was in that shadow of the sad man he had become. Actually, he sounded quite normal in conversations with Ma. But I had known the boy too well. I thought his answers were too glib, his eyes too bright, and his laughter just on this side of brittleness.

Much later, Ma sprung a surprise on me. Supposedly, when he had first left for the countryside, he'd spoken with Ma of his intention to offer for me when he had made something of himself with the farm. At that last visit, he asked her not to mention anything to me. "It is too late," he said.

He had no way of knowing that it had always been too late—a lifetime too late. I was never meant for him, having been born a dreamer as well as a bearer of responsibility.

The Orchard, 1963

President Diem, thought to be acting on advisement from his older brother, the Archbishop Ngo Dinh Thuc, issued a controversial proclamation forbidding the display of the Buddhist flag and celebration of the Buddha's nativity. Buddhist clergy called for resistance and organized student protests against this edict by the government.

A monk immolated himself, setting off a period of unrest during which the government imposed strict censor of Buddhist writings, arrested, or otherwise harassed protesters. Ba kept shaking his head, and Ma thought it was quite silly. Eighth Uncle naturally jumped on the bandwagon of the oppressed. I don't think he cared much about who did what to whom but simply enjoyed the drama. As for me, and also as expected, I took the government's side. What did it matter if a flag was displayed or not, or even if there was a flag? It was not like Buddhist was a country. If it had not been for our resident sage, also known as the Know-it-all Eighth Uncle, we would not have known what the flag looked like. And here I thought Buddhism was simply how we lived our life, the way my ma had taught me.

The showdown continued between the oppressors and the oppressed. The voice of reason was long gone as passion flared on both sides. The government's increasing unpopularity led to the inevitable—a *coup d'etat* ensued during which President Diem and his brother, Ngo Dinh Nhu, were killed.

Ma didn't care that President Diem was Catholic or if there were talks that he deserved such end by oppressing and killing Buddhists. Looking sad and troubled, she kept shaking her head from side to side and saying, "Toi nghiep qua."

It was not a coincidence that following the death of President Diem and the overthrow of his administration, land encroachment by Northern refugees came to a grinding halt. Eighth Uncle said the refugees had lost their champion and were now like a snake without its head. His pronouncement proved true enough; however, it was not just the Catholics who became leaderless. Flawed as he was, President Diem would be the last president of any worth we would ever have. The country would suffer through years of unfortunate leadership by largely ineffectual, egotistical, corrupt nonentity in the form of military generals.

The news of President Kennedy's death came soon thereafter. Ma didn't know what the world was turning into and thought for sure the end was near. I was sad. I had often seen pictures of President Kennedy and his wife in our newspapers and magazines and thought they were quite like the king and queen of my fantasy. Indeed, to me they had the royal look of kindness and benevolence.

龙

Third Older Sister, Aunt Phan's stepdaughter, found a good-looking suitor. A handsome woman in her late twenties, she had been considered past her prime according to the standards of the day. After all hope seemed lost that she would ever find a decent man, it happened. If it was too good to be true, it was. He disappeared on learning she was pregnant with his child, leaving her brokenhearted and shamed.

She gave birth to a baby girl whom she named *My-Lan*, or "beautiful orchid." It was the year of the pig—good for a girl. It meant the baby would have a life in which she could laze around with plenty of food thrown her way and no work. A lucky life! Definitely better than being born in the year of the horse, which would have foretold a life of back-breaking labor, or worse yet, the tiger, which was considered a "husband killer" sign. Mine was a cat, a sign that was not very good but not too bad either. Cunning and wise, cats, however, had to work for their food. Work, but not too much work, assuming mice were within catching distance.

I used to harp about the ignorance of peasant parents on the naming of children of my generation. Instead of getting beautiful names like rose, wildflower, orchid, drifting cloud, sparkling water, or river of fragrance, we got names like dragon, fortune, prosperity, or worse yet, bean, melon, jackfruit, mango, cucumber, or rat. Yet, even as I chastised Ma for my name, which meant dragon, I knew I was fortunate. She could very well have named me *"Meo"* for cat! And then where would I be? How could I look at anyone with that name?

Third Older Sister sure had a poetic side to her. She was not all that educated. Who would have thought she would come up with a pretty name like My-Lan for her firstborn?

Shortly after giving birth to My-Lan, Third Older Sister found a good job as a maid in the home of a French banker in the city. She left her baby daughter with us, coming home once a week on her day off. I was designated Lan's caregiver. For that, Third Older Sister was to give me money for breakfast and snacks, school supplies, plus one school outfit each year.

Every morning, just as the sun began its ascent from behind the roof of the meteorological station, which stood directly east of our house just beyond refugee row, I would carry Lan to the small neighborhood alley market to have our meal. Snack food vendors lined the road leading into the market, selling soups, sticky rice—anything one could possibly desire. Once, I could only look and salivate. Now, with money in my pocket, I could saunter down the road with my nose slightly turned up. Well, sauntering may not have been the right term to use in this case, since one could hardly call it that when the person who was doing the sauntering was thin and short, slightly bent, and off center by the weight of a robust baby on her hip. Anyway, it didn't matter how I looked, only how I felt. And I quite remember that I was "sauntering."

It hadn't been long since I'd started having money to buy what I wanted, but I learned fast how to assume that air of importance as I seriously pondered the selections, drawing out the moment of indecision, the sweetest, most golden moment there was—the moment before I announced my choice.

I shared my meager earnings with the boys via a process I would later know as subcontracting. I would ask Ngau, or his brother, Little Rat, to help put Lan down for a nap at noon or to wash Lan's and my dirty clothes. For the service, and the quality—judged by how long Lan stayed asleep—I would buy the provider a banana leaf twist of glutinous rice or the slightly more costly "jambon," or ham, baguette sandwich. Subcontracting freed me up to find other gainful occupations, like spinning cotton for one of the workers so he could take a longer siesta or running to the market to buy a half bucket of clams, wash, and put them to steam for those who wanted to celebrate their payday with a feast.

To stretch my allowance, I ordered only one portion of food for me and Lan to share. By doing this I would have enough to pay my "subcontractors" and still a little leftover to purchase something for Ba—a lump of glutinous rice, a section of baguette filled with pâté, or "*xiu mai*," ground pork stewed with tomato and mushroom.

I would stand proudly by his side as he reverently handled the treat. The light that shone in his eyes as he bit into each morsel of food and the pleasure that spread over his face as he savored every burst of flavor taught me the joy of giving.

From Ma I learned a different lesson: love and sacrifice.

She gave up her food so readily that it was easy to forget she also had needs. When I did buy something for her, she would do no more than take a taste before giving the food to Ba or dividing it among the boys—whoever was around surely needed it more than she. She would say, "*An roi*," or already eaten, and maintain her refusal even as Ba or I continued to press. Her stomach continued to shrink while mine swelled during those two years I cared for Lan.

So did my world, on one bright Sunday afternoon.

TWELVE

The Orchard, 1963

Third Older Sister failed to come home that weekend. Ma decided that I should go to find her at work to get my allowance for the coming week. There was no money for me to take a cyclo, so Ba offered to let me use his bicycle. Ma was to give me directions on how to get there since she had been to the place twice before.

Even though Ma had great faith in me at eleven years of age to find my ways around the big city of Saigon, Ba was not so sure, especially with Ma's bizarre directions. He shook his head in exasperation, as Ma *hmm*ed, and *mmph*ed, and *phmm*ed, confusing us and quite possibly herself as well. I was to turn to the left, or was it to the right? I was to turn at the sugarcane juice vendor, or was it the soybean wagon? One moment, she clearly remembered that I was to turn at the shoe shop; the next moment it was a clothing shop; but wait, she was certain the turn was at the shop whose metal shutters were green. Yes, definitely green. And yes, I could not miss it. There was a cobbler on the sidewalk in front of the shop. Next she took me to a street called "don," or "ton."

Ba could not help, for he had never been there. Usually imperturbable, he became more agitated by the second. He kept sighing and shaking his head. I heard him mumble, "Oh, she'll be lost. We will never find her. Lost, gone!" The possibility of that happening seemed more real all the more in his mind as Ma continued her litany, forward then backward, for he looked up suddenly. "Long-ne, can you find your way home? You know where you live?" I scrunched my face, amused by his discomfiture. "I know, I know, Ba. I won't get lost. Don't worry." For a brief moment, he seemed reassured. But out came Ma's jumbled words, and he looked as if he was in pain. Eighth Uncle came into the house. In a few short sentences, he made sense of Ma's baffling recollection and sent me on my way.

The bike seat was too high so I had to pedal standing up. Exiting the back gate, I went down the red dirt road. It took all my skills to keep the bike balanced on that deeply rutted byway before merging onto Cong Ly, a beautiful, tree-lined, paved road connecting Tan Son Nhat Airbase with the heart of the city. I rode furiously for a while then stopped pedaling and let momentum carry the bike forward. Leaning back against the seat, my eyes caught sight of a flame tree crowning the roof of a low, white-walled structure called a villa, home of the rich.

Ah, the flame tree, the tree of friendship and romance, a must for schoolyards. I had read dozens of poems serenading the scarlet blooms. If one were to believe in those celebrated verses, one would learn that only the best sort of love took place by those gnarly trunks. The poignant symbol of the tree manifested when petals burst free of their buds to announce the arrival of summer and school vacation, the season of heartbreaks and affirmations.

Here, the tree's dappled shade did not shelter the long black hair and white "*ao dai*," the long, flowing traditional dress of innocent young girls, or bear silent witness to the first love solemn-looking, studious boys held in their hearts. Instead of attesting to love, the tree extended its arms to shelter the stone bench on the far side of the wall, patiently waiting for the daughter of the house to come out for a soothing touch of a breeze. The tree, with help from the gentle wind, speckled the manicured lawn with its precious petals to ensure the continued good fortune of the rich with that lucky color of scarlet. While frangipani shaded the driveway and bougainvillea weaved a welcome coronet over the forbidding steel gate, the flame tree hovered in the background as a mere possession of the rich.

Houses of similar stature dotted the road and roused my heart all the way to the presidential palace, from where I turned left toward the Cathedral of Notre Dame. The tall steeples, redbrick façade, and colorful stained glass windows made the church look like a castle from the fables of another time. I sucked in my breath, totally enthralled by the breathtaking sight so foreign to my world.

Even the roads here were different—smoother and cleaner. There was no clacking of hooves, no rattling of wooden wheels, none of the usual sound of traffic from my part of town. I made the turn to go behind the cathedral, down a road where tall tamarinds stretched and arched as if reaching for the sky, while their fruits dangled and swayed. Ripe pods of tamarind lay forlornly every which way—on the sidewalk, on the street, near the gutters. I was perplexed by the view from atop my bicycle. *This is the place for the rich. No one want to pick fruits off the ground? Ha, arrogant rich. More for me then.* I rested the bike against a tree trunk and ran from tree to tree to pick up as many fallen fruits as I could. When the hems of my shirt could handle no more, I quickly took the shirt off and used it to wrap up my precious find and carefully placed the bundle in the wire basket on the bike.

My actions voided that proper look Ma had created by taking the time to fasten all the buttons on my shirt. She could not make the stubborn me change the tattered shorts for a pair of long pants, however. I had argued that the pants legs could get stuck in the bike chain and cause me to fall under an oxen wagon wheel and possibly kill myself. Oh, how that would make her feel sad for the rest of her life. Worse, how could she live with herself after causing my death!

I puffed up my chest, delighted with the fortuitous find. Racing down the road barefoot with the bike at my side, I held tightly on the handle bar, jumped up, and swung over the frame to land my feet squarely on the pedals, as agile as a Chinese acrobat.

Indeed, life was good! I lifted my face and smiled, as if saluting the beauty and abundance that was all around me. A breeze came through the tunnel between the lines of trees, scattering tiny tamarind leave petals around me and blowing soft bursts of cool air onto my half-naked body.

I pedaled alongside private cars, glancing at the deferential-looking drivers and their imperious passengers. Through a break in an ivy-covered wall, I caught sight of a young girl on a shaded driveway. She walked languidly as if on a road in heaven. In my version of paradise, there was no hurry, no worry about what the future might hold. Under the arc of frangipani blooms, she looked liked the vision my mind had sometimes beheld, the person I wanted to be—a princess with long black hair cascading down her back, embodying all the beauty and wealth I craved. Even from a distance, I knew she would have that soft, light skin of the privileged and those long, tapered fingers of rich young girls.

However much she had, I possessed that little. No wealth, no beauty, not even the manners of the well bred, even if Ma did try her best. We did not need wealth to have good manners, she preached endlessly. But having been allowed to run wild and left untutored for so long, I had morphed into a hardy, unruly creature unlike any other. I could curse up a storm and was vulgar as no other girls could be. There was no girl cousin my age, no classmate who was allowed to play with me after school—I was considered a bad influence—so I hung around my boy cousins. To hold my own against these kids born of hardship and poverty I had to be just as mean, though I was never as tough as I endeavored to be.

I rode on, but my mind remained on the girl in that driveway. I shook my head, blinked the ache out of my eyes, and pedaled madly to dislodge that curious, heavy feeling in my chest. After asking directions from a passing cyclo driver, who allowed me to hang on to the back wheel for a free ride, I arrived at Third Older Sister's workplace.

It looked like other villas, rich and forbidden. The wall was low, a play at elegance, as if the house belonged where it was, so forbidding in its exclusivity that there was no need to put up high walls to keep out intruders or prying eyes. But thick vines of bougainvillea twisted high above the wall, as effective a barrier as any concrete, while verdant leaves and thick blooms interlocked to shield the sight of German shepherds roaming the garden. I walked the bike to the gate and pushed the bell deferentially. Being the junior maid, Third Older Sister came to answer.

I followed her down the driveway, pausing briefly under the velvet dome of the frangipani. For those few seconds, I imagined myself that privileged creature I had seen. Acting as if this were my very own driveway, I lifted my head and walked slowly and serenely behind Third Older Sister, emulating that haughty look of the rich despite my partial nakedness. The fragrance of the blooms sweetened the air. High among the tamarind trees, the cicadas started their chorus. And I, I would forever associate the sight and scent of frangipani and the songs of the cicadas with the seemingly unattainable world of wealth.

I stooped to pick up a handful of the fallen white blossoms and added them to my bundle of treasures in the basket. Later, I would press them in that precious book I had of a young girl going from rags to riches to remember this beautiful driveway where they grew and that brief, incredible moment when I walked into my dream and found paradise.

We went to the servant's quarters, where Third Older Sister shared a room with the head cook. As she clucked her tongue over my state of undress, she poked her head inside the big, wooden wardrobe at the corner of the room and emerged with an old blouse for me to put on.

Noting that I was sweaty and out of breath, she left and, after a moment, returned with a glass of water.

The glass was shiny and clean, and the water was cold, ice cold, even if it did not have a single piece of ice floating in it. To my questioning gaze, Third Older Sister explained that it came from the "Frigidaire." When I continued to look puzzled, she took me to the kitchen and showed me the refrigerator, which she called "Frigidaire," and told me how it could keep everything cool. The water was better than any I had ever tasted—clean and delicious. I sat humbly at the edge of the chair, savoring every precious drop.

While my eyes took in the sparkling clarity of the water, I thought of its opposite—the water that was full of mosquito larvae in the drinking vat at home. When I was very young, Ba taught me how to tip the coconut shell ladle just so and to blow softly on the water to disperse the baby mosquitoes, or "*con lang quang*," before taking a drink. There was no lighting under the star fruit tree where the vat was, so when I got thirsty at night, I simply blew and hoped for the best. I reasoned the larvae were wise enough to swim in the opposite direction and away from the spout.

Third Older Sister returned with a bowl of rabbit stew and a section of baguette and hurried me along. "Eat, eat, so you can go home. I have to cook dinner." The food tasted like the water—foreign and delectable. To my impressionable mind, it tasted of wealth.

On the ride home, my thoughts dwelled on the flavors of wealth and class—the shiny white bowl, the worldly tastes. The food had a scent quite different from the familiar "*nuoc mam*," the fish sauce that was used in almost all of our foods. I wondered about the people who ate that food every day and about their world. Now that I had known wealth with all my senses, I was not so sure it would ever be in my reach. I felt suddenly, inexplicably afraid, for I knew I could not trust Fate to be fair. Generations of doing good deeds—first my grandma, her mother before her, then my ma, and for what? We have sown karmic seeds forever. When could we start reaping the blessings? I, the impatient one, didn't want to wait until the next life!

As the bike rolled down the road, I urgently recited the only Buddhist verse I had learned from Ma and asked Buddha and God to give me a better life than my ma's. Her feet cracked and bled, especially close to Tet, when the weather turned cold. The calluses on her heels grew so thick that she had to slice the ridges off with a razor blade, leaving the cracks still so deep that it took globs of petroleum grease to fill and ease the pain. I suspected the villas were beyond my family's reach, so opted for a humbler supplication.

If I could not have a nice home, could I have enough money for food, so I would not have to do what Ma had to do every day, going from merchant to merchant, begging to buy on account?

That summer of 1963 was the season of my awakening, to a world both real and unreal. It was real in that I had touched it, tasted it. But it might as well have been imaginary, for it was so lofty it would forever be forbidden to me.

Thirteen

In the news: 6/23/97 -
Cambodia–Guerillas
announce the capture
of former Khmer Rouge
leader Pol Pot, responsible
for the deaths of
millions of Cambodians
during the 1970s.

Suva, Fiji, 1997
The South Pacific

A VIP visit! We shook off the languor of sun-drenched days in the paradise of Fiji and leapt at the chance to return to Vietnam to support SecState Madeleine Albright's visit to Ho Chi Minh City, the "Saigon" of my youth and my heart. We could not turn down the honor of working a VIP trip, even if the frustrating experience of serving there was still shockingly fresh in our minds.

Returning to Vietnam for a two-year tour after Cape Verde was not quite what I had expected. It definitely lacked that warm and fuzzy sensation of homecoming. In that earlier lifetime, mercifully, I'd had nothing to do with the government. On returning as a diplomat, I would learn that dealing with the capricious, pompous officials was the stuff nightmares were made of.

Imagine suffering a cultural shock in one's own country. The northern speech again confounded. I had been away from that lyrical tone for over two decades, far too long, so that in the summer of 1995 and on my second day in Hanoi, I found myself standing in a somewhat befuddled state in the middle of a marketplace off Lang Ha Street.

The market peddlers suffered none of that perplexity. They knew exactly who I was, where I had come from. From my manner of dress, shockingly casual and perhaps even risqué, with a pair of knee-length shorts and an oversized T-shirt, they could tell I was either foreign to, or in defiance of, their ways. Tracing my speech to the south of Vietnam, they undoubtedly came up with the correct term for my particular species—Viet Kieu, or Vietnamese nationals who lived overseas.

The dialect was not the only thing that baffled. The people looked hard, grim, and countrified. How ever did I think they were more cunning than southerners! I supposed that to my child's eyes, everyone seemed cleverer in the arts of wheeling and dealing than my ma and ba.

I felt as though I had arrived in a foreign country, as indeed I had. In my youth, Hanoi was farther away than a foreign country. It was enemy territory, a land we'd never expected to transgress. As they pointed at me and laughed and chattered in that heavy accent, I remembered the first time I had heard the hoots, the laugher, and the strange speech, and something in me twisted and wrenched.

I missed my ba. The thought of him and a childhood that was lost to me sliced through my heart like a knife.

Nothing looked familiar. Some of the homes looked dilapidated, as if nothing had been done for them in a long time; others looked new and gaudy, which state was rendered even more garish by the rancid, decayed state of whatever lake or canal touted to be adorning their frontage. Hotels and restaurants shot up along many of the roadways in a rush to accommodate tourists who were first responders to the Hanoi government's new open-door policy.

Needs of the FS required that I take a consular job rather than stay in the administrative field. Not that it would have mattered. No job was simple during the difficult transition from foe to supposed ally. My entire tour was spent in a constant battle against the Communist old guards who did not seem to notice that the war had ended. And it was they, those cantankerous veterans, who populated the upper ranks in the government. Barrier after barrier were put up in belated retaliation as they conveniently managed to forget who the aggressors were, remembering only their hardships on the trail, the narrow escape from the firepower from the sky, the devastation of hearth and home and fallen comrades. The passage of time has helped them immeasurably, blurring the shapes of those lies they had told during the war, so that even they now had problem separating facts from fiction. They actually believed they were the aggrieved among those warring parties, that the south was at fault, perhaps for having the audacity to put up a fight, as well as the gall to enlist help from the United States.

Anyhow, they were in charge now and resented even the appearance of kowtowing to the Americans, regardless that their diplomatic overture was clearly an expediency of trade. Small-country complex, face-saving mentality, distrust between enemies, you name it, the relationship was fraught with it.

But the contentious nature of the bilateral relationship between the new Vietnam and America was what made an assignment here appealing to many in the FS, and I among them, who actually relished the chance to accomplish the almost impossible. Even so, the toll sometimes got too high. The stress came from all angles, including the private domain of our daily living. We were cautioned to be on guard since it was presumed that every movement, every notable incident in our lives were being reported back to the Vietnamese intelligence branch, where both our strengths and weaknesses would be analyzed and subject to exploitation somehow, somewhere, sometime.

I had certainly underestimated the pressure that could come from my ethnic origin, specifically on the important issue of comportment, which had always been a problem for me, having never been the conforming sort. My interactions with government officials had to be laced with a subservience that I had railed against in my youth. My hard-won new social station notwithstanding, I was reduced again to that beggar child, even though the goal was now for something nobler than food. I showed them the humility I sometimes did not feel, especially when it was expected of me, just so I could obtain a judicious hearing for a frazzled American tourist or secure that timely permission to visit American citizens who were languishing in prison hovels across the country.

Fortunately, I didn't have to wait very long for the blessed relief that normally came with an onward assignment—to Fiji at that. The new assignment required that my tour in Hanoi be curtailed by six months due to Embassy Suva's urgent need of an administrative officer. Thrilled with the prospect of leaving Vietnam early and of living in Fiji for the next three years, Acey and I plunged into the task of research on our new home, devouring every word of the State Department post report on Fiji, and going through the large stock of *National Geographic* magazines that we had lugged around the world with us, to find that issue on Fiji and learn more about those islands of palm-fringed sandy beaches and reef-protected lagoons.

Another adventure beckoned. At last, there I was, watching a dream coming together. My self-esteem and my career prospects had brightened perceptibly now that the test of Vietnam had been faced and overcome. Van, Shen, and Thuy were doing well in school and settled in their lives. Unfortunately, on matters of the heart, while Van had met and married the man of her life, a man strong of character and integrity and all other high-minded concepts I had never learned, and Thuy finally found the man who would be her husband, who was devoted to her and committed to working hard to build their life together, Shen seemed to be making the same mistakes I did, rushing love and looking for it in all the wrong places. My ma would have said it was karma—I had been careless with my affection, breaking hearts when I shouldn't have, and so my daughter would be treated likewise by heartless men. This she would have inferred from my girlhood, through my later reminiscences of Quan and Art, and Van's father. Given her pride in me, she perhaps thought I'd been so selective in finding a mate that surely I'd broken many a heart not deemed worthy.

She didn't know the half of it, never suspected the heartaches and frustrations I'd borne alone. Not that it would have mattered much. Compared to her lifetime of physical hardships and mental anguish, my self-inflicted pain on romance found and love lost would have seemed frivolous. To a then-novice to pain, my troubles were, however, significant to me, enough to make me wish that none of it would ever touch my daughters. I didn't have a choice in casting aside my youth and innocence, but my children did, and I wanted them to enjoy the kind of childhood and adolescence that I could only dream of.

Days before leaving Vietnam, we adopted Tyler, a two-year-old boy from a family of ten children, through his sister Trang, whom we had hired to care for Zu. He was a serious little boy, so solemn that he looked like a little old man. I remember when we first got him home, how my heart ached at the sight of his lying on the couch with one leg crossed over another, both bent at the knees, and an arm rested on his forehead, a posture of deep introspection. He wanted to grow up and make a lot of money to send home to his father, he said, and to "sponsor" his brother to come to the States to live with us. Whenever I saw him thus, a baby with a mountain-sized burden on his little shoulders, I would wonder if we had made the right decision in adopting him and quietly resolved that for his pain, he would have that better life we and his parents had wanted for him.

Ma did not visit me even once during my tour in Vietnam. She did not know I was there. She would have been so proud and would have found it "funny" to reside in the foreign city of Hanoi, living in that spacious four-story townhouse just like the one that used to loom over our gate. But my experience with returning Vietnamese-American citizens, and the economic and other hassles they suffered from a government that despised them even as it welcomed their tourist dollars, deterred me from entertaining the thought of having her join me.

It would have been a moment of triumph for her. I just didn't trust that the government would not come up with some charges against her just to blackmail me into committing espionage against the U.S. They could easily accuse her of trampling on someone's rice paddy in her haste to get to the river's mouth for that final boat escape from Vietnam with Brother Bong and threaten her with a prison sentence. I was convinced she was better off in Colorado with my cousin and his family. Certainly, that was a much more comfortable scenario for me, for it allowed me to devote all my attention and energy to that be-all, end-all, prestigious job I had.

The larger administrative position in Fiji gave me wide latitudes to exercise my considerable authority, and I did so with diligence, running the embassy the best I knew how and making decisions that would further our long-term policy goals and improve the staff's living and working conditions. It was a long way from implementing policies that had the power to lift entire villages out of poverty, but for that moment I found sufficient rewards in making the little differences in those lives on my path.

Away from work, life was at its most sublime. Fiji tantalized and seduced us as thoroughly as it had adventurers and dreamers for centuries. The days were of pleasures. The air was always warm and filled with intoxicating scents of a hundred different fruits and flowers. I basked in nature's bounty, rejoicing in the sun, the sea, and the fruits of the land, and now and again managed to retrieve the familiar enchantment that I'd once had as a very young child undisturbed by wants and needs, to savor fully the splendor in every breath of nature.

Inevitably, the wonder that stirred my heart also released an altogether familiar nostalgia...When new blooms opened on the bougainvilleas in their decorative earthen vases around the cabana; when scents of jasmines, gardenia, and roses filled the air and a passing wind skimmed across the pool, I would feel ripples racing across my heart, suffocating me with waves of longings for a wondrous life that was. And I would lift my face toward the heavens and let the fragrance fill my eyes with tears as I thought of the yard that was not to know the feel of these roots, the orchard air that never knew of these scents, and my parents…who never knew of such splendor.

When whitecaps raced across the sapphire blue sea and the flighty, frothy waves tugged the indolent, insolent sands from their beds, I would think of another sea and a wistful young woman on the rock alone, yearning and hoping, not knowing that Fate had the most incredible journey in store for her.

When I heard fat raindrops pelting down on the tin roof of our spacious, open-air island home, I remembered our rush to prepare the vats to catch the precious water that, according to my parents, was the best drinking water there ever was. When a rooster called for the dawn, the endearing sound reminded me of my crops of fowl—how my heart and hope soared at the sight of their maturity. When rainwater crested the rim of the grassy ditch outside the gate, I recalled the tropical downpours that flooded the muddy roads of my youth and the fervent hope that was resurrected anew in my heart when I penned my wants and sent them off to sea in tiny paper boats, praying that when the dragon next came to draw water for rain, he would find them and take them to God.

Whenever that cloud of a thousand memories came floating back, I would be able to taste the charm that was and know the loss of the richness that was my life. If it had not been for a heart so burdened with wants, I would have seen; I would have known.

The land on these blessed isles was fertile and rich. I saw ripe mangoes fall unnoticed on the ground and "*tsk*ed…*tsk*ed…" just the way my ma did. "What a pity, so much waste, no one wants this?" I would think then of another land from another time and my never-ending search for a sign of ripening fruits. Now I could sit at the table with my children where a dozen huge crabs, steamed and ready to eat, awaited our pleasure. We ate them as snacks in the manner of the haves, just because we could.

On many a languid Saturday, we anchored our twenty-three-foot boat, the *Princess Azura*, in any of those deep pockets of water in the lagoon and enjoyed a picnic onboard between snorkeling trips to the colorful world below. Sometimes, rather than going out to the uninhabited Nukulau Island, we would stop at the midway mark between the yacht club and the island and anchor at the sandbank, that delightful little blip of land that had been created by a tempest and quite likely would one day be obliterated by another. We would sit on the sand, half submerged in the warm water of the South Pacific, while Tyler ran back and forth to search for sand dollars and Zu shrieked in merriment each time the playful wind sprinkled seawater on her face.

Fiji brought incredible joy to my life, not the least of which was seeing Shen breaking free of the shackles of her boyfriend's manipulation. His callousness ended the relationship so that she finally was able to make her own way. At last, I learned the true nature of their relationship—how cheating was a norm for him. I gained little comfort in knowing I'd played a part in nurturing the boy who ended up destroying her adolescence and leaving enough scars behind to burden her adulthood.

As her heart began to heal, Shen abandoned her plan to study marine biology at the University of the South Pacific to return to Colorado—Suva was too provincial for her. Away from me, she looked to her father for love and attention, but he did not have it to give, still struggling from one difficult relationship to another. His needs came first. Come to think of it, mine did too, just in a different way. My narcissism was better camouflaged—it was called ambition.

Shen would return without fail to visit us every summer and Christmas, bringing Ma along. Ma was always delighted to come, but her exultation would last for only a few short days. Suffering from the onset of Alzheimer's, she would start nagging me to take her home in that belligerent, whining voice of a child. Even if my brother's wife had treated her like a burden, which made it necessary for her to move in with my cousin, I could not convince her to stay and make her home with me. With no apology and no regret, she said in a matter-of-fact voice, "I am poor. I not live with rich people. I not get along with rich people." My life, as she saw it, was gilded with wealth and comfort. There was no room for a consoler, a nurturer, the only way she knew how to be.

At my cousin's home, even if her wisdom went unheeded, she still retained a measure of usefulness—coaxing the storeowner to give her a good deal on those mangoes that were about to spoil or the fish that would not be too fresh anymore on the morrow. I understood her reason to stay near Bong—she was needed by him—but did not have enough love in my heart to want her to be happy wherever she was. My love was conditional, the way hers never had been.

I let her words puncture my heart and allowed the hurt to take me back to the years when, as a child, I had resented so much her preferential treatment of my brother. As an adult, I now knew the reason why he was treated specially. As a mother, I realized how mothers sometimes appear to favor one child over another. But I did not want to take the time to reconcile this newfound knowledge with that resentment from the past. I saved my sage reasoning and introspection for work and let the child's envy disturb my peace with Ma. A silly and fanciful child who grew up to be a foolish adult, I did not treasure my mother until it was too late.

Denver, Colorado, November 1999

I received news of Ma's death from my cousin. By the time I arrived, her body had lain in wait within the impersonal walls of the mortuary for four days, with only Shen in attendance from opening until closing times.

I looked at the body of the woman who had given me life, then helped me survive it, and felt the thoughtlessness and the envy slipping away at last. I touched the bony, big-veined hands that were folded on her chest, over the heart that was once filled with so much love that whenever I thought of childhood, I found only memories of tenderness and joy. I realized I was an orphan now, with all the significance that implied. The unconditional love and devotion, the single person whom I could always count on, was gone. Alone now, I finally knew the depth of a mother's love and my misfortune in having taken it for granted as if it were my right, as if it would always be there.

What broke my heart was the realization that she had never held my ingratitude against me. She had expected it. How many times did she recite this old adage in my careless youth, "A parent's love for her children knows no borders, no limits, but children account for each day they return that love."

I remember shushing at her silly lesson, claiming I would love her more than she had ever loved me, for I would have so much more to give. In my child's mind, that would be how I would show my love—more to give. She looked at me with a pride and wistfulness I didn't understand. Now I knew. She wanted my vow to be true, knowing it probably would not be. She needed to hear my affirmation, to know she had raised me right, that I would honor my duty and care for her and Ba and Bong when the time came, while praying I would come through on my promise.

Such was the irony of life.

There was never any doubt that she would be there for me; there was, however, every doubt that I would for her. She stayed in her familiar poverty while I flew high on wealth and privilege, busy charting my way to the top.

I looked at the plush room where she lay at rest, among the richness she had not known in life. There were beautiful landscape paintings on the wall, thick carpet below, and soft lighting all around to soothe the senses. All the same, I knew she would have preferred to have been laid out in the drafty upper room of that wooden house where her mother had lain before her. She would not have wanted to have garish makeup on her face to make her look like one of the leisure rich. She would not have wanted to pretend to be someone she never was, unlike her foolish daughter. She would have wanted to take her final rest in the poor section of that cemetery among the people of her class.

I followed her coffin inside the crematorium and told her I loved her, but the words sounded empty. How many times did I hear her preaching to a wayward child, "You not love your mother when she was alive, what good are your crocodile tears now?"

My heart convulsed with maddened pain as the crematorium workers closed the steel door shut. I remembered her fear and whispered hoarsely, imploring with her not to be scared, to move quickly out of her body, away from the flame. "We have to do this," I promised urgently, "so we can take your ashes home, to the temple where Ba's ashes have been waiting."

龙

I believed my ma's spirit stayed on in that little room until I arrived. She was not waiting for my brother. She would have known how his schizophrenia had gotten worse, that he could not even comprehend that she had died. At her last awareness, her sweeping love would have become even stronger for the delicate child who had needed her so much through his life and who needed her still.

Her spirit was with me when I opened her only remaining possession, the suitcase she had bought once upon a time to use on her trip to Fiji to visit me. There was none of the clothing I had made for her at every Tet—she had apparently given them away to those needier than she. I stared at the two outfits that remained and cried all over again for the modest life of the woman who had lived so well, who had given so much to others there was nothing left at her death. She had indeed left this life just as she had entered it—with nothing.

My cousin and his wife, mistaking my shocked silence for vexation over the disappearance of her belongings, rushed to assure me that they had no idea where most of her things had disappeared to, that there had been nothing there besides those few pieces of clothing.

So that was Ma... She had asked me for clothing at such increasingly more frequent intervals; I'd begun to wonder how she had gone through them so quickly and whether she had developed a penchant to accumulate more than she needed like many others in this new culture of ours.

I lifted a blouse and was overcome by the familiar smell of tiger balm, which she'd used to lather generously on herself to treat everything from aches to quivers to pains. Under it, in plain sight to all, was the little four-inch bag she had made to keep her money, which my cousin had said he could not find.

He and his wife gasped loudly. They were sure they had gone through every inch of that suitcase, even the lining, looking for that very item, but the stash bag was never there. They shook their heads, murmuring on how her spirit had kept that hidden from everyone's eyes but mine. I struggled to see through the veil of tears. Trembling, I counted every bill, all of which had been straightened and folded so neatly by my mother's hands, to a staggering sum of $2,215. Churned with agony, I clutched on the side of her coffin to pull myself up. I leaned over and touched her hands, the hands that had labored so hard to feed me. They were cold now, so cold and lifeless, nothing like the vital woman she had been. With a heart filled with remorse, I let the tears flow and felt my love for her coming through in torrents, just the way she used to love me. I whispered my apology, which came too late for me and her. I told her I understood what the money was for. "Ma, I have enough money to bury you. You not have to do this."

All this time, when she nagged me for money, squirreling away every dollar, selling this piece of jewelry and that which I had given her, I thought she was channeling it to my brother so he could go for another bout of drinking. But she was saving it for her funeral. I recalled clearly many a conversation we had had on the subject. "You know how you pay for my funeral? Land in American cemetery very expensive, you know. Send me home when I get sick. In Vietnam, land cheap. If too expensive in Saigon, take me to countryside where I used to live near Bong. Land very cheap there. Look for an old lady named Nhan. She has land. She my friend. She let you bury me on her family plot, maybe without charge."

I did not want to think about the gloomy prediction about her death, so discarded the talk as nonsense. "Ma, you are silly. I can bury you when the time comes. Don't worry." But she did. She loved me enough not to want to impoverish me by her death. She didn't know I could very well afford to buy all that her heart might have desired. The miser façade I had put up was to guard my possessions against the excesses of my wastrel of a brother. It didn't matter to me that his mind was not right

Her final lesson on love and sacrifice reached me from beyond and humbled me.

In a flash of insight, when it could no longer help my ma, I knew that I could have done much for both her and my brother. With the money I had, I could have set up a small shop—it didn't matter what we sold—on Federal Boulevard, the "Saigon village" of Denver. My brother would have felt useful, and Ma, Ma would have been proud to be a minor shop owner in ways she had never been with a gated villa and a circular driveway flanked with frangipani. Modest in wants, that shop would have been a sufficient reward, a venue for her to pay off her karmic debt, to return the kindness other shop owners had shown to her in the hard, hard days of my youth. Its patrons would have been the answer to her longing for the sight and sound of home. She would have allowed the poor to keep a ledger with the shop; she would have been kind.

Fourteen

In the news: 11/1/64–Viet
Cong attacks major U.S.
base, destroys six B-57.

The Orchard, 1964

In a modest emulation of the northern entrepreneurial spirit, Ma borrowed money from Little
Second Older Sister to increase her herd of pigs.
She crammed the twelve piglets into her baskets
and took them home to the little pen Ba set up
at the corner of the existing sty. As they grew
bigger, Ba expanded the sty, building an addition
over the ditch. The proliferation of food stalls
and restaurants helped enable Ma's latest venture. Deferential and helpful, she was liked by
everyone, so it was easy enough for her to obtain
permission to put a slop bucket at this restaurant
and that stand to collect food for the pigs.

Twice a day, she walked through the sites,

emptying those buckets into bigger tin cans that she carried by means of a bamboo cane and ropes. I could tell how heavy the load was simply by watching her. With her back bent from the weight, she looked much shorter than her five foot height. The cane rested on both of her shoulders rather than one, and she walked more quickly, as if fearing she would lose her balance if she were to slow down. Sometimes she asked Ngau and me to come along to help with cleaning the bucket and wash area. We would jump at the chance, for this was an opportunity to do one chore or another for the shop owner to earn a half a bowl of soup each. Ma was always happy when this happened; it meant we could save food at home.

While we ate, Ma would wash the dishes, sweep the floor, soak and wash basketfuls of fresh basil or chop up green chili peppers to show the owner her gratitude for our food. Whenever he thought of it, the owner would offer a bowl to her as well, which she would take but a few bites then divide the remainder between me and Ngau. It didn't matter that she gave us her all—I always turned greedy. I would sit on the edge of the chair and watch the distribution while saliva pooled in my mouth. A helping of noodles for me, one for Ngau, a spoon of broth for me, one for Ngau…To prevent her making an error in his favor, I would call out our names alternately so she would know whose bowl she had last filled.

Every pig sale was a celebrated event. The sale negotiation usually included so many kilos of meat in addition to an agreed-upon monetary price. We would get a pig's head (never one of our own) and about five kilos or so of hindquarter meat. The treat never lasted very long in a large household like ours. The dry period between the rains—that familiar famine—was usually so long that our appetites became insatiable. Pork stew, with plenty of fat, was the rave. After the meat had been reheated for several days, the fat would literally dissolve on contact with the tongue. It was the taste of plenty.

Naturally, Ma had to share this largess with the extended family—a generous hunk for Eighth Uncle, another for Older Sister Phuong, and one for Third Older Sister. Others could be selfish with what they had; she always had to do the right thing.

The main treat, the pig's head, would be boiled then offered whole to wandering spirits. Afterwards, Ma sliced the ears and some of the fatty meat to serve with heaps of fresh lettuce, corianders, bean sprouts, and moistened rice paper, for a round of "*an choi*," or "snack." What remained of the head was then added to the hindquarter meat to make a stew that could last up to a week.

Out of the sale proceeds, Ma made sure she set aside enough money to buy sufficient quantities of basic staples such as rice and fish sauce to feed us for at least a month, just in case worse came to worse. The salt jar and the lard bowl were also filled to the top. She did not trust her heart not to feel sorry for Ba and give him more than she should of what was left.

Thanks to the sale, we would have a few days of feast before the famine would again descend upon us. New piglets would arrive in the same week, as Ma tried to time the next pig sale to coincide with the arrival of Tet.

Every pig sale was Ma's victory. To make sure it was grand, she prepared carefully for it. Before the sale, she would frequent the coffee shop where rumors of all sorts could be picked up. She sought tips on current prices and on pig brokers—who was good or who was not so reliable. It was through this venerable rumor mill that Ma learned about *Anh Tam*, or Eighth Older Brother, who was reputedly the best of the best in pig brokerage.

He was tall, unusually handsome, and a smooth talker to boot. Forever respectful to Ba and Ma, he earned their affection almost immediately. The first transaction he handled for us garnered a higher price than Ma had expected. Even the wizened men were impressed. "Very, very good deal," they said.

The rumor mill sang his praises. He gained a few more customers and the attention of Third Older Sister, who happened to be home during one of his chance visits. She made the trip home more often, which usually coincided with his coming to call on Ma and Ba. He began to give her a ride back to work on that three-wheeler of his, which he operated as a public conveyance whenever he needed the funds on whatever route that took his fancy. Next they started going out to eat. Then came the strolls along the bank of the Saigon River at dusk. This was the thing for lovers to do—"catching the breeze," it was called. They would park their motor scooters, or bicycles—in the case of impoverished lovers—along a river or lake or at the edge of a rice field just outside the city to catch the breeze at sunset. A courting was definitely in progress.

Proper and wise, Eighth Older Brother started to bring gifts for Ba and Ma with each visit: one day a kilo of the meatiest roast pork, the next a succulent road duck and a few baguettes to go with it, and still the next a dozen pork dumplings and a few plastic bags of sweet beans, or dalo and glutinous rice pudding.

His generosity and correct manner went a long way in dispelling any misgivings Ba and Ma had had about him, which I'd overheard during their morning coffee. Eventually, they disregarded that inner voice telling them something was amiss. Eighth Older Brother, after all, seemed a respectable sort who made a good living, very unlike Third Older Sister's first love, who had drifted in with the wind one day only to go out with the rain the next.

Proper he may have been, Third Older Sister became pregnant before the year's end. Ma and Ba waited for the right words from Eighth Older Brother. Surely, they would plan to be married, or, at the very least, start living together. Anyhow, a formalizing of arrangement of some sort was expected, not a wedding since Third Older Sister was no longer a young girl.

An announcement came, though not quite the kind my parents had in mind. It happened late one afternoon just after we had finished the evening meal. I was the only one who still lagged behind in the kitchen to snatch a pinch of the leftover stir-fired long beans for another mouthful. As I washed the greasy evidence from my fingertips at the washstand, a breeze came through. I smiled and lifted my face to cool while playfully urging the wind onward. "*Gio oi* (hey, wind), no lovers here, go play somewhere else."

I heard the squawking of a hen then a series of wild flapping of wings. Making my way out to the yard, I thought to scold Ba for his lack of finesse in stealing eggs. There was a way to get eggs without agitating the hens, and he knew it. But Ngau came running up the path just then, panting. "Third Mother, Third Mother, Eighth Older Brother's wife is asking about Third Older Sister. She's at the gate. Old Lady Hai (the grocer who lived by our gate) tell her our house's here. She come right now."

Before Ba and Ma could utter a word, a woman alighted from behind the palm tree, her steps purposeful as if heading for battle.

A commotion ensued. Cries of anguish and obscenity and threats were hurled on the unwitting heads of Ma and Ba. In one hand, the woman held a sharp-looking knife. Its blade shone menacingly, to which Ba had only the softest words of consolation. Her aggression withered in the face of his humility. Eyes closed, she wailed and sank to her knees. The knife dropped with a thud on the packed earth. As Ba picked up the knife, Ma squatted beside her and listened to her ranting between heart-rending sobs.

I was entranced by the unfolding drama. So this was a "jealous assault." I had heard about these but had never witnessed the real thing. Here, the scene ended a little differently; the woman wronged sought vengeance but found sympathy. Her body was wracking with sobs rather than delivering or receiving blows, which turned out to be what she needed, as she calmed in the soothing tone of Ma's words.

Scenes like this were part of the dramas of our lives. It even had a name—"*Danh ghen*," or jealous assault. Eighth Older Brother's wife did not go home a peace-loving, repentant woman by any means, even if she did cry on the shoulders of the other woman's mother. Threats were left in no uncertain terms—acid thrown at the face was the method of choice. "Leave Eighth Older Brother or else," were her scathingly issued parting words.

Eighth Older Brother's embarrassment, or "loss of face," was mitigated by the vehemence of his wife's threats. Ma tried to talk Third

Older Sister into leaving him so he could return to his wife, but it was much too late. Eighth Older Brother rushed about to find a place for Third Older Sister to live, or hide, rather, until he could resolve matters at home. The situation was progressing as expected. Here was a wayward husband moving at a frenetic pace to hide his paramour. From one house to the next, this would go on until the wife accepted that the other woman was here to stay. Third Older Sister was lucky. I heard Ma say so one early morning. "She not get beaten. She not watch out, one bottle of acid, finished."

Eighth Older Brother turned out to be a skillful juggler, as adept in that task as he was at courting and winning Third Older Sister's affection and ours, even if it did take several moves to various safe houses to accomplish. The drama finally ended when his "big wife" accepted the fait accompli. After all, a child was on the way, and Eighth Older Brother had promised to be fair to both houses.

Years hence, we would learn that he had another house set up elsewhere in the city.

His wife settled into her new station as "principal," or "big" wife, even if she was still bitter and would remain so for many years. Third Older Sister moved back to the room Ba had set up for her at the corner of the lower house. There she would stay and bear five children with Eighth Older Brother.

FIFTEEN

IN THE NEWS: 6/29/65–U.S.
FORCES AUTHORIZED TO
FIGHT IN VIETNAM.

The Orchard, 1965

Another summer rumbled through. Dragonflies lanced through the field, buzzing over grasshoppers, which hopped, stalked, and munched their way slowly through the grass. Crickets sang their tunes from caves and among the weeds, celebrating the season of abundance. The land hummed with new life, while the heat simmered and scorched and humidity deepened. Rainstorms came in deluge, inundating roads and burying bicycles in shin-deep water, as the village's primitive ditch ways struggled to accommodate the rushing runoff. After the drenching, the following day's heat would be welcomed as it dried up muddy sidewalks and alleyways, then again scorned as it peaked at high noon. Relief would arrive once more in the form of torrential rains.

The weather may seem unchanging to visitors foreign to the land. To the fresh-faced soldiers who came to Vietnam many moons ago, summer might as well have been the only thing that was. Heat and more heat, they moaned. They would remember the rain that never seemed to stop and the mosquitoes that came when it did. Misery on top of misery, they struggled to cope with benevolent forces of nature while trying to survive a malicious war waged by misguided men. Not only did they not have the home-field advantage, but for all the strangeness of the place, they might as well have been on another planet.

Meanwhile, I roamed from one growing season to the next, closely watching the blooms in the orchard, then the mango tree, hoping for a bumper crop. From pig sales to coriander harvests, Tet to Tet, we lived off the fruits of the land. I never knew the narrowness of the margin to which we clung for survival, or the precariousness of such an existence, or the sweet simplicity of such a life. We trudged faithfully through the cycle. From joy to sorrow; from the feast following a harvest of pigs, flowers, or collard greens to the famine when neither was matured enough; from the joy of Ba's winning at the games to the stormy disappointment at his loss; from the unrelenting heat to the rain that never seemed to let up; we went through the cycle so many times I knew the ups and downs of both extremes and all the shades in between. But I would remain ignorant of the wisdom and necessity of opposites. I only knew how ecstatic I was during the upswing of feast, not realizing that the feast would not have been termed such had it not been for the famine.

The cycle of life, of nature, is perfectly orchestrated with all its causes and effects and contradictions. And there is beauty and perfection in all of it. Take the rain—I remember how those life-giving but bothersome afternoon rains could spill into the night under a cloud cover so low and thick that it was impossible to tell when day became night.

However, more often than not, the downpour would stop before the sun could slip away. Against a brightened sky, the sun would descend in all its glory, including that last-minute splash of gold to showcase remnants of the storm—those thick, dark patches of clouds across the sky, and turn that sunset into the wonder only writers and poets could render justice. Therein lay the brilliance of the interplay. If the heavens had not stirred, the clouds would not have gathered, and that dramatic backdrop would not have been there to set off the majesty of the setting sun. Surely the scene would have arrested, but not stunned, the senses.

If I could have known that each experience would add form and color to my existence, I would not have worried and grieved so. If I could have believed in the all-knowing and benevolent God with the conviction Ma had, I would not have struggled so hard to break away, to seek happiness on the other side of that proverbial hill. I would not have burdened Ma with scorn for her life and ingratitude for what she tried to do for mine. But it was the beginning of a senseless war, and I was but a foolish and ignorant child who thought not of the misery and cruelty of war but only of the excitement for the new and extraordinary.

In early childhood, sometimes I went to bed hungry in spite of my best scrounging efforts. Over time, my imagination and resourcefulness sharpened as I, like the adaptable creatures in Darwin's world, adjusted to the environment around me. I became better at foraging on the field, in the orchard, and on other people's kindness. Survival was the name of the game. Only it was not a game. All around me, everyone was practicing these survival skills, including the wandering soup peddler, whom I had envied for the longest time. I resented her children for all the foods I'd supposed they could eat—the variety and abundance of it all—a different soup each morning, another kind of sweet pudding in the afternoon. I did not know such was all she had, that her family's livelihood rested on her shoulders. A slip at a pothole or a fight over space in a crowded alley would have obliterated her capital and so hardened their struggle.

As a child, I idolized Ba because he was quiet and kind—an island of calm in the sea of turmoil that was my ma. I stayed away from the shouts, the curses, and the cane, avoiding Ma and the hateful tasks that I was sure had been designed to keep me from doing pleasurable things such as reading and daydreaming. It was so much easier to gain affection and favors from Ba. With little effort, I would earn a smile, which could later translate into a bill discreetly stuffed in my pocket when he returned triumphant from a game. All I had to do was find a ripe lime in the sometimes-barren orchard to make a glass of fresh lemonade when he came in for lunch, or if there was not a lime to be had, a ladle of cool water from the rainwater vat.

It would have taken far too much work to please Ma.

Ba was thoughtful and considerate, except for that lapse of reason caused by his love of gambling. Knowing how that flaw contributed to Ma's pain, he tried to make up to her in other ways. He listened to her, comforted her, and shouldered many of the chores. Before heading out in search of a game, he would make sure there were sufficient firewood and kindling neatly stacked near the stove, pig slops cooked and left to cool, and clothes washed and hung on the lines to dry.

A pacifist by nature, his serenity lessened the turbulence that could have been. It were as if because he himself could not give me the dreams—he didn't know how—he gave me the peace I needed to dream. That was to be his gift. He would gently shush Ma. "Our child is still too young. Let her play for a while longer."

That time came when I was about nine. I could not remember exactly when or how it happened, but suddenly I was left to Ma and my responsibilities. It was supposed that I had matured enough to learn my place in the household and to help shoulder some of the burdens. I was ready to be a participant in the business of making a living.

Gradually, with the responsibility of an adult, I began to see Ma with the eyes of a child grown. I saw the perennial hardships that continually bore down on her shoulders and the sadness in her heart for failing to provide for us. In my future, a perpetual struggle such as that could lead many an otherwise responsible adult to a melancholy so debilitating that it could lay waste to all movements and thoughts extraneous to the nurturing of misery. It did none of those things to my ma. She would allow herself mere minutes of indulgence—counting off to Ba all the merchants that she had owed too much to ask for another purchase on account or wondering out loud what to do, where to go for the day's meal. Unshed tears would glisten in her eyes for a few moments. Then it was over. She was ready for life once more.

Her love for us had no bounds and knew no conditions.

I used to enjoy being ill. I didn't even mind being bled for days on end, because it meant I could have all the attention I wanted and more food, the best food there was, so I could get my blood back. To this day, I still didn't know what it was that had ailed me. Whatever, for several long weeks, the neighborhood nurse rode her little scooter, the "Mobylette," to our house every afternoon to make incisions on my back with a jagged piece of shard and let the blood run into a dozen little suction jars. She judged me better after each visit by the sight of brighter blood at each letting.

Ma didn't seem to care that her ledgers around town got longer after every bout of illness. She was forever hovering over my bed, touching my forehead with her rough, callused hand to see if the fever still raged. "You want fish soup? Get up just for a moment for a bowl of soup. No like fish soup? How about chicken Pho? You are weak still. Ah, too weak for beef, hard to digest. A wonton soup? I think… mmm… How about it?"

She alternated the different dishes to whet my appetite so I could eat more to regain my health, and rushed about to get her work done so as to return to my bedside to monitor my recovery. It did not matter that I just had a cold; she indulged my every whim.

By and large, Ba was spared the task of foraging for food. Mindful of our never-ending needs, he would stop and pick a few handfuls of young potato leaves if he should happen to spy the sight of their exuberant reach above the staid, dark green patch of leaves that had been young once but which he had missed and now were altogether too tough for good eating. Ma would make *nuoc mam* the way I loved it, with plenty of fresh garlic and spicy chili and fresh lime juice as a dipping sauce for the crispy-steamed leaves.

Ba's expertise was in catching frogs.

His time to shine as an accomplished hunter was in the middle of the rainy season, right after a rain, where parts of the field were inundated with ankle-high water and the croaking of frog punctuated the stillness of the night.

When I was about ten, he began to bring Ngau and me, and sometimes also Little Rat, along to help. Why not Big Rat or Bong? Well, Big Rat was considered smart, an intellectual among us, so he was frequently left alone to study for this test or that exam. As I remember, Bong was a fairly good student as well, but the main reason he was exempt was because Ma feared he would get sick from the cold.

As we ventured into the field, the tall grass would brush against my chest, making me wobble from fear of caterpillars. As I stumbled, the oil lamp in my hand would swing wildly in tandem with the sloshing sound of water under my feet. Little Rat, Ngau, and Ba, favoring a more stealthy approach, would branch out ahead of me, far enough to find those intended victims still undisturbed by, if not quite unaware of, the noises I made, but close enough to see by the luminescence of the light.

Our rainy night forays into those watery depths did not stop until I got to my early teens, when we finally had more money to buy food and were no longer reliant on frog meat to supplement the meals. Our adventures did become more stable in later years on our acquisition of a flashlight.

Ba's catches were always substantial, a feat that was made more spectacular by the fact that he didn't even have the proper equipment such as a fish-trapping basket that peasants normally used. He simply aimed, jumped, and grabbed the frog with his hands. Given that we kids were still very small with little hands, we had to employ a different method of catching frogs—leaping and falling on the frog, using the mass of our bodies, what there was of them, to pin the frog down. Being extremely ticklish was definitely a liability in this frog-catching business. Between the frog wiggling to escape and Ba snaking his hand under my tummy to find a frog that didn't want to be found, I would squeal and roll and sometimes lose my catch.

We would have a delicious meal, usually frog curry with thin vermicelli noodles. A thoughtless carnivore in those days, I loved the meal, even if I thought the sight of skinned frogs lying in a row looked humanoid.

For a time, our compound remained that oasis of calm and simplicity amidst the widening desert of concrete opposite our gate where jasmine, tea, and vegetables had once flourished. With American aid, the roadway beyond the compound had ceased to be a dirt road. It was now a paved thoroughfare where the few remaining horse wagons and oxen carts vied for the right-of-way with cars, military trucks and jeeps, motor scooters, and three-wheelers running their routes to and from the marketplace. A row of modern villas rose on the other side of the street. Although these did not have the sheltered look of the older ones in town, they had the promise of dignity, since the requisite frangipani and bougainvillea had already been installed.

One of the villas belonged to a lawyer turned political activist. I learned this from Eighth Uncle, who read everything that was fit to print. And what they did not print, he got from the coffee shop. Anyway, this lawyer *cum* agent provocateur eventually ran for election against President Thieu under some sort of anti-government reconciliation with the Viet Cong banner and ended up being jailed for something or other. Eighth Uncle followed the celebrated career path of our esteemed neighbor with a slight bias. Given his dislike for the establishment, any establishment really, Eighth Uncle was the man for the underdog— definitely the right man for his time. What with the Buddhist clergy crying oppression, the Viet Cong denouncing American imperialism, and the people against government corruption, surely the Americans could be blamed for all of it.

I didn't much care about our neighbor or his politics, although his controversial rhetoric did liven up my meal and bedtime debates with Eighth Uncle. I noticed only the little girl who lived in that house, a girl about the same age as I, whom I used to watch from our gate. My eyes would glue to her, this light-skinned, moon-faced girl with a school uniform of blue skirt, white shirt, and clean brown sandals. I knew she must be going to one of the uppity French *lycees*. All the rich kids did. It was not only a status symbol; it was a means to ensure their privileged lifestyle. A sort of insurance in case the Fate turned capricious. This was how it went, as Eighth Uncle once summed it up for us. Higher education in France, then with wealth and connection already in place, a rich kid returned to assume a mandarin type of job in the government—the next generation of lords in the making.

Untouched by trivial things such as hunger, she sat serenely on her fancy white swing, reading as she waited for her chauffeur to get the car ready and time to leave for school. Close to the gate, bougainvillea vines tightened their gnarly grips on the wall, even as paper-thin scarlet blossoms unfurled to meet the morning breeze. Several frangipanis lined the edge of the lawn; their fallen blooms littered the path to cushion the footfalls of the rich.

The fragrant blossoms held no value for that young girl. They did not warrant even her merest of glances. Before the sun even cleared the rooftops of refugee row, the boy gardener would have come around with his short broom and stooped to the task. Thus hunched, he would turn this way and that, swinging his broom to the right, then to the left, then right again, to rid the lawn and driveway of fallen leaves and blooms. In no time at all, the silky blooms would be relegated to a garbage heap.

Meanwhile, she remained oblivious to the toiling around her, to those waking sounds of the poor, evincing a calmness that was the opposite of my own teeming envy and frustration. The difference hence illuminated the distinctness of our paths: hers, peace and contentment; mine, anything but.

She would look up occasionally at her chauffeur and the passing traffic. Her face, angling just so, looked proud and disdainful. The fragrance of frangipani wafted across the street to where I stood, caught on my tangled, matted hair, lingered for a moment, then sailed away with the capricious breeze, leaving me feeling strangely bereft. Curiously, the blooms' sweet breaths did not soothe but caused my eyes to burn and my stomach to clench. If someone had seen me and asked why my eyes looked watery and pained, I would have said...

Now, in my mind's eye, I can see us again—that little girl on the swing, a picture of perfect tranquility in the soft morning light, and me, standing on the opposite side of the street, holding so tightly to the vertical bar on the gate that my fingers turned bloodless. So strong were these emotions of old that in summoning the images, I could almost smell the fragrant air once again and remember the painful force of my want.

龙

Finally, American dollars reached inside our compound to expand the little-known department into a well-staffed agency, charged with helping farmers protecting their crops. Progress arrived, with water that traversed from our ancient well through little steel pipes to the house, ending at a leaky little faucet over the wash stone, and electricity. The house looked bright and joyful with the amazing neon lights. Ba would sit on his divan, glance at the bright tube high above our heads, and smile proudly, as if *he* had just invented electricity.

We no longer did our homework by the warmth of an oil lamp or candlelight. Dazzled by the bright lights, I soon forgot about flickering flames and dancing fireflies. To find again the twinkling magic, I would have had to venture deep into the orchard. Once upon a time, the sight of dancing lights in the orchard used to stir my imagination, evoking my resolve to triumph like the fabled poor peasant who was too poor to even afford a lamplight but who nevertheless rose to be a respected mandarin in the king's court by studying within the luminescence of the fireflies.

The grassy dike that cut through the middle of the compound became a gravel road. A big villa was erected at the end of the road just inside the back gate for the boss engineer. It looked like all the villas I had seen, only newer. Two half-matured frangipanis had been planted along the driveway. Dark purple, white, and red bougainvillea rose from big ceramic vases to twist around the pillars and wreath the front portico.

At the opposite end of the path, construction then began for a new warehouse, as well as a glass-enclosed laboratory and two buildings of offices, all of which would be used to house and further the work of agricultural engineers and biochemists. The orchard was silent no more. Where once there were only the lullaby of the wind and soft stirrings of insects, now a jarring cacophony of man-made noises—hammer banging, tin sheet clanging, and bawdy chattering by workmen from atop rickety scaffolds—filled the air and stifled all lives within it.

Like the insects in my paradise, my senses were jolted by the violent intrusion. The time for dreams had effectively ended. I moved on with the universe and the wheel of Fate.

I was thirteen years old and already a veritable breadwinner. I roamed the construction site to scavenge for empty cement bags and scrap metals to sell to scrap buyers—women with canes and baskets who came through the neighborhood to buy everything from broken glass bottles to duck and chicken feathers, to discarded newspaper, scrap metals, and empty cement bags.

This was not a simple matter of collecting unwanted items. I had stiff competition from the watchman who also wanted that additional income. My raids thus had to be done at dusk when he was out having the evening meal or at a card game. Not content with his own loots, which were entire bags of cement and wheelbarrows upon wheelbarrows of sand and gravel diverted at delivery, he wanted the scrap metals as well.

I used to curse him and his accomplice, the appointed foreman of the new warehouse, naturally a northerner, for the way they treated my ba. Ba was so pure and untainted by the corruption, a bystander amidst the madness. But they were worried about discovery, so tried to edge him out by saying he was too old to be working still, that it was not right for too many people to be living in our house, which sat on government land. The usurpers were not there when Ba defended and cared for the property during the brief but brutal occupation by Japanese forces in the waning days of World War II. They saw him as a barrier to their scheme, not realizing the full extent of his pacifism. Live and let live, he was aware of their illegal activities but never breathed a word to anyone, not even to my mother.

Thanks to his benefactor, the resident engineer, whose fancy house stood like a beacon at the end of the lane, the matter was dropped before it got too high up the hierarchy. We became even more beholden to this man. Ba and Ma made themselves available to serve him and his family. If the cook was away and there was a pigeon to be plucked, or if there were coffee beans to be roasted, a flu-stricken fowl to be moved, or an after-party cleanup, they called on Ba to help. Afterwards, they would reward him with a little something from their table or the larder, which he proudly took home to us.

I had to scavenge in the dark, even though the night whispers terrified me. Only the fear of getting caught could override my fear of ghosts. I kept to the protective deep shadows as I ran from pile to pile of construction materials—from sand to rock to gravel—eyes darting all around for that little bit of iron, before searching for the bonanza of all loots: the stack of empty cement bags. Sometimes the watchman would return all too soon, and I would be forced to flee. He would see only a flitting shadow but was smart enough to know that it meant a loss of income, so would start hurling rocks at the moving target with ferocious intensity.

Clutching the precious plunder close to my body, I would run along the fence until the chase ended, either by his giving up or my breaking away unnoticed. After stashing the goods in a hiding spot along the wall behind the lower house, I was ready to join the family again. But first, I had to get rid of the evidence. I washed the dirt off my feet at the faucet, breathed in and out deeply to calm the wild thumping of my heart, then sauntered into the house with the ambling, nonchalant mode of the innocent rather than those quick strides of the hunted.

However clever I thought I was, Ba seemed to know. More than once, as I tried to control my galloping breaths, he simply said, "It not worth it. He beat you up if he catch you. Don't do it." Rather than feeling chastised, I would fix my eyes on the multitude of shadows on the wall and press my lips together in a tight, grim line. I was simply angry at the watchman's greed.

I resolved to have my revenge. Following a vicious rock throwing, I snatched his valued hen and ran all the way to Old Lady Nam's, a poor old woman who always had a fruit for me whenever I came with Ma for a visit, and gave it to her. The man searched high and low for the lost hen, even risking offending my parents by extending his search to the proximity of our henhouse. Ma and Ba suspected but were not sure if I was the culprit until much later, when Old Lady Nam thanked them for the gift of the precious hen.

When the peddler came through a week later, I had enough of a scrap heap—metal, bottles, duck feathers, and cement bags—to earn enough money to buy feed for my fowls, a day of market for Ma, and several days of snack food for me.

SIXTEEN

IN THE NEWS:
3/31/65–MARINES LAND;
BOMB RIPS SAIGON EMBASSY.

The Orchard
Saigon, Vietnam, 1965

Third Older Sister's pregnancy became more advanced, a good enough reason for Eighth Older Brother to make her quit her job. Ma presumed jealousy was his motivation and thought it was silly that Eighth Older Brother actually thought suitors would swarm around Third Older Sister for her attention. After all, she was a simple, middle-aged pregnant woman with ordinary looks. Ma couldn't understand how someone could forego such a good job. "To go home and wait for a guy to bring rice home. If he go back to his wife, then what? Silly woman!"

So Third Older Sister came home to stay. She

liked to play cards, especially the game of *"Tu Xac,"* a game we co-opted from the Chinese, which used cards barely an inch wide, three inches long, with Chinese characters similar to those on our chess pieces. The cards could be played in several different ways, all complex as far as card games went, and therefore of great fun. With her and Ba in residence, we had two players, enough to begin hosting card games at our house.

However the winds of fortune shifted for the players, the house pot was never empty, since each winner had to surrender an amount equaled to one unit—equivalent to the game's stake—to the house pot at the end of each hand. Often, we had to subtract Ba's loss from the house collection, but even with that, we stayed ahead, earning enough money to put food on the table every day.

The compound was government property and therefore considered a safe place to play—safe from police raids. Ma did not have to worry about Ba getting caught. As for me, I knew *I* didn't want to get caught. As a child of five, I almost got arrested with him once at a supposedly secured house; the host had been paying "coffee money" to an informant at the police station, whose job was to inform his patron if a raid was planned. No one anticipated an impromptu raid prompted by an errant, eagle-eyed policeman who noticed the unusual comings and goings and decided to gather a few of his hungry colleagues to check things out.

Catching card games was a lucrative endeavor for policemen, since they could siphon most of the confiscated money for themselves. It suited the players to have most of the money vanished in order to keep the fine low, so no one ever complained about the often vast discrepancy—a definite win-win situation for both sides.

Anyhow, as the police rushed in and called for all to halt, I swiped the pile of money in front of Ba, jumped over the panicked crowd, and ran out the back door. Fortunately, no one thought it important to chase after a terrified child. Meanwhile, Ba was taken to the police station, along with a dozen or so players and spectators. Thanks to the money I seized at the last minute, he did not lose his seed money, and we were able to pay the fine immediately so he did not have to spend the night in jail.

Besides the income gained through the house pot, I made money running errands for players—getting cigarettes or snacks, even taking some of the winnings home to someone's wife for market. Whenever the games continued through the night, I swatted mosquitoes for those who wanted to pay for the service. During the day, I performed pedicures with an old, rusty razor blade or extracted their facial acnes with my thumbs.

The household came alive. Ma hurried through her chores so she could help me with doing errands or cooking for the players if I had arranged to cater a dinner for them, a service I would offer only to well-heeled or generous players—profits were greater with no complaint.

I moved just as quickly through my own daily tasks—school, sweeping the house or the yard, helping Ma or the boys scrub clothes, or collecting clothes from the lines and folding them—so I could get on with the business of making money.

It did not take long before we made enough money to pay off all of Ma's accounts around town. For my part, I had built a good enough nest egg with which to buy a few fighting cocks; they fetched higher prices and had tastier, if tougher, meat (in case a flu came through). I also bought a piglet to add to Ma's new herd and thought again about that calf…

Our larder was always full now. That year, when Aunt Phan's death anniversary came around, there was money to put on a feast without getting into debt. The day was celebrated with more food than previous years. At cockcrow, the womenfolk were already at the wash stone scalding chickens and ducks for plucking and rinsing rice and beans for soup and cakes. Voices echoed through the house as cooks and helpers gossiped and chatted their way through the preparation of curry, glutinous sweet rice, rice cakes, bean cakes, chicken curry, duck soup, and salad.

As was usual, helpers brought their children along to enjoy the feast. I was too old and busy to play anymore, but I enjoyed watching them chasing one another into one door and out the other, cackling all the while. The sound of merriment would lift the air already lightened with the delicious aromas of special foods. Those were the scents and sounds of happiness and abundance.

龙

We took in a boarder, which was nothing new. Over the years, we had frequently done so, providing food and lodging for a small fee to batch after batch of newly graduated agricultural engineers, six or seven at a time, who had come through to cut their teeth on the insects in our field before going on to their respective postings—agricultural offices in the Mekong delta and the highlands, tending to outlying rice fields and cotton fields, gardens and orchards, and coffee and rubber plantations.

Seventh Older Sister would be our first regular boarder. The location of our house was perfect for her. Along with its peaceful surroundings, it was a short walk to Old Lady Hai's intersection, where our boarder kept a cigarette and fruit stand under the faded canvas awning of the coffee shop. Since she was a woman, and therefore needed more privacy than those male engineers, Ba boarded up one end of the verandah to shield at least part of her bed from public view.

The rent was minimal but better than nothing. Besides, Ma could not say no to this woman's plea for a place to bed down. I got to cash in on the new opportunity, getting paid for laundering clothes for her and providing relief at the stand when she needed a break. Eventually, I came to enjoy the selling so much that I could not have cared less about being paid for my labor. Instead, I hustled to show her my usefulness so she would let me substitute more often.

I traded my love of reading for a chance to sit behind a wobbly cigarette case and a glass cabinet where wedges of papaya and pineapples cooled under thin blocks of ice and treasured every minute of it. I carried out all my tasks with the greatest of care; there were no seeds remaining in the inner pockets of papayas; each eye of the pineapple skin was taken out with the utmost caution to preserve every bit of the meat.

Sitting behind the little stand, I was every inch an ambitious proprietress, always ready with a smile to attract potential customers. Old Lady Hai, the owner of the coffee shop, was kind to me, for my parents were well known there. Ma usually stopped in several times a week on her way home from the vegetable patch to help with washing dishes or waiting on tables. For a few hours of work, she would earn a few spoons of freshly ground coffee beans—enough for about two days of morning coffee for her and Ba, or several loaves of two-day-old bread to take home for Ba to steam for breakfast. Steamed stale bread lathered with chopped green onions and lard and dipped in *nuoc mam* was one of my father's two culinary specialties; the other was roast chicken done the rich people's way—whole—chicken rotisserie it was called. He had learned this last from a chef at some French household when he was a young boy. But he would have only one chance to make this for us, back when I was very young. Typically, any chicken we had would be cooked poor people's style—salty—to make it last longer.

The coffee shop was my favorite spot for another reason: a boy at the Chinese noodle soup wagon. He was older than I, seventeen or so to my thirteen. For a small rent, his family was allowed to park their wagon on the other side of the coffee shop. Busy with school, he came out to help only when his mother was occupied with other things: attending a wedding, a funeral, or visiting relatives. I would keep my ears peeled on the shop gossips Ma brought home so as to be there when he would.

He was handsome and quiet, speaking only when he needed to confirm a customer's order or to ask his little sister to fetch more lettuce to garnish the soup bowls. But every one of his precious words was a balm to my soul—the voice low and warm, that of a man, which stirred up all sorts of strange longing within me.

We rarely talked. Whenever he did address me directly, it was to relay an order for a plate of fruit for dessert or a pack of cigarettes to go. He hardly ever looked at me, but this did not bother me in the least. I was very comfortable with my one-sided crush, for I knew I had no right to him, not at all. I was too thin, and my family too poor. What would he want with me? Even if he did have feelings for me, his family would never agree to ask for my hand. My face was too long, not at all pretty. It did not invoke any appearance of health, of abundance, or good fortune.

His family was Chinese, which meant they were even more superstitious than we were. The moon face, the face of gentleness and mercy, was much preferred and that which I didn't have. It was quite a hopeless situation, but I was happy simply to have someone to love.

I heard of his marriage when I was seventeen, to Old Lady Hai's daughter. By then, I no longer frequented the stand but still caught sight of him now and again. The news brought back memories of those blistering afternoons when I sat under that tattered awning behind the glass case hoping to catch his eyes; one look would sustain me for a week; a smile would take me to two. He never did know how I used to sit in my classroom and stare out at the flame tree at the corner of the schoolyard, dreaming of a future for us, sounding his name on my tongue first tentatively then more certain, and loving the sweet resonance of it.

I did not know of his offer for me until many years later.

Ma was making bean dumplings for me and my children in the kitchen of our home outside of Denver, Colorado, one Sunday morning. Out of the blue, she wondered out loud whatever happened to "the Chinese noodle soup fellow."

"Who?" I asked her.

"You know, the boy who sold '*mi*' at Old Lady Hai's intersection."

"Ma, I wouldn't know. I have been gone for more than ten years, remember?"

"Ah, I wonder what happened if you married him."

"But I could not have married him. There was nothing between us."

She continued to beat and shaped the dough between her palms. "Hmm, his parents came to ask for you, did you know?"

"Wh…what? No, I didn't know. You never said anything."

"Oh, I forgot. They came after you got job at embassy. No-good life for you—selling noodles, his parents' wagon at that. If his own wagon, maybe fine. But no wagon, no good. I told them you too young to get husband. Just pretend, you know."

She giggled at this, no doubt thinking how clever she was. Over her bent head, I could see aspen leaves twirling exuberantly from the line of trees along our back fence. Beyond them, in my mind's eye, I found the tender memory of those times I waited for hours just to catch sight of the object of my adoration.

But the memory hardened quickly enough at the intruding images of weary cyclo drivers, tired women bent under their canes and baskets, and peddlers balancing the whole of their livelihood on flimsy, wobbling bikes.

I shuddered at the thought of the children he and I would have had, and how those emaciated, little figures would have meandered through lanes and alleys narrow and wide with two bamboo pieces clanging loudly in their hands—*clackkety… clackk… clackkety… clackk*—advertising the soup and bringing orders back for us to fill. Against that tableau I saw images of Shen and Thuy prancing down the clean streets of our neighborhood to the green-lawn elementary school where there were no more than fifteen children in the class, of the well-stocked public library that they and I frequented every weekend, of the food-laden table in our kitchen, and silently thanked Ma for her interference.

SEVENTEEN

IN THE NEWS:
11/30/00–BALLOTING BATTLE
FOR THE U.S. PRESIDENCY.

Saigon, Vietnam, November 2000

I returned to the land of my birth in style—traveling with the President of the United States. Sitting in one of the two straggler cars at the tail of the motorcade, I stared out the window at the passing landmarks, familiar still after such a long passage of time and circumstance. Cong Ly Street still followed the same course, though it did not look so stately any longer, having been reduced to an inadequate roadway by the explosion of population that came with peace and another northern invasion. It looked like a worn, old woman now, having seen and experienced more than enough of its share of life.

This suburb, like all of Saigon's suburbs, had indeed changed in the years I'd been away. Wide stretches of open space around Tan Son Nhat Airbase had been divided and allocated to heroes of the war: Communist old guards and their families from the north, and those treacherous southerners credited with either having caused the highest death tolls or committing the most notorious betrayals. Houses and shops fit snuggly along both sides of the road. Garish neons lit up the signs for karaoke bars and al fresco eateries, while dim little light bulbs cast shadows in those establishments called "beer *om*," roughly translated "beer hug," with pretty waitresses available for the "om" segment of the service. The villas were still there, along with their ancient bougainvillea vines.

How many times had I ridden on this road, revving up the fifty-cc engine of my blue Yamaha motor scooter for all its worth, speeding away from or catching up with the catcalls of American troops passing by in convoys of GMC trucks?

Air Force One had barely been on the ground for an hour, yet we could already tell the visit would be a success. It was a day to be an American, especially an American diplomat charged with helping orchestrate the visit. The pride I felt as Air Force One glided to a stop almost equaled the honor that swelled in my heart at my swearing-in more than ten years ago as a Foreign Service Officer. The sight of the star-spangled flag at the tail of the aircraft and the bold lettering "United States of America" at its side brought back memories of the days when America and Americans were very much part of the southern landscape.

Except for a small logistical snag before Air Force One's arrival where the Vietnamese guard at the airport gate challenged the authenticity of the seal on our permit to enter to greet the car plane that was bringing the president's and first lady's limos and SS vehicles, hoping for a generous greasing of the palm, everything went smoothly. The wily manager of the New World Hotel motor pool was able to requisition all the vehicles we needed for the motorcade. A hustler, he sure had the natural instincts to make a fantastic general services officer for one of our embassies.

The hotel's general manager had taken personal responsibility for the visit, working closely with the advance teams to prepare for the daily arrival of more and more American diplomats coming to support the visit.

Not only did we have POTUS and FLOTUS, "First Lady of the United States," but D/POTUS Chelsea Clinton and M/FLOTUS, "Mother of the First Lady of the United States," as well. Nothing was overlooked or left to chance. Everything was confirmed once, twice, thrice, to make sure the visit would go flawlessly.

It looked like it would. If nothing else, the president and his family would find the welcome heartwarming. Starting outside the airport gate, they lined the road—at some spots, seven or eight deep—to welcome the return of a former friend. The late arrival of Air Force One did not seem to have deterred the curious and the faithful. By their enthusiastic reception, one would not know this president was the leader of a former foe; perhaps because he was not—not to the South Vietnamese.

The memory brought tears to my eyes and took me back to the time that was...

They and I had shared a lifetime of change—a few years of uncertain peace in our youth, a tumultuous adolescence, then adulthood in what was easily the most extraordinary decade of our lives. We lived purely through instincts, one day at a time, singly but together in that shared quest for survival. Until the end...when I fled the country on fire, and they stayed to face the proverbial music, those deadly tunes of vengeance drummed out by ruthless victors.

My musings strolled past the yellow streetlights of the present to the young girl of those maddening years. With hope in her heart, she hopped on the back of her father's bike three nights a week for the hour ride to an English class. She could have ridden the bike to class alone, but she was getting older, old enough to be bothered by wild-riding hoodlums who roamed the streets at night to harass lone young girls. So her mother decided that her father would take her. Down Truong Minh Ky Street, which became Truong Minh Giang, with its pot-holed, lopsided shoulders, they approached the bridge under which the tepid, sluggish water of a tributary of the Saigon River flowed. Huts on stilts spread out from the bridge atop patches of thriving swamp cabbage down under.

To get them over the bridge, the girl jumped off the bike and gave her father a push up the steep incline until the bridge leveled out. To prevent a loss of momentum, he did not stop the bike for her to get back on but merely slowed down. His daughter was as agile as a monkey; he knew she could jump back on without missing a step. And she did. But he didn't know how quickly she squinted her eyes shut after embarking, holding tight on the back of his seat for the heart-stopping drop on decline, which danger was made more real by his wobbling hold on the handle bar.

A gaunt, shrunken man with a concave chest, looking at least a decade older than his age, he would rest his bike against the opposite wall of the school, a remodeled villa in a neighborhood of villas, and sat down to patiently wait for his daughter.

Sometimes he had money to buy a glass of sweetened iced coffee to while away the time, but often not. Whether he had money to buy or not, his polite and gentle ways assured him of a seat on a stool beside the stand. It would have gotten him a glass of coffee as well, but he always declined the offer. A thoughtful man, he could not infringe on the poor street vendor's kindness, eating into the latter's precious profit. He figured he did not need the coffee that much. He simply watched the gate and waited for his little girl to emerge two hours later.

Neither the girl nor her father knew how knowledge of the language was going to help. They had no map to guide them, no promise of the pot of gold at the end of that rainbow. They only had her infectious optimism.

He was a modest man, both in his outlook and way of life. All he knew was that he wanted his daughter to have a good life. For that to happen, she needed to break away from her lot. If she said learning English was the way to do so, then that was the way. Even as he believed, sometimes he could not help but feeling a bit befuddled. He was used to being a spectator of change; that his recalcitrant daughter thought she could become part of that sweeping tide totally boggled his mind.

But his ambivalence did not have a chance. His daughter was simply too adamant, too sure. A gambling man, he bet on her conviction, surrendering the entire lot of his winnings, including the seed money to pay for a three-month course, twice. That meant he had six months within which to come up with another sum to take her studies to the end. How long was it to the end? Would she know enough English in six months' time? Know enough for what? He didn't know, but he was certain she did. He would leave it up to her.

He sometimes thought there must be some wisdom in those English language books that would explain the determined and sometimes faraway look in her eyes. She was forever burying her nose in it, sounding out exotic words with seeming proficiency. He watched her when he thought she was not looking, saw the determination on her face, and believed.

Their dreams would be realized years hence, and it all began with his leap of faith that took her from the rickety old bike to the gleaming white Mercedes in the motorcade of the President of the United States...

I shook off the nostalgia, blinked away the tears, and stared out at those well- wishers who showed up to greet my president, their hero. They were old, young, and all ages in between, coming out to bear witness to a moment of triumph. And it was that. Looking at the people of my generation, I saw my elated feelings mirrored on their faces. They had come out to welcome back an old friend, the towering symbol of their former comrades in arms. For that moment and through the days of the visit, we who were there would feel a height of euphoria akin to victory. It did not matter who won that war long ago, by means fair or foul; we were finally vindicated.

At last, the charisma, the earnestness of the man, and the majesty of his office impressed on us the greatness of the country that went through so much with us, the country that did the wrong things for the right reasons.

Presidential advisers and political commentators termed the visit cathartic and essential to America's ability to finally close that painful, bloody chapter in its history. But it was more than that. To the southerners who were left behind, it was redemption long overdue. The glorious symbol of the commander-in-chief of their long-ago comrades indeed obliterated the shadows of that tragic end.

On those eager, excited faces, I saw the familiar, endearing sights of my youth—the ravages of war and poverty on roughened visages and wise, sorrowful eyes. They came out to show us that all was well. Theirs were the faces that had haunted me during my exile. Cunning though they had to be to survive the viciousness of war and the cruelty of peace, they did not have the ruthlessness and arrogance I had seen in some of the new rulers at the new capital of Hanoi.

Forced to realize the exchange of relations for economic reasons, the Vietnamese tried to manage a measure of face-saving by dragging their feet on every request, every procedure, thus giving new meaning to the term "bureaucratic red tape." Their behavior kept the fledging relationship adversarial, at least at the working level. It was a continual parry of will and power, a stressful situation for American diplomats on the scene. To be sure, we were not alone. Our colleagues in China and the former Soviet Union and elsewhere had to manage the same hostility, under that thin veneer of diplomatic niceties.

It was a lopsided bilateral relationship, and one that once again showed how well the Vietnamese knew America. The decision had been made to exchange diplomatic relations. From the American side, it was to ensure full accounting of American MIA and to facilitate American business entry into Vietnam's investment and commercial markets, then thought to be among the most lucrative and profitable. Hanoi knew that any bump on the road was not going to alter the direction set by Washington, just as they had had in the months and years preceding the end of the war. Then, before the ink was even dry on the peace agreement, they had moved men and materiel into position in southern cities to prepare for the takeover betting on the fact that the die had been cast—the Americans had washed their hands and would not be around to call them on any violation.

Now, eager to settle an old score with their nemesis the Americans, insofar as the latter had finally come within reach, they fluffed their feathers and devised ways to harass anything American, which term was soon expanded to include most foreigners. They had a special bone to pick with overseas Vietnamese, who, in their eyes, had dared to flee on the dawn of their victory.

The joke in Vietnam at that time among expatriates was the would-be motto by the Vietnamese Tourist Board: "Send money, don't bother to come." It was not far from the truth. The Vietnamese government would rather have had tourists stay home and simply send their tourist dollars to the country. Likewise, they would have preferred American diplomats to remain in Washington to facilitate trade agreements, for-eign aid, and whatever else was needed to further Vietnam's interest.

In my role as head of the American Services unit in the Consular section, I saw my share of these capricious maneuvers. My fluency in Vietnamese was a blessing and a curse. I could often interpret the speak-er's undertone—his arrogance, his hatred, and his complex—which made it hard to pretend that all was well. However, I did eventually earn the trust of those whom I despised. Interestingly enough, I earned it by being blunt, a character trait not usually associated with me—the sophisticated me that was, or particularly condoned in the business of diplomacy. I encouraged the Vietnamese to consider halting the petty harassment of hapless tourists for inconsequential, imaginary offenses. Through casual, off-handed remarks, I reminded them how the big picture—that trade agreement they had been after for so long—could be negatively affected by a disgruntled visitor's penning a scathing letter to his or her congressmen and senators on returning home.

Economic scams were everywhere. It was a feeding frenzy. The gate had been closed for so long that the influx of gullible foreigners now drew a gathering of the most avaricious, unscrupulous feeders from the top down, the bottom up, and everywhere in between.

Even though successes, such as regular quarterly visits to American citizen prisoners and fewer hassles for tourists, filled my heart with pride, the stressful living and working conditions eroded the highs of those accomplishments. I remember our first R&R trip out of the country and how at liftoff, Acey and I looked across the aisle at each other in complicity then expelled harmonized sighs of relief.

As we sped toward the New World Hotel in the heart of the city, I felt a bit smug. This was a much more pleasurable way to visit Vietnam—with President Clinton, the President of the United States.

EIGHTEEN

The Orchard, 1966

Buddhist monks had accelerated their campaign to mobilize students and the faithful to protest against religious oppression by the government. Strange how they continued to be persecuted even after the reviled Catholic regime of President Diem had been toppled. A devout disciple of the Buddhist way of life, Ma thought it was silly of them to make a big deal out of "Buddhist rights."

"What else we need?" she mused. "No pagoda, stay home and pray. Buddha not mind." She thought it stranger still when the clergy demanded that Buddhist candidates be admitted into government positions.

In retrospection, I believe the Buddhist monks were truly motivated to act on the basis of suffering and oppression they had seen. Unfortunately, once they embarked on the path of resistance, they got caught in the fervor of the fight and turned un-Buddhist-like by invoking the ego and attaching results to everything they did. They were as naive as the Communists were cunning, as uncertain in their aims as the latter were resolute. And so it was that their struggle would be exploited by the hardened northern Communists, just like many other apolitical southerners before them.

Psychologically conditioned by our long history of armed struggles against foreign domination, these southerners were easily swayed by the well-crafted Communist propaganda and failed to differentiate between the colonial colors of the French and the ideological bent of the Americans. They let rousing words of heroism and idealism blind them to truth and to virtues of love and compassion, believing that if they followed the path to sacrifice, they brought honor on themselves and served the people. They did not stop to think that not all sacrifices were noble, nor nobility was always good or true.

The same old pattern was then repeated—that of human beings acting out their darker emotions under the guise of morality.

As for my family, we were unknowing like the rest of our countrymen, so preoccupied were we at snatching a piece of the good life. Cashing in on the buildup of American forces, Big Brother Si finagled a contract with the BOQ (Bachelor Officer's Quarters) near Tan Son Nhat. His laundry shop had been expanded and could handle the ironing, but they had no space to wash and dry such a large quantity of uniforms. With our spacious yard and available labor force, we became uniquely qualified to take over the washing and drying for a monthly fee.

He provided scrub brushes. Ba came up with several half barrels of old oil drums for soaking, rinsing, and starching. My arms were too weak to scrub or rinse, so I helped Ba with the starching—turning the clothes over and around with a pole. I was particularly useful in sounding the alarm whenever rain clouds approached, running from one end of the compound to the other, calling out to Ba and the boys, then rushing back to set empty baskets under the lines for them to fill.

Folding the oversized, heavy clothing was a noisy family affair. One afternoon, as I went through my usual routine of making play out of work by prancing around in a huge pair of military fatigue pants, Eighth Uncle turned on the radio to look for music for us to toil by. His hand paused, incidentally, on the American Armed Forces station.

I caught the beautiful, seductive sound coming at me like streams of rhapsody and was lost—lost in love with the warm male voices and the strange tongue that evoked feelings of forbidden romance and exciting adventures. For the first time, I was consumed with a want greater than that of food. I wanted to feel that exotic sound coming from my own mouth; I wanted to be the recipient of the warm cadence that came through all hours of the day, sometimes hard and fast, but often soft and alluring.

Not convinced that the once-weekly English class in the high school was sufficient to enable my comprehension, I began exploring available options, taking my bike to different English language schools to find out about their courses and fees. With many jobs available on American bases, in snack bars and restaurants with American patronage, English classes had mushroomed throughout the city.

When Ba returned victorious from the track one day, as I had expected he would sooner or later, I asked him for money to pay for the tuition, promising it would help me get a good job working for the Americans to help our family.

The language would keep me busy for a long time. I would lie on my canvas cot and listen to the sound of it on the radio, not understanding but a few words of what was said. I studied and studied. Still, nothing made sense. In class, I parroted after the teacher, at first with complete ignorance, then with seeming fluency, but never really comprehended much of what was said outside of my textbooks. Meanwhile, Ba and others in the household were convinced I had become fluent and therefore could serve as their bridge to the foreign world of English and the

Americans. I continued the charade, sounding loudly words I knew, even those I didn't, to impress them.

Big Brother Si, a wheeler-dealer of northern roots—there was no other kind, not really, although those produced by the central region came a close second—stumbled in our house one day, almost tripping over the threshold beam in his haste to show us his gift: a small black and white TV, part payment for our washing that month. With exaggerated reverence, he plugged the cord in the outlet, turned a knob, moved the antenna backwards, then forwards, then sideways. He wiggled it some more, turned the knobs again, then stepped back and rubbed his palms together in anticipation. Nothing happened. There was nothing but white flakes on a dark screen.

He smiled ruefully, scratched his head, looked around, then handed the instruction booklet to me. I approached the TV as if it were a firing squad. There was no way out of this. I looked at the booklet. The words were totally unfamiliar; they didn't even look like the language I had been learning. I flipped over the pages, hoping for a glimpse of providential guidance.

Everyone waited. There was no escape. I went through the pages slowly once more, comparing the now vaguely familiar words with the drawings on the pages, then twisted and turned this knob, then that one. All my guardian angels must have been summoned to the scene. That was the only reason for the television to work. But work it did, to the *oohs* and *ahhs* of the gathering audience.

"*Con Long gioi qua, gioi qua* (very good, very good)." Big Brother Si clucked his tongue in praise. I stepped away with only the faintest smile on my lips, a look one could have assumed as modesty. If Ma wondered where the roll-of-the-eye and the rocking-of-the-heel cockiness were, she didn't say. She could not have known I was scared to death of being found out, or that the look she thought was uncharacteristic humility was actually one of fear. I simply wanted to hightail out of there before the pictures disappeared from the screen. The show that came on was "Combat," starring Vic Morrow, who would forever be my hero.

It would be my favorite show, for it was what I saw in that moment of my first triumph.

The orchard watched as I left the comforting world of dreams behind. The old orange tree stood like a loyal sentinel, bearing silent witness to my impossible journey.

The incident with the television convinced Ma of my mastery of the language. She boasted of my accomplishment to all who would listen and consequently snagged a job for me with a rich cousin who operated a snack bar inside the American Embassy.

There was only one thing wrong with the job—it required that I clean tables and chairs like a maid, like one in servitude. That bothered Ma. She had tried so hard for so long to keep me from that lowly place, and there I was, in the thick of it, after all my supposed exalted schooling.

However, she was convinced I was on the right path. Ma didn't need any formal education to guide her in the ways of the world. Having navigated against the tide for so long, she had become wisdom personi-fied. Before the term "getting your foot in the door" was perhaps even coined, she had plotted that course for me. "Try to endure this. Work hard so your betters (meaning the people who staffed the offices at the embassy) like you, then they help you get desk job, comfortable job. Not cleaning tables and chairs. Bah…you better than that."

In a society where connections meant everything, Ma knew we needed to get me in the door, even if it was a kitchen door. She had no idea that I was ecstatic with the job; I would get to be close to the Americans and practice my English. I was far from thinking it was beneath me.

The snack bar opened for business at five in the morning, five days a week. That meant workers had to be ready for pickup by three a.m. Ma and I would walk the deserted street to Old Lady Hai's intersection, where we sat on a wooden bench across from the coffee shop to wait for my ride. As we watched life on the street stir to a new day, Ma taught me about patience and about acceptance … of whatever life put in front of me. She believed that she and Ba had been kind enough throughout their lives to yield sufficient karmic blessings on mine. All I had to do was behave likewise—kind to all and the rewards will come.

Whenever I complained of being yelled at for being slow or forgetful, she would smooth my hair and gently console; if only I would try to endure the hard times, the good times would come and I would be free of their tyranny.

Thanks to Ma, Flower, daughter of Mr. Little Foreman, one of Ba's workmates, also got a job working with me as the second waitress. She and I would wipe down tables and chairs and set up salt and pepper-shakers, tableware and napkins, while the cook prepared her famous beef stew and a tasty pork broth for the equally praised Chinese noodle soup, together with bread and cheese for toasts and omelets.

The American marine on duty at the booth inside the gate was always friendly. I guessed our arrival meant his breakfast was forthcoming. For embassy staffers who wanted to avail themselves of the delectable offerings but did not want to leave their offices, Flower and I took turns making deliveries. I didn't have to try very hard to follow Ma's advice to ingratiate myself with my "betters," for I discovered that I quite liked the praises I got from the staff for getting their food there quickly, prepared and served just the way they liked it.

I painstakingly committed their personal preferences to memory: how much chili the local guard chief liked to have in his noodle soup; how little butter the American personnel officer wanted on her toast; or how the budget officer preferred to have wedges of tomatoes served with his cheese omelet. Some extra ham in the bowl of Chinese noodle soup would earn me a smile from the Vietnamese personnel assistant and a good tip of five dong, so I convinced the cook to add a few extra strips for the nice lady in personnel.

The cook, Second Older Sister, was kind to me, even if Older Sister Lieu, her stepsister and the owner of the snack bar, was less than generous.

Sometimes Second Older Sister would give me a bag of soup bones at the end of the day to take home to my mother for our table. One day, Older Sister Lieu came by just as Second Older Sister was putting the bones in the bag for me. She promptly scolded Second Older Sister and told her to save the old bones to add to the next day's broth.

Second Older Sister looked at me apologetically and shook her head in reproach at Older Sister Lieu's retreating back. I returned her kind gesture with a half smile to let her know it was all right, that I understood who the boss was. But as she put the bones away, I touched a hand to my mouth and swallowed back a sob. A pain rose from my stomach to my chest then formed a lump at my throat. I could not take my mind off the pork bones, which would have been so tasty. I could see my ba digging out the marrow and sucking on it as if it were the best food on earth.

I turned to another end-of-day task—stacking empty bottles into the wooden soda keg as my eyes burned with self-pity. If anyone had seen me with tears in my eyes, I don't know what I would have said.

I gave all of my meager earnings over to Ma for market. She would take care of my needs first since I was then a regular wage earner in the household, a status that earned me some respect. From time to time, I would get a new blouse, a pair of western slacks, or a new "*ao dai*" for school.

The job gave me something more precious than money—hope. The world I'd once dreamed about, and then discarded as out of reach, had again become a possibility. I breathed the clean, filtered air within the white, spotless walls, took in the foreign smell of butter and cheese— that scent of wealth—and felt the stirring of a dream long dormant.

I listened to English spoken every day and got to practice the language, albeit in short phrases. The Americans—soldiers, civilian contractors, embassy staff—were delightfully different, both in looks and the way they ate their food, even how they took their coffee. I never tired of watching them and marveled at how physically different they were from us, how refined their manners. There was no slurping of soup, no sucking of teeth, and no spitting or tossing of bone and unwanted foods on the floor.

But my joy was ephemeral, like smoke in the wind. The odd, tingling sensation in my body and the stirring in my heart on hearing the intoxicating sound of laughter from the handsome young men would disintegrate at the arrival of Older Sister Lieu's youngest sister.

She was about eighteen years old with the world at her feet. She came to work at about ten in the morning, in the family's black Mercedes, driven by the family's long-term chauffeur, not in the back of a truck atop bags of onions and potatoes as I did. She would waltz in on gliding steps, in black or white tights and a gossamer, colorful blouse or an expensive-looking knit sweater. She looked every inch a rich girl, with rose-tinted skin and lustrous brown hair, a pretty face, a beautiful figure, and well-made clothes. She was perfect to her fingers and toes—the nails looked properly manicured, even before manicuring was popular.

I used to watch her every move. As soon as this privileged girl put her purse down under the high seat at the cash register, Second Older Sister would have a bowl of Chinese noodle soup, made special with extra meat, or a hot omelet with slices of crusty baguette ready for the "princess" to partake. But often she would take only a few bites before pushing the food aside. Second Older Sister would offer the leftover to me and Flower after she had refreshed the soup with an extra ladle of steaming broth and a few more strips of ham and allow us to take a short break in the mesh-enclosed outside dining area to enjoy the food.

While Flower chirped on about the Vietnamese women in the embassy—how this person had a new "*ao dai*," how that one looked arrogant with her fancy pearl necklace, I ate my food in silence, wondering if I would ever have so much food as to push perfectly good food aside after a bite and say "no more."

Not only did my glamorous cousin have the looks, she also had a winsome personality, both of which drew men to her like flies to honey. They would hang over the counter to speak to her for what seemed like forever, while she responded with the same fluency. Her ease with the language reduced my fledgling competency and confidence to total insignificance. I became so tongue-tied and insecure in her presence that I could not even manage a well-rehearsed sentence with any degree of proficiency. To my ears, my voice sounded wooden and crude, while hers a perfect blend of velvet and elegance.

With certain attractive-looking men, she would take the conversation to one of the tables. She had no compunction about leaving the cashiering tasks to her stepsister, Second Older Sister the cook, who was already swamped with kitchen duties. This girl, whose name I cannot even recall, would sip on a glass of white iced coffee while she conversed with her admirers. The concoction, unusual to some foreign palate, then became a conversation piece, as if she needed help in that area. Sometimes her momentary companion would take a sip of her special drink, an intimate gesture that usually caused my heart to ache.

During a pause in the talk, she liked to make a point of calling out to me as I cleaned adjacent tables in a careless, condescending manner of gentry to serf, in the solicitous spirit of *noblesse oblige*. It was a difficult time in my life. I could feel the men glancing at me then away, as if dismissing my insignificant presence, and yearned so desperately for a miracle that would transform me into a creature of beauty and class.

I advanced steadily to the top at the most prestigious English language school in the city, the Vietnamese American Association. Before long, I passed the highest test available, the Michigan English Proficiency. As I prepared to leave school, for there were no other classes for me to take, I received the highest accolades possible from the teacher, a Vietnamese man who was well educated and extremely proficient in English. He told the class that I was the epitome of a student of a foreign language who had "made it." He said I had lost my Vietnamese accent, thought in English, as opposed to thinking in Vietnamese and translating my thoughts into English, and was conversing in a very unique American accent. He thought that it might have come from the northeast region of the United States. I suspected he was being fanciful, that perhaps he was a fan of the handsome President Kennedy. But again, he could very well have gone to study in the United States and recognized the accents from the different regions. However, that still did not explain how I might have acquired that accent from New England.

NINETEEN

Saigon, Vietnam
The Tet Offensive, 1968

I dreamt of the warm fire in the library at Thornfield Hall and woke to the cold kiss of war. Impressions of the heartbreaking love between Mr. Rochester and Jane Eyre were still clear, making me feel befuddled in the incongruous surroundings. The scene was all wrong.

My limbs felt heavy in the disorienting, heavy darkness. I became vaguely aware of a disembodied voice telling everyone to get on the floor. Then it came. The familiar thudding pushed through the haze, jarring me to instant wakefulness. Like a seasoned soldier, I rolled off the bed, bringing the duck feather pillow along to cushion my head for the drop, then crawled over the fifteen feet or so of dirt floor from Ba Ngoai's old bed to the upper house. I saw Ma on the wobbly high chair, where she did not belong, not while the thudding still resonated. I knew she was praying for our safety, as well as that of Bong, who had just finished his officer training at the military academy in Thu Duc and was now at artillery school. Also for Big Rat, who was in his first year at the National Political Military Academy in Da Lat. Ba was flitting here and there, gathering beddings and handing them to Ngau.

Everyone else—these days that meant Little Rat, Cousin Mai, Eighth Uncle and his wife, Third Older Sister and her two children, Older Sister Phuong and her three children—was already in the designated indoor shelter, that empty space under the thick wooden divan at the corner. As I scrambled to their side, the tempo of the sound changed—closer together, too close—as if another gun or two had been added. Ba shouted for Ma to get down and for us to put pillows on top of our heads for protection against straying bullets and shrapnel. There was no protection necessary in case of a direct or close mortar hit.

With my cheek pressed against the cold, packed earth, I listened intently to the different sounds, trying to identify what each was and how far it was from us. I thought I detected the rougher sound of the AK-47, the weapon of choice of the Viet Cong, rather than the smoother M-16, which was ours.

I could tell Tan Son Nhat Airbase was under attack. The siren from the base was howling for help against the barrage of incoming mortar. Then came the welcome *pop pop* sound of flares being launched, and at last the hurried takeoff of fighter jets. Seconds later, a series of explosion followed, silencing mortars and men. That silence after the thuds would become one of the most comforting sounds in my memory.

Ba rose, and we silently followed suit. Even though the immediate danger of a stray mortar was gone, our steps were halting as we traversed the short distance to the yard. The spectacular flare-spangled sky lit up before us. Against that backdrop were bulky shadows of helicopters hovering over billowing columns of smoke. We were held spellbound. One by one, we lined up behind Ba like a row of ducklings to get on the rickety ladder to the rooftop for a better view of battle, while fighter jets continued to streak overhead.

Ba and Eighth Uncle contemplated what they knew, which was not very much, and conjectured what they didn't, which, as always, was quite significant. The gunfire gave them a hint of a *coup d'etat*, which had become commonplace in the years following the overthrow and killing of President Diem. Even with the daring attack on the base, a coup d'etat was still a possible scenario, though not likely. While the air force might have fallen under the authority of a non-conforming general and therefore had to be silenced or suppressed, no coup plotters would dare harm the Americans, many of whom lived or worked on the base. That would be sheer foolishness, if not downright suicidal. Who would finance the new government and help it fight the Communists?

What was happening then? The probability that remained was unthinkable but had to be true. War had finally arrived at our doorstep, for this was no isolated mortar attack.

"If the Communists were brazen enough to do this, they must think they can win," Eighth Uncle said in a familiar, know-it-all kind of voice. Ba agreed that this might be the beginning of the end for the Viet Cong, or us. As we watched, more helicopter gunships lumbered across the sky, then halted atop their targets and spit out traces of fire. If this had not been mortal combat, the scene would easily have been considered appropriately festive to welcome a new year. The sky lit and guns crackled from afar, just like the booming sound of firecrackers celebrating the arrival of Tet. We would learn that the Communists indeed had timed their attacks just so to mask the initial sound of gunfire with the familiar *pops* and *booms* of firecrackers.

For that reason, following the Offensive, a ban would go into effect. Firecrackers could no longer be lit to bring in the year; henceforth the age-old tradition would be sacrificed for the expediency of war.

Ba and Eighth Uncle did not think a Viet Cong victory was in the cards. "Just think, their mortars have already been stopped. They can't fight our air force. We too strong for them." But Ma did not want to take any chances; she asked me for the notice I had received a few days before, on an American Embassy letterhead offering me employment, to be effective on March 15. She twisted it into a flute and fed it to the flame under the wailing water kettle. Good kindling it was—and definitely good sense. We would have less to worry about in case of a Viet Cong triumph.

By day's end, the sound and sight of battle had retreated, at least from our view. Earlier, the Viet Cong had taken the radio station, the target of choice for all aggressors—coup plotters of late and now Communists. The intent was to confuse the populace and government force defenders—demoralize then conquer. But on this occasion, they failed to make a single broadcast. At the end, facing defeat and capture, the infiltrators chose to blow themselves up, thus sacrificing all for the shadowy promise of glory.

The mortars had disappeared, although jets continued to thunder past, leaving Tan Son Nhat for destinations unknown. Eighth Uncle left to scout for news, only to rush back a few minutes later, so shaken he could hardly speak. "Mortar, mortar, come see, come see." He pointed to the area left of the orchard and stuttered unintelligibly. We ran after him, only to halt abruptly at the sight of a gray tail of a mortar by the path. Ba yelled for us to get back, that it could still explode. After some confusing moments, he and Eighth Uncle decided to venture out to find a police or military patrol to inform them of the metallic problem that was anchored deep in our compound.

I stepped back from the path, my gaze automatically drawn to the sentry position on the rooftop of the U.S. 3rd Field Hospital. The usual guard had acquired two reinforcements. All three of them were in heavier battle gear than normal—flak jackets and thick strands of bullets crisscrossing on their shoulders. The rifles were now in the crooks of their arms, in the ready position, rather than standing at rest against the knee of the sentry as done previously.

The sun flared brightly in descent, a dark red globe hung over a city in chaos, a portent perhaps of more bloodshed to come. Turning to go back to the house, Ma did not take her usual long and quick steps, but sidled hesitantly, her eyes focused on the scarlet omen. She made a *tut-tutting* sound then muttered, "*Chet het* (everyone is going to die)."

龙

I showed up for work at the embassy on a bright morning in March. My place of work was at the Old Embassy Annex by the side of the Saigon River, rather than the new embassy on Thong Nhat Street, which was a good thing. I would have seen the site where several American MPs and marines had lost their lives defending the building during the Offensive and would have felt sorrow rather than joy on my first day at work at one of the most prestigious places in the country, the American Embassy.

The dust from the Offensive had settled, at least in Saigon. For the graceful, often-serenaded romantic city of Hue, the nightmare was finally and mercifully over. American and government troops had taken back the city from the Viet Cong. Now the search could begin for the missing and the dead, casualties of a short but bloody and ruthless occupation.

Police and military checkpoints now dotted Saigon. Their sentries shared a grim look that I had not noticed before. Fresh American troops were still arriving; their faces showed looks of bewilderment and apprehension as they sat side by side in convoys of trucks heading toward the bases at Bien Hoa and Long Binh.

The atrocities in Hue, on the streets of Saigon, and elsewhere gradually faded from our minds. Life had returned to normal, at least in Saigon, whatever normality meant in the time warp.

At the embassy, my long fascination with Americans blossomed at closer proximity. The language continued to sound like music to my ears. So it was that I had one crush after another with those faceless voices on the American Armed Forces radio network, a frustrating experience as far as crushes went, until I learned to match those faces on the convoy with the voices on the radio and managed to achieve a degree of realism.

I watched the soldiers coming to the embassy cashier to cash a check and stop at our snack bar for a taste of home—a hamburger, French fries, and a Coke—and felt my heart flutter at the foreign, captivating sights of beguiling blue eyes and golden hair the color of corn silk. On some of their boots was the red dust of the highlands; on others, the black silt of the delta. I had heard enough of their habits to suppose that one of their stops would be along that strip of bars on Tu Do Street.

Naturally, I could not help my impulsive and irrepressible self. I would take that route home sometimes just to see them swaggering in and out of those darkened doorways, some with scantily clad Vietnamese girls clinging to their arms. I would hear the lively music blaring from within, wonder what fun went on inside, and feel a tinge of envy toward the girls who looked so glamorous and seductive. It was something I would never know. I could never laugh that loudly or freely or dress and act with such reckless abandon.

But I wanted to. What if I should die without knowing? With all my senses, I reveled in this new world that war and the Americans had created. So many things had changed—the city, the way we lived. *Better*, I thought, *except for the war. Oh, if only we could take one without the other…*

However, as long as the war stayed away from the city, we could enjoy the spoils. I especially loved the rhythm of the Western music, which seemed to touch my very soul so that I could often feel the cadency of my heart—my entire being, actually—move with the beat. *How perfectly appropriate was this music of our time?* I would later wonder. How much it reflected the unspoken needs of our psyche—jaunty notes for us to jig away in defiance of death and soulful tunes and mournful ballads by which to whisper our last farewell to life.

While I tried to forget about the war and focused on living, the soldiers did the same, coping however they could, through drugs, alcohol, women—those pleasures of the flesh. But they would get only a short reprieve from the madness. The cancer from the treacherous war would return time and again, and the poison would spread and eat away at their souls. Some carried their afflictions outwardly in the cold stare, the vacant look, or the devil-may-care attitude; others buried the pain deep within.

It would be years before I would learn of their struggle to survive the physical and psychological horrors of our war or know of their aversion to us, the marginal bystanders. Of course, the term "bystanders" did not apply to all of us, though we dressed the same, talked the same, and, to a certain extent, looked alike, at least to a westerner. Like the Americans, I did not know who the enemy was among us. Ma frequently had to remind me to hold my tongue when outside our home just in case any Viet Cong was within hearing. Not that it would have mattered. By my employment with the Americans, I could not expect mercy when the enemy arrived. With that ever-present apprehension, I sometimes found myself scanning the faces of my thirty-odd Vietnamese colleagues in the office, wondering which one of them was a Viet Cong sympathizer or infiltrator.

For the soldiers, the confusion had to be baffling at best, for the price of error could mean instant death. At every patrol, the blurring lines of battle and shape-shifting nature of the enemy must have become more pronounced, turning frustration to fear, to hatred. All their thought processes, actions, and reactions had to be geared to that one fear— dying, and that one desire—surviving. However flawed their reasoning was due to this narrow focus, their conduct would be judged, even if we couldn't presume to know what they had gone through, what they had supposedly done or why, not having been where they were. *What did we know about being in the throes of confusion, fear, and hysteria?*

We would condemn them nevertheless for giving into temptation, for turning themselves into drug-crazed zombies and thereby weakening the war machine.

It was a difficult time. The drugs—perhaps I too would have surrendered to their lure if I had had the money and known it could help pass the time and numb the fear. It was fortunate for me that I didn't, for I needed all my mental acuity to plan my escape, just as it might have been fortuitous for some of those who did, for it could have given them a measure of solace, a reprieve from the fear.

But this was then, and I was unaware of the psychological turmoil that was all around me. In blissful ignorance, I stared at these strangers from afar with interest and infatuation and gratitude for their coming to help us. Yes, I believed they had come to help, regardless of the Communist propaganda that decried America's intent to subjugate the Vietnamese people. My parents, and especially Eighth Uncle, who was actually more an agitator than a Communist sympathizer, thought I had an American soul. How else could they explain my strange opinions, ideas, my independence and restlessness, or why I agonized more over American dead than ours.

I did not have any deep philosophical answer, then or now. My reason was simple: It was not their fight; they should not have been asked to make the ultimate sacrifice for us.

The soldiers' childlike ways beguiled and charmed; however, the more they did, the sadder I was, for I knew that innocence would be gone soon enough. That painful realization swarmed my emotions, but the feeling was so foreign and personal I could not share with anyone. No one would understand anyway. So I turned my thoughts inward as I always had and became tormented by the haunting images of their broken bodies being readied for the final flight home. Every time I heard the whirring sound of choppers arriving at the 3rd Field Hospital, I would feel a heavy weight on my chest.

But these were not normal times, and ordinary behavior had no place in them. Away from death, I would forget about shattered lives and lost innocence and let myself be swept into the seductive waters of womanhood, wooed by the good looks and exuberance of the living. Compared to these demonstrative "aliens," we were like old people from an ancient land, so jaded through the ages that by birth we had already lost our enchantment for life.

The Americans were everywhere—in cars, on foot, on every roadway, in every neighborhood from Saigon to the China town of Cholon, to the suburb of Gia Dinh, and by our very gate. I could not recall when they were not there and could not imagine when they would be no longer. They had become part of us, in many ways intrinsic to our existence.

On the way home from work, I sometimes stopped at the corner of Nguyen Hue and Pasteur Streets for a snack. Sitting astride my motor scooter, I would enjoy a plate of green papaya salad mixed with thin strips of beef jerky and linger over a glass of sugarcane juice to watch the objects of my affection browsing through the souvenir shops on Nguyen Hue.

The peals of their laughter would float by, and I opened my heart to them like a scorched earth to the first rain of the season. Like the parching soil, I let myself be drenched with the earthy feelings of well-being and abundance as those young men took time out from death to celebrate life. They smiled, cajoled, and played around with the "dust of life" street urchins and cyclo drivers; so ebullient and playful, they made my heart hurt for the precariousness of it all.

I still remember the first time I laughed loudly in public, which was not a thing for a lady to do, at a scene extraordinary perhaps only to me. On the crowded sidewalk, a GI turned up the volume on his cassette recorder, handed it over to a buddy of his, and proceeded to show a group of street kids some of his dance moves by gyrating and sidestepping to a tune. I grinned then burst out laughing as his movements became more exaggerated. I could not help myself. I had not seen an adult acting so free and uninhibited, in public at that, in all of my life.

Seduced by the superficial, I did not see the shadows in his eyes or suspect the horrors that might have been hidden in his heart. My young mind was busy questioning the fate. How was a person's place of birth decided? From where I stood, it more or less determined whether a person would have a life of plenty or one with the barest subsistence; if one would be bestowed with a love for life or burdened by tradition and responsibility. What was it about America that gave its children such confidence to be as they wished, as individual as they came, and a collective surefootedness that bordered on arrogance?

My obsession with these strangers from afar would change my destiny, or, as Ma would have said, it was my destiny that spurred the obsession.

Aid dollars continued to flow in, so fast the government could not keep up with the pace of spending, though many government officials did their best to fill their pockets. Corruption went amok. The audacity and horrors of the Tet Offensive seemed to have opened a floodgate of good will, or perhaps more accurately, strengthened America's resolve to rid South Vietnam of the Communist menace. The aid was to build infrastructures and empower the people economically to win their hearts and minds, thereby giving the Saigon government an edge. I did not understand the concept of aid very well, the whys and wherefores of a rich country's policy of foreign aid. But it worked for America in my case. Then again, maybe that didn't count, given that I already possessed a Western, or an "American," soul … In any event, my heart swelled and my throat constricted every time I saw a bag of grain or fertilizer, the cover of which was imprinted with the trademark handclasp of the U.S. Agency for International Development and the lettering "United States of America."

From the laundry shop at the street corner to a cyclo driver to the secretary at an office at MACV (Military Assistance Command-Vietnam), we all gained from the inundation of aid money, directly or indirectly. Before long, in addition to the commercial aid program, through which items such as TVs and motorbikes were imported and sold at relatively low prices, another source of aid was created—the black market. Everything available in the American PX could be had on the backstreets of Saigon, courtesies of corrupt procurement or warehouse officers, wily guards, or malleable GIs and contractors and the Vietnamese women behind them who pushed for the maximum limits purchase at the PX of TV, radio, cassette recorder, stereo equipment, and china, and cigarettes at duty-free prices. Seemingly, there was no effort to stop the trade; there was no reason. Everyone benefited. A great many homes were modernized over a period of months. While it was not intended as AID money, it did go into many pockets of the poor.

A creative USAID official could have considered any such ware-house losses as American aid. The money from the black market went to help the masses, as AID money was intended. With so much aid, and even more opportunities to reap untold riches from a runaway economy, high government and military officials did not begrudge the poor of their deals; they were busy lining their own pockets.

Unfortunately, little of the windfalls extended to the far reaches of the rice fields, whose muddy water was turning redder every day from the spilled blood of peasants, victims of both the Viet Cong and government troops.

We did get to cash in on the rush, both in the war efforts and the black market, thanks to our homegrown, crafty northerner, Big Brother Si. From subcontracting his laundry service, we did earn a TV, a small tape recorder, and food on the table every day. Ma no longer had to borrow money, although she still kept her pigs and the vegetable patch as insurance against that proverbial rainy day, the day the contract would disappear. That was as much advance planning as had ever been possible for us to do.

Death seemed to come more frequently on battlefields far and near. Consequently, we did not harbor any illusion that the end would be any different for us. The Viet Cong had taken their campaign of intimidation to the city. Bombs were going off all around—in cars, at the central post office. To calm the fear, we surrendered to Fate and accepted that death was inevitable, not inevitable in the abstract, metaphoric sense, but definitively, absolutely, and real, as in predestination. So we left the business of death to God and concentrated on living, on making our lives a little better while they lasted. We would live through the war this way. It was not courage that took us to the end. Courage was a conscious resolve. This was more a subliminal conviction that everything had its time.

We coped so well that some of our men managed to forget completely about the war. They focused instead on the baser issue of their manhood. The issue of Vietnamese women in the arms of American men raised its thorny head and disturbed my quiet fantasy. I defended the underdog, the women whose voices no longer mattered to anyone. Why? Because I could see myself doing just that—falling in love with a foreigner. This was not hard to conjure actually, since I had been half in love with truckloads of American soldiers anyhow, albeit from afar and terribly one-sided.

Before the Americans, there were the French. One would think that by the time the Americans arrived, the Vietnamese men would have gotten used to losing some of the women to the more urbane, liberal Western men. But they indeed had difficulty with the issue, even as regards the prostitutes who were only plying the trade. Many prostitutes maintained Vietnamese boyfriends—the reasons for which I discerned but could not accept—and turned their earnings to those men. For that generosity, or rather foolishness as it turned out, they got back neither genuine affection nor love but, in many cases, violence whenever money became short.

The crudest jeers and sneers, however, were reserved for those women who did not appear to belong in the trade, but who were nevertheless found in the arms of the Americans. It was chauvinism, and nationalism, at its worst. Somehow the Vietnamese men felt that the good and pure, or at least the desirable, should have been reserved for themselves. *Tsk, tsk,* such a waste! "A waste of what?" I asked and hotly challenged the detractor with all my youthful passion. If nothing else, the strength of my conviction usually won the day, but only because no one suspected the secret in my heart—my fixation with America and the Americans—and judged my argument to be objective.

Not that I could not have argued the point just as effectively and fervently, having had enough practice debating with Eighth Uncle since I was a child. He and I would argue the ills of communism late into the night from our respective cots. Neither of us would relent until Ba told us either to quiet down or take our argument outside so others could sleep. I had the advantage of being a child, and being me. When I ran out of facts and exhausted every clever conjecture and supposition I had garnered from the wizened men and the newspapers, I would turn belligerent, even militant, so as to get the last word in before we were forced to shut down for the night.

The American experience produced a cultural enlightenment that was to be repeated often in my journey. If one could not understand the language, the natives somehow assumed that one was less intelligent, less human. I would listen to the same nonsensical comments from my cousins and turn aflame at their hypocrisy and ignorance. There they sat, in front of their TV sets, riding around on motorbikes courtesy of American aid, enjoying heaping trays of food bought with money gained through American connections. When their stomachs were full, they would shoot the breeze with talks about women who prostituted themselves with Americans. Somehow, "second" or "third" wives or "concubines" of Vietnamese men, or even Chinese men, were considered a nobler breed than consorts of American men. Newspaper commentaries joined in to lament the women's pitiable descent to a life of decadence and the rending of the societal fabric by the mighty American dollar.

The acceptance did come, gradually, if only to reasonable, enlightened minds. Meanwhile, fallen or virtuous, our women persevered in their sacrificial roles—just like my ma—to help their loved ones survive the war that was on our path, the war we'd unwittingly created through fear and greed and a gross misconception of courage, heroism, and conquest.

TWENTY

IN THE NEWS: 3/2/68–48
GIS KILLED IN AMBUSH
NEAR SAIGON.

**American Embassy
Saigon, Vietnam, 1968
Following the Tet Offensive**

The Americans continued to feature promi-
nently in my life. Hoang, son of Big Brother
Si, burst into the house on a Saturday morning.
Clearly agitated, he told me and Ma that he had
just left a scene of perhaps a murder in Cowshed
Alley. An American soldier had gotten stabbed
in the gut by several hoodlum friends of Hoang,
who made off with a wad of dollars and a watch
they took from the fallen man.

I stared at him in shock. The distant sound
of choppers arriving at the 3rd Field Hospital
at that very moment churned the blood in my

A DRAGON'S TALE   221

veins and whipped it into a storm of uncontrollable fury. I seethed. I could not help the deaths on the battlefield, but here, for a watch and few dollars? Such senselessness! The poor, poor American…What did he know of my land and the ignorance and lunacy of some of my people? Fuming, I shouted at Hoang, "I am going to tell the police on you! Maybe I will get the American MP to beat you up." My mind whirled in panic as I turned to Ma. "Ma, what do we do?"

She had already grabbed her long-sleeved blouse off the nail peg on the wall and picked up the tattered cone hat and turned to Hoang. "Come, show me." Left alone, I dropped down on the canvas cot, stretching out like a corpse. I tried expelling my anger through heavy breaths, but it didn't help. Such stupidity! My insides trembled and quaked at the waste of a life.

Ma did her part. She flagged down an American MP jeep and took them to the site. She believed they understood her, she said later, because she talked very loudly, to which they said, "Okay, okay," calling her mama-san, which was the only thing she remembered. The accompanying Vietnamese police praised her for getting help for the man. Later, Ma proudly related that she had taken care of the soldier as well as she could—lifting his head and placing it on her hat to keep it off the dirt.

The fate of that stranger continued to haunt me. There was nothing I could do about those who perished in those faraway jungles and rice fields, but how could it happen on a benign street of my hometown, by those harmless boys of my youth?

In the embassy, I was the youngest in an office of about thirty-five people, mostly women, mostly older. Inevitably, as the fighting intensified, war casualties extended to their own sons, fiancés, and husbands. A wail would rise above the *tac-tac* of typewriters and whirring of calculators and adding machines. The elders would gather and collectively issue a buzz of tongue clucking. "*Toi nghiep qua.*"

One more number added to the death toll; another mourning scene. It would either be a full mourning—complete black or white dress, or the diminutive black or white cloth pinned to a shirt lapel.

The war had been on for all of my life and most of theirs. Somewhere along the way, our value of life must have changed so that these scenes of sorrow blended quickly into the landscape, and the unbearable pain of loss seamlessly absorbed in the psyche. After the shock came the offering of sympathy, then back to the imperatives of living, until the next time. What was more tragic about the losses was how seemingly normal they had become.

A mythologically grounded people, we subscribed to all sorts of legends and folklore and made fortune telling a popular pastime. Among the most susceptible were the young, the romantic, and the hopeful. There were three of those in my office, Ngan, Diep, and I, who were bound together by the commonality of youth and *naiveté*.

Romanticism, curiosity, and insecurity drove us far and wide to search for that all-knowing fortune-teller. The best ones supposedly received their advice directly from otherworldly spirits. Regardless, all had something to say about that kind, handsome, and wealthy stranger. Tall was not often added to the description, which was just as well since Vietnamese men were not known for their towering stature. Neither was "dark," since that was the color of the lower class.

From having our horoscopes charted to palms read to summoning spirits through their colorful mediums, we wanted to know. Would we be richer? Would we live long? Would we find love and kindness? Yes, always that all-essential kindness.

Rejoicing in my blossoming girlhood, the likes of which none before my generation could have envisioned, I listened to Ma's tale of hers with sympathy. Poor Ma. She never had the opportunity to indulge in frivolity; her entire life had been one of duty. She could never understand the frivolous things I did—spending the day taking pictures at the zoo or going to the movies alone and watching a film twice.

Not only did I waste precious time that could have been devoted to helping her deal with the practicality of living, but I began to make daydreaming a regular pastime and a source of pleasure, thereby spinning a web of misery for all the days to come—the misery of wanting what I didn't have.

Diep and Ngan took to flirting with the American marine guards on duty. Their audacity knew no bounds when the three of us were together. There was only one problem. Neither of them understood or spoke English as well as I did, so I became their interpreter by default, delivering little one-liners every time we came through Post 1, the main entry to the embassy. I was the most inhibited, which made the scene look rather comical. There they were, the bright-eyed girls, sending those come-hither smiles then pointing to their interpreter, a solemn-looking beanpole. As laughing eyes and anticipatory looks shifted to me, I managed to find the right words for the impromptu translation but could never quite manipulate the delivery to convey the spirit of the message. My tone was a little too leaden, my face too grave, which were in complete discordance with the intent.

Diep was the one to whom the marines were drawn; she with a curvaceous, full body of a married woman and mother; she with the dark, sultry eyes and that knowing look and confidence of a woman. I had traveled far to get to where I was, but I still lacked that self-assurance these girls were born with. Not yet a woman, I was a gangly, awkward creature with none of the sensuousness or self-assurance they had. I would have given much to be carefree, to be vivacious, if I had only known how.

TWENTY-ONE

IN THE NEWS:
4/10/00–VIJAY SINGH OF
FIJI CAPTURES MASTERS.

American Embassy
Suva, Fiji, 2000

The months leading to our final departure from Fiji were decidedly burdensome. Dark, ominous clouds overshadowed what should have been a glorious, exciting beginning for another adventure. News articles of suicide bombings in Sri Lanka began to appear at regular intervals in the *Fiji Times*. It seemed as though the Tamil/Sinhalese conflict had just started. But we knew better. It just happened that we were on the upsweep of an on-again, off-again campaign of bombings by the Tamils to sustain the decades-old struggle for autonomy.

Everyone in the embassy, from Ambassador

Siddique on down, was worried about us. When they could stand our insouciance no more, they asked pointedly, "Things are getting bad in Sri Lanka. Have you read?"

"Oh, we have. We will be okay. The bombings normally take place near military installations or police checkpoints. As long as we stay away from those places, we should be safe."

Their concerned looks and solicitous remarks niggled at our confidence, even if we had complete faith in the U.S. government to protect us. If it had been that dangerous to live there, surely the State Department would have designated Colombo a danger post with all that would entail—a financial incentive called danger pay and a requirement for employees to safe haven their families in the States or elsewhere.

Much like Saigon at war.

I remembered the city that was forbidden to dependents of U.S. government employees and chided myself for worrying unnecessarily about the unsafe situation in Sri Lanka. *If I did not feel the danger in Saigon with car bombs, the riots, and the tear gas, why should I be fearful now?*

We had read all about Sri Lanka, described as the "teardrop of India," and dreamt of "the enchanted land that time forgot," according to a travel magazine. It was called "Serendib" by early explorers. The assignment to that embassy was a natural professional progression for me, from the mid-size, three-American administrative officer position at Embassy Suva to the four-American administrative counselor position in Colombo.

To prepare for this new posting, Acey devoured information on golfing and fishing for trout in the highlands and eagerly psyched himself up for the place, suicide bombings notwithstanding. He would later find that trout fishing in the hills was long gone, quite possibly way back in the colonial days. While his enthusiasm became temporarily dampened, my expectations remained undiminished. If I could get a promotion from this tour, then an ambassadorship was an almost certainty in the not-too-distant future. I could retire then.

Acey and I had talked about leaving the FS for years, back to when we were in Hanoi. Much as I loved the job and enjoyed the lifestyle,

I had developed a longing for a home I could call my own rather than simply residences, luxurious and grand though they may be sometimes. Most of all, I yearned to reestablish that connection with my children. The biannual home leave or once-a-year Rest and Recuperation (R&R) trip to the States were no longer adequate. The last time I had any sort of meaningful conversation with my daughters was when we gathered at a coffee shop in Denver following their grandmother's funeral. I certainly didn't want our next heart-to-heart to be at that of my own.

It didn't take long for my children and Acey's parents to join the throng of opponents to the assignment. Their anxiety stirred my apprehension. Perhaps we had been too jaded. Perhaps we should worry. In a reflective moment, I recalled the crazed city of my youth and thought wryly, *I didn't survive Vietnam to be decapitated by a suicide bomber on the streets of Colombo.*

Then I remembered. It was not I who distinguished herself in getting through the war. It was not as if I had survived through sheer courage or ingenuity or endurance. It was not as if I had not tried so hard to escape. It was my ma who actually deserved all the credit for shepherding me through the hardships of war and poverty, the heartbreaks and the confusion. One reflection led to another. What did I do to return my ma's love?

I abandoned her to the inhumanity that was called peace.

The Vietnam War meant the loss of innocence and reality for many, including my parents, who had supposed that it was simply another violent conflict, one that would fade over time like all others they had known. They thought they would weather this the same way, by "*chay giac*," and then return when the guns stopped. They didn't count on becoming part of the casualty. They had always been the insignificant little people, so believed they could simply retreat and resurface when it was over.

It didn't happen quite that way.

But it was not war that destroyed our family. It was peace that managed to divide us in ways wars never had. No wonder, for it was a sham of a peace. That was the only reason for the suffering to go on and on in the land that had been largely decimated by the long, murderous conflict. Those of us who had been spun far and wide from the splintering of the family were spared that horror. But my mother remained and bore the brunt of it all, handling that ordeal the way she'd cared for us, almost single-handedly.

She had to be sad. She had to be in deep despair. She had to be terrified. But somewhere in that shrunken body was a will of steel. She found the strength to go on virtually undaunted.

During the post-1975 years of upheaval when there was widespread starvation, peasants like her had to pay a high government quota of rice for each "*mau*," or acre, of land they farmed, which barely left enough for them to live on. She managed to increase the yield by planting rows of seedlings on the sides of the dikes. She gained still a few more kilos of rice by asking Brother Bong, then a merchant's son-in-law, to increase her monthly allowance. She would consume even less so as to have more to smuggle into the city for Third Older Sister, her five children, and other relatives. If she had been caught, the penalty would have been imprisonment and hard labor. But she thought little of the consequences. To her, saving others from starvation was worth any risk to herself.

She made a body pouch, filled it with rice, then tied that around her middle before getting on a check-point-riddled, harrowing bus ride to Saigon, the city under siege, to ease whatever suffering she could. The vicious purge was on. Southerners were given the untenable choices of starvation in the city or relocating to the so-called new economic zones in the mountains and the jungles where deadly malaria awaited.

Even as the survival rate for "boat people" plummeted as pirates began to ply the sea looking for the would-be refugees, fishermen in the Mekong delta and others continued to risk death by putting their often-not-seaworthy vessels out to sea rather than staying to face the petty, deadly vengeance of the northern Communist government.

That was how my ma spent the autumn of her life—not by the warm hearth of home in the companionship of her husband, children, and grandchildren, but in a lonely thatched hut in the middle of a rice field, collecting and storing precious grains of rice and drying the fishes she had caught illegally in the river in order to feed others...

Colombo, Sri Lanka
The Indian Ocean

We arrived in provincial Colombo on a typical sweltering summer day. One look at the airport told us what we'd already known: Sri Lanka was a poor, developing country. The place looked worn, the air stifled with heat and red dust, quite the opposite of the open-air freshness of the international airport in Nadi, Fiji. Another look at armed military men and women guarding every entrance convinced us that we had arrived at a country at war.

The last of my enthusiasm fled at the sight of pot-holed roads and poorly garbed vendors at roadside stands with their scruffy children. It had been so long since I had seen poverty like this. Fiji was not rich, but it was far from being this poor. I tried to remember if Vietnam at war had been this bad.

Sensing my disappointment, Acey gave me the usual pep talk. He was used to this. On coming to a new post, any excitement I'd had prior to arrival usually eroded to disappointment rather quickly. The expectation was so spectacular and intense that reality just could not deliver.

I settled down after the talk. I simply needed to be reminded and to adjust. I knew this would be home for the next three years, and we would make our time here happy and memorable, just as we had done at even more unlikely places, places as desolate as Praia or as angst-ridden as Hanoi.

While I waited to be charmed by our new home, I found pride in my true home away from home, the U.S. Chancery, which stood resolute and imposing against the backdrop of the roiling waters of the Indian Ocean. While it was still not comparable to its sisters—those mammoth structures in Paris, London, or Lisbon—it was more impressive than any Acey and I had ever worked at.

However remarkable, none could replace in my memory that Chancery on Thong Nhat Street in Saigon, by which other embassies would be measured and found lacking. It stood foremost in my mind, that young girl's mind, not for its architectural design, which detractors had bemoaned from the beginning as an ostentatious disturbance to the quiet dignity of the most prestigious and beautiful road in town, but for being the tantalizing rainbow that guided my youthful dreams, and a reminder of the ultimate sacrifices by those young American soldiers who walked into hell simply because their country had asked.

I hit the ground running. That was the term frequently used to describe the speed and zest Foreign Service Officers bring to their jobs. We had only two to three years at a post in which to make a difference, so we aimed to accomplish and even surpass that expectation, proud as we were of our capabilities and the nobility of our mission.

But the land of Serendib did not enchant as it should have. Colombo was a city in despair. At its head was a president who believed she was born to rule. Daughter of two prime ministers, she touted her superior bloodline as if there were such a thing as that. Her children followed the colonial practice of old and went to school in England. Assuming they had political ambitions, there was little doubt they could return to claim their mother's seat. Pedigree counted for something here. They could win, if only by that name recognition, as if their mother had created such a legacy of goodness over the land. Benevolent she most assuredly was not.

This woman successfully parlayed the Sinhalese arrogance against the minority Tamils and others and sowed so well the seeds of ethnic hatred. The grievance of the past could have been forsaken for the greater good, but she held on to it because for her, it was her *raison d'etre*. Without her war, she would have had to work harder to ease the suffering of millions of her poor subjects, which she neither had the love nor the compassion to accomplish.

I followed the pattern of our nomadic lifestyle, settling in swiftly so we could enjoy the post before it was time to move on. In a matter of weeks, we had already identified good places to shop and eat and tourist sites to visit on long weekends. Colombo was more and less. It was more like Hanoi than Saigon in that it was lethargic rather than energetic, but lesser than both because of the war that continued to divide and destroy not only livelihood, but also hope. Its many beaches remained mediocre. Squatter huts formed shantytowns that littered and polluted the shore all the way from the capital of Colombo to the fort at the southernmost city of Galle.

Things continued to go well for me professionally. A bigger embassy meant bigger challenges, which, to me, simply meant more opportunities to shine. There was no doubt in my mind that I could overcome just about any obstacle put before me.

It was ironic that Vietnam, which lay at the root of my insecurity, ended up being the very place where I overcame the darkness of doubt. Those hard-won successes from the hostile corridors of the Vietnamese bureaucracy were exactly what I needed. Against some of the most stubborn, narrow-minded, complex-ridden men I had ever known, I finally gained the confidence that had long eluded me. In the place where I'd lost a large part of self-esteem, I came to know the comfort of self-worth.

I was promoted after the first year in Colombo and became the third most-senior officer in the embassy. In that capacity, I would have occasions to serve as the acting deputy chief of mission and also as *charge d'affaires* when both the ambassador and his deputy were out of the country. It was a heady feeling to lead country team meetings in the embassy's bug-free "bubble" room, looking around the table at men who used to be deemed "my betters" filling every seat, who diligently noted my request for information or asked for my concurrence or direction.

I rode in the ambassador's vehicle with the dual American and ambassadorial flags flapping from the hood to the Foreign Ministry enough times to be impressed with the office I held and the power and pride of representing the United States to other governments. What I didn't count on was, while within sight of that ultimate goal of many FSO—the glory of an ambassadorship before retirement, I would feel a curious indifference, a subtle letdown of sort.

There had to be more than this. The idea of bending, compromising, and catering to sometimes cruel, indifferent, or ignorant world leaders, to accomplish those intangible American policy objectives that were contrived not by benevolent, godly individuals, but by egotistical, misguided humans, somehow felt wrong to me.

There was also the matter of my misdeeds that continued to dodge my steps from post to post. It had started out as an act of compassion, misplaced as it was. Over the years, it had morphed into something else, something that could take me down from the height of my success by the speed of a single breath. To get out of those invisible shackles, I suspected that I would have to leave the prestige of my perch and forsake the material comforts and adulation that came with it.

Subsequent ruminations led me to another place—a role audacious even for my usually bold imagination, not for the grandeur of its cloak, but for the good that could come. It was that of the United Nations High Commissioner for Refugees. I had already learned how to bend, cajole, and beg well enough within the U.S. government bureaucracy. I was certain I could do that on a world stage for the millions of faceless refugees. Once, I had imagined I could make a difference by joining the Foreign Service. To a very limited extent and in very personal ways, I did.

What my Foreign Service career did for me was propel me to the highest mountaintop and give my baser needs more than a little boost. My successes also gave me something else, something definitely precious—the freedom from the bondage of wants. Now I was ready to do something worthwhile, something that would ensure someone out there could eat a little better and suffer a little less.

That thought hardened into a promise so real it gave me the motivation to remain in the job for which I was slowly losing ardor. To realize the dream, I figured I had to make a name for myself; an ambassadorship would not be a bad entry in my curriculum vitae. With eyes on the future, I moved forward on my current path, believing all would be well until I reached that metaphorical fork on the road, when Fate would steer me toward my destiny.

TWENTY-TWO

IN THE NEWS: 4/3/69–
U.S. DEATHS 33,641,
PASS KOREA TOTAL.

American Embassy
Saigon, Vietnam, 1969

Diep's husband returned from his duty station in Qui Nhon for a visit and brought along a fellow military policeman from his platoon. In his early twenties, Quan was easily the best-looking Vietnamese man I had ever met: tall (in relation to Vietnamese men) with dark, soulful eyes, a legacy from an ancestor with Indian heritage.

It was love at first sight for both of us. A courtship began with all the usual frills—going out for ice cream, to the movies, and the ultimate...to catch the breeze along the Saigon River.

The relationship realized all my romantic fantasy except one: I could not introduce him to my parents. In my time, a girl could not bring a boy home unless he was in every way suitable and willing to commit to matrimony. Quan was polite and proper and, from what I knew, of a good family—no problem there. I believed he would be ready for marriage when the time came, so that was not it. The problem was me. Since I was about eight years old, I have known that a normal marriage was not for me. Because of Bong's delicate mind, my parents had entrusted in me the duty of caring for our family. I was to take care of them and Bong. Later, Cousin Mai was added to the list. On listening to my parents' conversations over the years, I had gained a good idea of what was expected of me.

They didn't want to lose me, but rather hoped to gain a son-in-law. For this to happen, my intended had to be an orphan, or a third or fourth son of a not too wicked or selfish mother who would not mind releasing him to go to our household. He had to be hard working with a good trade. It would be best if he had a good-size shop of some kind. Yes, Ma said she could see me sitting behind a cash register. Ah, such a good, leisure life.

In watching other women's lives unfold around me, I knew I had another alternative: I could be the second or third wife of some rich, old man.

Those were the only options available to me since the usually traveled path was forbidden; traditions dictated that I leave my home for my husband's, and everything I owned would be his and, by extension, his parents'. To me, this would never do.

Until I met Quan, I had thought that those erotic images and enchanted feelings from the magical world of romantic novels would never be part of my reality. As an only son of doting parents, Quan was wrong for me. But I didn't want to think about the future yet; I wanted to experience all the excitement and sweetness of a first love, to know the joy of holding him in the deepest part of my heart and to act on all the longings that had festered within me since … well, since that disastrous first crush at adolescence.

I had come a long way surely. I remembered sitting on our divan night after night to watch the singer/soloist in the band my Brother Bong, a drummer of note, had helped create, hearing nothing but the liquid gold of his voice, and saw little else except the hypnotic movements of his fingers sliding sensuously on the guitar strings. "The House of the Rising Sun" had never sounded so warm or romantic. After months of being hopelessly entangled in the seductive coils of my own making, I promptly fell out of love, all because he had a smear of ice cream on his chin at our first date, which I had to look at through the longest hour of my life, under the bright neon light of the shop.

It was different with Quan. My heart fluttered and danced when he was near and pained when he was not. Unlike in my daydreams, where the stirrings simply roiled then disappeared in the vastness like waves in an ocean without shore, I found in Quan a perfect and willing receptacle for emotions that were both gentle and explosive.

I put my heart and soul in the romance and wrote to him every day. I told him of the sun and the moon, which lost their luster, and the shadows that gained when he was not by my side. I told him I would send my love with the next wind and to think of me when the cloud slipped across the moon, for such was I—cold and lifeless like the darkened moon when he was away.

During the year in which we pledged our hearts to each other, our love remained chaste. That was the norm and the tradition, which was all well and good. But I did not count on those vague yearnings within my body, how they roused tingles and aches merely at thoughts of him. The strange stirrings drove me mindless until I decided I wanted to know more. Since there was to be no good and advantageous marriage, I figured I did not need to save myself for that nameless, and quite possibly domineering and cruel, someone.

Diep and I cooked up a scheme to go visit the men. I told Ma I was going upcountry with Diep to see her husband, conveniently omitting any mention of Quan. Unaware of my audacity, Ma helped me prepare for my first plane trip. She was so eager for me to experience that which she had never known—gliding across the sky like a bird, seeing a place so distant from her world. She had no mental conception of what it was like. None at all, except for the tasty marinated fish that was supposedly among the best in the country. "Buy '*mam*' (marinated fish) to bring back," she said. "Qui Nhon near sea, your Eighth Uncle say 'mam' there very fresh and tasty." If I had not been so consumed with anticipation for the forbidden, I might not have gone through with the plan, for her generosity made my duplicity ugly and obscene.

Diep and I settled in a small hotel, which looked less like a hotel than a large townhouse. The thick, wine-colored drapery and scarlet velvet bedspread added to the outlandishness of my adventure, which was made even more titillating by a haunting. No, this last did not come from my imagination. Fertile as it was, ghosts were not what I thought to immortalize that weekend.

Surely it had to be because of the drama that Ma had weaved around me. Of all the little hotels in all the towns, Quan had to pick that one. He had no way of knowing of course. It didn't look haunted; there were no ivy creeping up to the window, no towering banyan with vines like a hangman's ropes, no drooping pines hovering at its side, no soulful bamboo to house wandering spirits.

However, at the end it was a combination of ghostly terror and Quan's sense of honor that enabled me to keep my virtue. He wanted to save that special act for our wedding night. He kissed me and breathed tender words of love, telling me his love was to be for a lifetime, then held me at his side until our hearts had calmed and the soothing night air cooled down our heated bodies.

In the morning, we found out that the haunting was real—so real that the owner had begun to go home at night, abandoning guests to their own peril. Apparently, the ghost was a Korean soldier who had killed himself with a hand grenade after his Vietnamese girlfriend had left him for another, an American GI. "How sad! *Toi nghiep qua!*" Diep shook her head as the owner clucked her tongue in agreement. As for me, and quite perversely, I didn't think of the tragedy of the soldier's death, but only of the romanticism of his act. I wondered if his girl had been beautiful, and if any man would ever care enough about me to sacrifice his life over the loss of my love.

Ma was impressed with my ghostly encounter and, of course, started to spin the tale as if it were her own. I had to embellish the story some, deleting all references to Quan. She didn't have to know that the incident took place while I was flitting about in a hotel room in nervous anticipation of a would-be lover. I could not have done that to Ma. I would have denied to my dying breath if she had ever suspected and questioned. As long as she didn't get the confirmation from me, she could still hang on to the hope that I was wise, that I knew what was what, that I would not have shamed my family in that way.

It was a confused girl that got off the Air Vietnam flight from Qui Nhon to Saigon two days later. The embers that had smoldered within me through days of longing and sizzled during my search for the most beautiful words to describe the basest of desires had been snuffed out at the edge of combustion. Ironically, they withered at the manifestation of one forlorn, romantic ghost.

The sky that saw me home was a harsh blue, seamless, limitless, completely devoid of romantic wisps of white.

While my honor remained intact as I deplaned in Saigon, other consequences of my stay would plague my sensibility for a long time. It caused the death of two innocent men, who were caught in the macho of the moment, fueled by the madness of war. It started on the first night of my arrival.

The men from Quan's platoon had just dropped us off in front of the hotel after dinner when several Vietnamese Special Forces men walked by and issued a few whistles and flirtatious remarks to me and Diep. As expected, Quan's friends responded with a few threats. A week later, the men ran into one another again at a bar in town. This time, ugly taunts were thrown all around that escalated to a violent confrontation. Two men, one from each side, later died of gunshot wounds.

The trip became a watershed event in my life, even if I didn't lose my virginity as planned. In Quan's mind, the relationship had been taken to a point of no return; it was thus incumbent upon him to take it to its natural culmination. He said he would ask his parents to offer for me. In our case, no intermediary was required since we already knew each other.

I listened to his plan for us, how I would live with his parents until he could get an assignment in Saigon, then we could rent a house somewhere nearby, even though he would prefer that we stayed with his parents. As an only son, he had the duty to look after them. He knew I would be a good daughter-in-law, "respectful and obedient."

His plans left me cold. Worse, it offended me, for it would have left my parents with nothing. After all they had sacrificed for me, raised me to the day where I could help make their lives a little better, how could I then take my precious earnings and affection to another household, to someone else's parents? It did not matter that such was the tradition; I would have none of it.

It was Quan's misfortune to fall in love with a girl whose duty was just as large as his. My fury shocked him. He could not understand why I would say no to his proposal of marriage. He became angry at what he thought were my "delaying" tactics. How could I not want to marry him? After all, wasn't that what courtships were all about? Not terribly perceptive, he gave me an ultimatum. His parents had demanded that he marry soon. If I didn't agree, he would have to yield to their wishes and marry someone else of their choosing. "They are anxious to have grandchildren," he said.

Two months later, he married a girl of his parents' choice. He told Diep of his loveless marriage and why he had to do what he did. If he could not have me, he didn't care whom he married. He came back again and again on leave. Each time he did, he maintained a vigil outside the embassy, waiting to speak to me.

I gave in to the pressure and finally agreed to meet. On the afternoon when we did, I remember walking across the divide that separated the embassy walkway from the road, taking the long way around instead of snaking between the metal rail fence to get to him, the way I used to in my eagerness to reach his side. I waited as a train chugged along the fence line toward the multi-lane roundabout at the market, howling piteously as if echoing the pain I saw in his eyes.

The sound made me feel cold and sad. I wondered where the racing pulses and light-headedness had gone. While Quan hoped for the chance to apologize and to mend, my heart had gone and emptied itself of the warmth and tenderness it used to know. It no longer flipped and spewed poetry at thoughts of him.

It seemed as if our love had never been. Now he was a stranger, a ghost from the past. I listened to his words of love, offered in beseeching my forgiveness. He didn't know that it was I who should have begged his pardon for trampling on his heart.

He wanted to know if we could continue to see each other since he didn't have any feeling for his wife and that the marriage had been a horrible mistake. The plea renewed my fury. If I didn't want to be his wife, what made him think I would consider being his "*meo*," or cat (a word for girlfriend or mistress)?

My indignation dissipated soon enough, when his gentle, loving eyes roamed my face, searching for a glimpse of the love we once had. I felt like weeping then. Indignant no more, I had to steel my heart lest it weaken. But I didn't need to worry. It seemed that once my mind had made the decision not to abandon my parents, my heart followed that dictate faithfully, immediately banishing any feelings that could have led me astray.

It was his fate to fall in love with someone whose filial duty was as consequential as his, a so-called "only son," and to have found the restless wind that was my spirit, just as it was mine to roam the world, living the life of a nomad with no thoughts of safe harbor until the universe shifted, and I, like the wayward wind, was forced to turn toward home and away from the glory and treachery of foreign shores. Wonder of wonders, my wind and I would find that the peace and joy we had been searching for in all the world had been there all along, deep inside our turbulent hearts.

Quan's love was gentle and noble. It would have withstood any change of time and circumstance. It could have given me the emotional stability to better manage life's challenges. For my betrayal, he would become a bitter man for most of his.

TWENTY-THREE

American Embassy
Saigon, Vietnam, 1969

The war continued to rage, even as American resolve steadily weakened by increasing anti-war protests across the United States. The wizened men monitored these events in amazement, wondering how a people could impact a powerful government's decisions on matters normally considered beyond the working man's influence. The bad thing was that the Communists now understood, as we did, that time was on their side—the American people at home would help win the war for them. All they had to do was continue inflicting further casualties on the

Americans and wait for public outrage to escalate and force an end to the war on whatever terms they desired.

Taking full advantage of these serendipitous developments, they stepped up the campaign to decry the immorality of the war, using words that carried no significance, or even meaning, to them and watched the American public flinch and turn against their own countrymen for atrocities committed in the name of war.

Unformed as my mind was, I thought the generosity of spirit shown by the Americans was unusual. I was puzzled that they could empathize with the pain and suffering of their own men as well as hapless villagers whom they had never met. With no ulterior motive, to me they exemplified selflessness and compassion that was lacking on all indigenous parties of the Vietnam civil conflict.

Much later, after I had embarked on the path to self-awareness and at last understood what unconditional love was, I would know that if one was truly merciful, one could not limit that humanity to one's home or national borders, that love and compassion were qualities unquestionably inclusive and universal. On that discovery, I began to search my memories for impressions of the war in order to reconcile the remarkable sense of familial duty and responsibility that supposedly defined our people—Communist leaders and their southern spies included—with their shameful surrender to the dark side of pride.

The glaring discordance convinced me of the conditionality of their feelings. If they were truly selfless, dutiful sons and daughters, and responsible, sacrificing parents, they could not have launched conflicts that inflicted suffering and death to millions of other sons and daughters and equally responsible, sacrificing parents. Their loving spirits would not have allowed it. They would have paused to consider the human costs of their ideas. The Communists' famed Uncle Ho reputedly once said, "You could kill ten of my men for every one I kill of yours, and I still win." How shameful that body counts did not matter to him, that winning did. If he still lives, I wonder if he would now reflect on the counts that didn't matter at the time and could finally admit that it was a nonsensical war.

In reflecting on the falsity of the warmongers' professed brotherly love, I would arrive at a vile contempt for even the most idealistic of men on finding that behind their fiery rhetoric and proud righteousness was that need to satisfy the ego, a need so consuming they willingly surrendered their souls.

These insignificant little people, from presidents to kings to all their men and women to revolutionaries, touted the nobility of their ideals since, to them, it defined who they were. How tragic is it that they think themselves nothing beneath those ideals? Idealism is what idealism does—not much without humanity to go with it. So it is with the intellect. Without heart, it reduces would-be men of significance to ego-ridden men, men who, when stumbling onto those so-called great thoughts of other men, did not have the heart to let it merely inspire them to inject love and compassion into the world, but rather undertake to perpetuate fear and greed, in reckless and complete disregard for the human costs that entailed.

To the heartless among them who claimed they did it for the people, I would agree with Ma, who would have said, "Bah... all for you." A political scientist she was not, nor a self-proclaimed humanitarian. But she knew well enough of the dark side of human nature to remain skeptical of any aggrandized avowal of selflessness. She preferred to stand in solidarity with the nameless, those humble makers of peace.

But this was then, and I was young and impressionable, half delirious at having broken through the barrier of class to the uncharted middle ground where anything was possible. I reveled in the high-paying, prestigious job at the embassy and showed gratitude to Fate and my employer by devoting my all to it—working hard, learning how to use calculators and adding machines with a speed that incited envy from slower hands and reluctant minds. My payroll sheets were always immaculately prepared, the sums perfectly balanced.

My workmates respected me for my English language skills and envied my quick mind. I could decipher the most circuitous routes taken by the most errant FSO travelers and equally complex travel authorizations, amendments to authorizations, amendments to cancel amendments, to determine the appropriate authorized per diem allowance.

However, they did not think much of my modest background and thought even less about me, for they did not quite know what I was all about. I was that unusual breed, an extreme introvert and a dreamer who lived mostly within my mind, except for the vocal expressions of my pro-American, anti-Communist sentiments.

They didn't know why I kept learning English, why I took every opportunity to attend any and all classes offered by the U.S. Mission, and continuing night school. After all, I had already gotten what was easily one of the best jobs in the country. What else did I want to do? I didn't know either. I simply moved to the call of Fate.

In the week I came to the ripe old age of seventeen, Diep and I went to lunch at the embassy cafeteria, which was located across the bridge from our offices in the Old Embassy Annex building. Unlike the snack bar where I had once worked with its pristine white American corridors, this new eatery had the tropical ambiance, rightfully so, for it was built to belong. With part of its wooden frame hung over the heedless water of the Saigon River and walls of mesh, the large, square dining room often enjoyed an unfettered flow of air even at the noon hour when moving air was in short supply—a fact of life in the tropics, where the ever-present stifling heat had the power to reduce all living things to listless zombies, including air.

By the riverside, the lively air danced through with vigor, engulfing all on its path with a unique, musty scent of life from the busy waterway. No languid water here. The rushing current seemed alive and inexorable, dutifully gathering scenes of life along its path, a path of blood and tears and pleas for deliverance. Amidst the gabbling and the laughter, the water gurgled and churned with the burden of its charges as it rushed toward the nurturing folds of the sea.

Across the crowded lunchroom, over the bobbling sea of black hair, I saw wind-tousled hair the color of sunset and a pair of sky blue eyes whose gaze was directed at me. Thanks to Quan's devotion, I no longer felt like a gauche girl. *If my somber face and serious eyes could elicit a love like his, then perhaps I am not so bad after all.*

My heart lurched. I sucked in my breath as the bearer of those eyes sent a heart-stopping half smile my way over the shoulders of his lunch companion, an older man whom I recognized as the American supervisor of the building and maintenance section.

Over the course of the following week, we met several more times at the same spot, mainly by contrition on my part, for it had not been my habit to frequent the cafeteria more than once a week. I had to see him again. I wanted to be sure I had not imagined the ardent look of adoration and interest.

When at last we came together, the romance started off immediately sizzling and intense, shades darker than my relationship with Quan. I was courted and seduced thoroughly, even though Art was basically a shy and gentle person. You might wonder why gentleness held such importance in my consideration. You see, it is and always was one of the most treasured, sought-after personality traits in our culture. Having a quick temper or a mean streak was considered a weakness, a flaw generally associated with low breeding.

A product of my culture, his sensitivity and shy smiles impressed me as no slick maneuver ever could. Meanwhile, Diep was determined to resist his charm. The blossoming relationship between Art and me made her hurt for Quan as though he was being betrayed all over again.

An electrical engineer from Australia, Art was on contract with the U.S. government to provide technical services to the embassy, overseeing electrical work in the main Chancery and its annex buildings, including sensitive areas of the Ambassador's Residence. During the war, the American government hired many such third-country nationals, notably citizens of the Philippines and Australia, to occupy jobs that were too sensitive and technical to be given to the Vietnamese.

We followed the trail other lovers had gone before, no matter that he was foreign to the ways of my people. We would drive to Bien Hoa, the closest countryside, or more accurately, the safest countryside, and sit by the side of a rice field. Unlike more inhibited Vietnamese couples, we ended up catching more kisses than breeze. I would discover that what I thought was passion under Quan's tentative touches was but a gentle breath of air compared to the earth-shattering tempest of Art's unrestrained ardor.

We spent every lunch hour side by side, met again after work, then remained together until long after dusk had settled. I started making excuses to Ma about working overtime, about having a new girlfriend in the embassy. I was not afraid to bring Art home to my parents, for in fact he represented the perfect solution to my dilemma. Marriage to him would enable me to meet my filial obligations as well as fulfilling my romantic fantasy, but I could not risk shaming my parents if perchance the relationship did not work out. So I waited.

It was only a matter of time, I thought, before I could tell Ma that I had found the perfect solution. Just imagine—I did not have to settle for one of those pitiable options. I could have it all—love for me *and* the financial wherewithal to take care of them. I had heard and read enough about the Western affluence and knew I needed only a fraction of Art's or my income to send home to keep their lives comfortable. Art was kind. I was sure he would let my parents and Cousin Mai come and live with us.

Unfortunately, for the time being, I could not even talk about him. Girls from respectable homes just didn't have friendships with foreigners, not girls from my station anyway. If I had been a rich girl studying at a French lycee and living in one of the closed-off villas, my highbrow neighbors would not have cared. Being rich meant they must have had some connection to the French colonial government. That affiliation would have brought with it a kind of progressive thinking on the matter of association with foreigners. Moreover, rich girls would not have been presumed to be selling themselves to foreigners for money and thereby debasing themselves, as I was.

No matter. I was too in love to be bothered with what others thought. My heart was light; my every nerve was alive. My future had suddenly become so blindingly brightened that it was almost frightening. Silently, I thanked the Fate for being kind. Surely I could not be this fortunate: being in love with a handsome, wealthy man who was as besotted with me as I was with him.

I was ecstatic when Art finally took me to meet his brother and sister-in-law who happened to be in Vietnam and actually lived in the heart of the city. The gesture indicated to me that he was serious about our relationship. In the days that followed, we would stop by his brother's house to visit and stay long after they had retired for bed, availing the use of their yard as a sort of lover's lane. It was the only place we could find a measure of privacy and be away from scornful eyes.

Still, the judgment came, from the lone night watchman who walked by our spot more often than was called for, clearing his throat and muttering under his breath derogatory remarks about fallen girls, worthless girls, girls who forgot their honor and breeding and coupled with foreigners. I tried to ignore his cruel remarks, but the condemnation was so virulent that it made me recoil with shame. I would shake off the indignity after the man passed, focusing instead on Art and our forbidden passion. There, on the fragrant, petal-strewn lawn, shadowed by my beloved frangipani, I became lost to the world, in love.

Diep continued to grumble about my foolishness of leaving Quan and blamed me for Quan's presently loveless marriage. On the subject of Art…"He is not even an American, probably poor. You see the beat-up truck he drives, and how about his clothing? If you had to couple with a foreigner, why couldn't it be a rich American officer from the embassy?"

It was true that Art cared little about what he wore, usually sporting a pair of corduroy pants that had seen too many washes and shirts that always managed to look slightly askew. Somehow, his careless manner of dress and loose-limbed, casual gait managed to convey a self-possession that made him endearing to me. He wore a crisply new blue shirt to take me to lunch once. I took one look at those blue eyes dancing in amusement at my startled response to the new shirt and lost my heart all over again.

Detractors of these interracial, international unions at the time questioned how two people could fall in love if they could not communicate with each other. The implication was that to lose one's heart, truly and absolutely, one had to know one's mate well, and this knowledge was only possible with full communication and understanding.

It was certainly true that in those early years of my girlhood, I was not quite proficient in English to understand the depth of Art's feelings about more complicated matters. All I knew was that my heart melted with tenderness on hearing the affection in his tone, the warm meanings of his words, spoken in the language I loved so well.

If there was a void in our relationship due to the language barrier, I did not see it. I knew he cared about me. As for me, I loved him, for reasons dictated by my culture—he was gentle and kind and could help me fulfill my filial duty. I was in love with him, for reasons of the heart—the torrents of longing and desire that flowed and crested when I saw him and the pain that tore at my heart whenever we said good-bye.

I remember when I first realized that I had lost my heart to him. We were having lunch at one of the most exclusive places in town—a cavern-like restaurant hidden under a modest sign on Nguyen Hue Street, a short distance from the Central Market. In the half shadow of candlelight, I watched his shyness disappear and his face animate as he talked about his boyhood in a wild, beautiful place called Tasmania and the turbulent sea around it. His pale blue eyes shone in the darkness like the stars of my childhood, beholding me as if I were the most important person in his life. By the time lunch was over, I had fallen in love with the man and his wistful blue eyes and rough, blunted worker's hands.

The days passed by in a blur. I was happy in love and heady with the unimaginable future that was now within grasp. *I did it! I would marry well, for me and my family.*

Meanwhile, I knew Ma was having a difficult time fending off those busybody cousins of ours who had started to gossip about me. They lived in the house, so naturally knew of my comings and goings; arriving late every night was not quite the conduct of a "good" girl. Added to the fact that I worked at the American Embassy and therefore would have plenty of opportunity to form illicit liaisons with Americans and the assumption of guilt was absolute.

But they didn't know my secret. I could just imagine their faces when I could announce that I was getting married. And how about those smiles on my ma's and ba's? I hugged those priceless images close to my heart and patiently waited for that sweet moment of victory.

Art and I returned time and again to that spot by the rice field. He eventually found a dirt road that took us even closer in, so I could touch the soft, young rice seedlings as they bent in line with the wind. I marveled at their golden tint of youth, which was refreshing in the largely unchanging world of dark, sad green that populated our landscape. I used to liken that vibrant green to the Americans, all westerners really, and the dark, despairing aging leaves to us, which looked rather like we did, old and burdened. In those magical afternoons by the field where the color of hope reigned, I wrapped myself in the scent of my love and let his touches take me away from the fear and the uncertainty.

At the suggestion of his brother, Art and I planned a trip to Da Lat, a lovely, haunting city in the highlands, where we would be together, really together, for the first time.

I lost my virginity in a small lodging villa called Sans Souci, which sat at the edge of a pine forest outside the city. Even if the act turned out to be an unpleasant, painful physical experience, my love for him transcended the pain and allowed me to find delight in the merging of our bodies, believing that finally he would love me as I did him. It was such that I felt no regrets afterwards, but only a sense of belonging.

Later, as I looked back to "the morning after," when my heart was full of love as my eyes beheld his across the breakfast table, I wondered if there might have been a glimmer of doubt in his eyes that I hadn't wanted to see. If I had looked more closely, perhaps I would have seen that while I loved, he only desired.

We cuddled in bed and out of it, holding hands at breakfast and lunch and dinner and all the times in between. I floated about with joy for my fortunate lot and for the chance to be in such an elegant city, both of which were clearly too good for the lowly me.

The city had the right to be out of reach of mere mortals surely, for it looked decidedly mythical. I had never seen fauna and flora of the kinds growing in this gem of the highlands. The surrounding was so lush; it made my orchard seem a scrawny, stunted patch of poor old trees. That realization made me a little sad; I didn't want to think of my sanctuary that way. I didn't want those happy memories of childhood blemished by this emerald sea of paradise. I didn't want my orchard to be reduced to insignificance, the way I was, by the opulent world beyond our humble home.

Nevertheless, the beauty was so otherworldly that I wished my parents could enjoy it with me. Just once, I wanted them to know something other than the heat and humidity of the south. I wanted them to see how roses look in the mist—mists that drifted and swirled throughout the day, then thickened and lingered long after dusk to color darkness gray.

Art and I took long walks on the trail through the woods and along the rim of a little valley, stopping now and again to steal kisses behind hedgerows. We woke up early and strolled through the lodge's garden, snaking between rows of dew-sweetened roses on our way down to the center-city lake. His arm closed firmly on my shoulder as we scampered down the wet, grassy bank to the water's edge, tightened even more as we leaned forward to view our entwined reflection, gray and solemn in the stillness of the morning. From a hill behind us, among the pines came a melancholy whisper. Filled with the pleasure of the moment, I couldn't tell it was the sound of coming sorrow.

The inevitable ripple came a week after we got back to Saigon and shattered the peaceful reflection we had imprinted on the lake's surface at that one moment in time. She was abrasive and loud, and had the look Eighth Uncle said came from the street. As soon as I alighted from the embassy entrance, she started shouting obscenities, accusing me of stealing her husband, of being a home wrecker. They had a child together, she said, and threatened to beat me, kill me, throw acid in my face, whatever it would take to protect what was hers.

I veered away, thankful for the rail fence that helped keep her at a safe distance from me. My senses were numbed; they barely registered the roaring of a vehicle heading toward us. Art tore across the bridge in his blue pickup, jumped out of the car, and packed her into the cab. With a regretful look at me, he drove off.

I stood among the chattering of my workmates. Several approached and offered me words of comfort. The sad thing was, in that moment of utter devastation, I didn't think of the repugnant scene that was still palpable enough to foul the air I breathed, but only how much I loved him, and how unbearable it would be to go on without him.

I talked to Art once more. He explained that she was his wife, but in name only. He no longer slept with her; in fact, he had not for a long time. He was thinking of buying a divorce from her, a prostitute he used to see and ended up marrying after she claimed she was pregnant with his child. The child turned out to be pure Vietnamese, and the brother she'd brought to live with them was actually her boyfriend and the baby's father. Art had considered not doing anything about the situation, thinking he could just leave her when it was time for him to depart the country for good.

I wanted so much to believe him. But fear, blood-curdling fear, got in the way. I didn't want to end up like that sweet-faced engineer in our compound who spent the rest of her life hidden away after her face had been destroyed by acid. I wanted to explain my fear to Art so he could find a solution but thought he was too gullible to handle a woman wise in the ways of the street as she was. He would fail somehow, and she would make me pay.

I ended the relationship, for I could not risk having anything happen to me. Who then would take care of my parents? Besides, I was offended. How could he have touched me...after touching that filthy trash of a woman? I couldn't stand it, knowing that the caresses I'd treasured were so tainted. Proud, I believed I was better than she was. For my rebellious nature, I was still very much part of that class-conscious society. Even the poorest could find a perch from which to look down on others. In this case, my relative purity compared to her immoral occupation.

Brushing off his entreaties, I let fear and wounded pride destroy whatever chance we might have had.

As days turned into weeks, my thoughts became as bleak as the future that now stretched endlessly before me. My days were haunted with thoughts of Art. I missed him. Whatever was going to become of me? Where there used to be love and joy, there was only this aching void within me. I was thinking of him all the time and knew I mustn't. I had to be strong. After all, what was done was done.

龙

Another Tet came and with it, traditions. The season's hope momentarily lifted my despondency as I accompanied Ma to Ba Ngoai's grave for the yearly ritual of worship.

Grandma's grave sat in the poor section of the same cemetery that was a stone's throw from the old schoolhouse of Master Hunchback. Wealth had come here also, to the world of the dead. The rich frontage area, that which was close to the village street, had expanded over the years and crept past the demarcation line between the poor and the rich. Cement tombs now stood imperiously among multi-hued green weeds and dirt graves, lording, it seemed, over the peasant poor in death as they had in life.

Some of the tombs proudly featured pillars and roofs, crosses and angels, and pink and white impatiens blooming in narrow ledges around the tombs. These symbols told me the tombs were of the up-and-coming northerners; southerners would not have used them. It was strange how I associated impatiens with the northern Catholics. It was just that I had never seen them until the northerners came south, and then only in cemeteries. We in the south would have used the ten o'clock blooms, the rooster's crown, the trang bush, or chrysanthemum.

Grandma's grave had sunk drastically since the previous year, for which Ma wept and apologized. Under her breath, she cursed the worker who had repaired the grave last, how he should have found clay to mix in with the dirt so the mound could have withstood the rain better.

We squatted down and quickly tackled the rambunctious, hardy weeds that had taken over the entire plot. Ma went to the end of the field with her little spade and brought back large chunks of dirt, which we broke up and, with the heels of our palms, worked the loose dirt onto the mound. Before the sun reached its zenith, the grave had attained its previous elevation, the weeds cleared, and the headstone scrubbed and washed with water that Ma had brought along in a tin bucket.

She placed tangerines, bananas, and dried dates (Ba Ngoai's favorite), and two rice cakes on a piece of banana leaf, opened a bottle of *xa xi*, the dark soft drink that Ba Ngoai used to like, poured it into three little cups, set a bunch of white lilies in an empty jar, and placed that against the marker. We sat on the ledge of a cement tomb nearby and watched as smoke twirled heavenward from the burning joss sticks.

Ma complained about Ba. "Not know anything. Why he not remind me to take care of Ba Ngoai's grave? Whose fault grave look like this? Watch out, Ba Ngoai come back and break his leg or something."

"Ma, you talk nonsense."

"You not know, Long-oi, you not know how mean and ornery your Ba Ngoai is."

"You mean, like you?"

She silenced me with a mean side look.

Her eyes shifted back to the grave and the still-lopsided marker. Touching the cement coolness of our seat, she said wistfully, "I not know when we have money to cement Ba Ngoai's grave."

I was way ahead of her. "Ma, next month and the one after that, I work overtime, and we save money to do that." The promise brightened her eyes immediately. She smoothed her hair back, straightened up to assume a more serious pose, and immediately whispered that promise to Grandma, saying my name out loud so Ba Ngoai would be proud of me, but also to show me that she was not trying to take the credit for herself.

Just then, three dark-skinned, grubby boys with tattered shorts and open shirts wandered toward us with hoes and spades in hand. *They have to be hungry to come here. The better place to work was the rich sec-*

tion, closer to the entrance. Motioning to the weed-free grave, Ma smiled regretfully. "Already done. Go on home."

I called out just as they turned away dejected, shoulders slumping forward like little old men. "We need some more dirt and a few bits of rock to push up the marker, can you do it?"

"*Da, Co, Da, Co, tui con lam duoc* (Yes, Miss, yes, Miss, we can do it)." Huge smiles split their faces. All three approached the grave, bent, and shifted the marker back and forth to gauge how much propping needed doing, stepped back, and consulted like professional tradesmen they were not.

Two ran off to the edge of the cemetery to collect dirt, while the other, with one arm akimbo, lifted a hand to shade his eyes and scanned the area for remnants of gravel and stone from some newly cemented grave.

I followed his eyes … to the past, when I used to work the graves in this very same cemetery.

I was never quite as aggressive as the boys, even though I had often fancied myself to be one of them. At Tet of another time, I would arrive at the cemetery just before dawn. Few family visitors came this early, but I wanted the few who did. Once the worker boys and men arrived, all the business would go to them. After all, they were thought to be stronger and better workers. I tried to lower my fee to half of what others would charge but still found it hard to find enough work. I was too young, in addition to being a girl. Another drawback was, except for the one year when Ngau and I joined forces, I worked alone rather than in a gang of two or three who could finish the work in half the time, thus allowing the family to finish their prayer and offerings early.

After a few years of going home at the end of the day with barely enough money for even a day of market for Ma, let alone snack food for me, I came up with an idea.

In what was the last year of my graveyard-weeding career, I arrived earlier than usual. Even though my legs were a bit unsteady, and my heart was beating a tad too fast for fear of troublesome spirits, I was determined to stay and test on an idea that was bold even for me. After deciding on a good, rich-looking section of tombs, I went to work. One tomb after another, I weeded, cleaned, and scrubbed. By nine in the morning I had already finished a good part of the row and settled comfortably at the base of a grave to wait for my customers.

Some of the families came as expected and paid well, even though they really didn't have to. I had no bargaining leverage; the work had already been done. It was my luck that none wanted to get out of paying or to haggle over the price. I had bet on the fact that none would want to show their miser side when their deceased ancestors were watching. However, for me the day was a success. I earned more that day than all the years I worked the graves. Ma was proud when I arrived home with my pocket filled with bills.

The boys worked diligently while I reminisced. I could see they were giving the task their all, patting more dirt on the grave, pressing to make sure it stayed, and doing so reverently in order not to offend both the deceased and the living. I remembered how hard I had tried to impress my patrons in order to earn a good tip over the agreed-upon price.

I gave the boys more than three times the going rate so they could share and still retain a decent wage, which set their hearts afire. They whooped, leaped into the air, and took off chasing one another through the maze. I could hear Ma mutter, "Silly boys, they break their legs yet." The scowl notwithstanding, the light in her eyes and that half smile on her face told me she was proud that I was kind, that where it counted I was really her daughter. The boys' laughter tugged at my heart from across the graves.

TWENTY-FOUR

American Embassy
Saigon, Vietnam, 1969

Despair tightened its grip. I felt smothered by hopelessness and rather deadened by the anticlimatic end of the much-heralded event of becoming a woman. In more sobering moments, I was shocked by my audacious actions. I had done it now. I had experienced romantic love and rushing passion, even the accompanying heartbreak. For those emotional milestones, I had paid with my honor and purity and was now paying still with doubts and regrets.

While in Cambodia, mobs started to kill Vietnamese residents in settlements near the border and even in the capital of Phnom Penh. The headlines reached every household in Saigon, resurrecting the long-held ethnic hatred. The Vietnamese called for revenge against the "*moi*," or "savages," the dark-skinned Cambodians. Ma made fun of Ba, telling him to lie low lest he became a casualty of this latest outbreak of violence between the two former foes, given that Cambodian was his heritage. She was jesting of course. Everyone in the village liked and respected my ba.

I paid little attention to these tragic events, consumed as I was with my personal tragedy. It didn't help that while my young heart was shriveling, new romance blossomed all around. Art's boss had begun an enduring romance with an older woman in my office, and one of my bosses started seeing yet another workmate of mine. Both men, like many other U.S. government civilian employees, had their families safely tucked away in peaceful Bangkok, which was only two hours away by air, definitely within weekend visiting distance.

Saigon was a dangerous place to house dependents, so the U.S. government gave its employees a special allowance called the Separate Maintenance Allowance to allow them to maintain their families in safe neighboring capitals like Taipei, Hong Kong, Singapore, or Bangkok, or as far away as Sydney. Besides housing and other expenses, the allowance also covered airfare for frequent visits by the employees. Comfortably lodged in whichever city, the children attended American Embassy or international schools, as their mothers passed the time in the company of other wives from the embassy community at their locale while some of their men availed the use of Vietnamese women to warm their beds for companionship in between visits.

Was it so difficult a time to hang on to virtues? I wouldn't know. I thought I had only one virtue left anyhow, that of honoring and caring for my parents.

Thrown together by the worst sort of human folly, the land in turmoil brought out the best and the worst in all of us. Even the United States Foreign Service, an unanimated object, did not escape the forced metamorphosis brought on by the war. To hear old FS hands tell it, the FS had never been and would never again be the mammoth, omnipotent entity it had been during the Vietnam War. Why, it even had its own airline for employees to travel to temporary duty stations throughout the country. Admittedly, Air America was used by the CIA for other purposes, but it was also made available for use by other U.S. government employees, both Vietnamese and American, to cities up and down the country from I Corps in the northernmost highlands near the Demilitarized Zone to IV Corps in the deep southern delta.

In the office, there was still a whisper of gossip about me, but by and large the busybodies had found better targets in those newer romances. The two women who were going to their beaus' apartments every day for lunch became the butts of the raunchy gossips…"Huh…what do you want to bet that lunch involved amorous activities? Heh heh heh…cackle cackle cackle…you mean…umm, that…for lunch?" Given the popular verdict on the sensual, lusty nature of American men, the supposition was accepted by all as fact.

The American presence enlightened us in ways I was certain they had never expected. From the way Vietnamese men talked, I learned that Americans were extremely sexual creatures, incapable of few other emotions besides satisfying their basest physical needs. Certainly, they were incapable of the higher love Vietnamese men reputedly were born with.

Not surprisingly, Ma quashed this line of talk almost with demonic glee. "Hah, the Vietnamese louts should be ashamed of themselves. Bah…the liars, the cheats."

From what I had seen and heard all my life as far as straying men were concerned, I had to agree with her. Surely Vietnamese men could put Americans to shame. Rather than having affairs, they formalized dalliances, turning paramours to second or third wives. A different string of children here and there did nothing to impair the moral righteousness of these men.

Ma could talk all day about the peccadilloes of Vietnamese men and defend the Americans as hotly as I was. "*Noi bay qua*. Nonsense," she would declare in a ruthless end to the discussion with any man who dared to prolong the debate.

Diep remained close to me throughout this time, even though I had closed up and become more incommunicative than ever. With acid being the weapon of choice by scornful first wives, she reminded me of the threat from Art's wife, just in case I was softening and thinking of a reconnection with him. But I was young and fickle. Soon, other men and newer faces crowded my dreams, and Art's sad eyes retreated to the deep recesses of my heart.

But I did not foresee that I could not return to the life I had known. I had now become a woman with a past, one who was once a target of an almost-jealous assault. The scandal had branded me a fallen woman, and there was no going back. Fortunately, I still had the defiance and fearless-ness of youth to carry me forth, if only to lie on the hard bed of shame I had made for myself. No longer worried about the reputation that was in tatters, I resolved to live my life however I wanted…just as Fate contin-ued to fan my fixation with the Americans and teased it to life.

龙

The sky was hard and the air heavy as I returned from a visit to yet another back alley seamstress one Saturday afternoon. The narrow roadway of Truong Minh Ky was clogged from shoulder to shoulder with all kinds of conveyance, from the modern to the archaic, to the most ancient of them all: pedestrians and peddlers. The noise deafened, and fume and dust rose from the street to seep down my throat. Spotting the familiar alleyway and spying the drink stand in its mouth, I made the turn.

After inching my motor scooter into the full shade of the faded awning of the stand, I settled back on the seat to enjoy a fresh coconut drink. Wandering peddlers passed by on foot and bicycles, advertising their wares. Two small urchins, a boy and a girl, careened toward the stand. Dirty from the top of their unwashed heads to their scrubby bare feet, they chased each other down the alley, screeching to a stop at the American soldier who was sitting on a wooden stool on the other side of the stand. They stared at him unabashedly. With hands clasped behind their backs, faces solemn, and heads slightly tilted, they looked like two midget elders examining a modern-day Gulliver in the land of the little people.

"Heh…heh…heh…" They looked at the sun-washed hair on the American's arms and giggled. The girl stared at the foreign face with fascination. As if testing the water, she broke out a shy, beguiling smile, to which the American returned with equal charm. To all the worlds, they seemed equally engrossed in each other, so alike in their looks of innocence.

The boy jabbed a finger at her shoulder, breaking the endearing moment of hero worship. He shoved her at the soldier and urged, "*Ro di, so ha?* (Go ahead and touch, you scared?)" Her lips pressed together, as if summoning courage, but her feet betrayed those determined lips and stayed firmly anchored where they were. I could easily see myself being that fascinated by an American at her age. Why, I still was at almost eighteen.

Bemused, I asked, "*Chau muon ro gi?* (What you want to touch?)" Embarrassed, she started to twist the hem of her ragged shirt and was about to take the dirty flute to her mouth when the boy helpfully supplied, "She want to touch the arm of Mr. American to see if the hair is soft."

"Hmm…" I turned red with embarrassment even as I moved to translate. Eyes dancing with humor, the soldier extended his arm toward her. "Come on, you can touch." She reached out tentatively and smoothed her fingers over the hair on his arm, up and down, up and down, barely touching the skin. She fluttered her lashes and looked up at him through half-shuttered lids—a look as coquettish as the most accomplished bar girl, one that completely charmed him and reduced me to a jealous idiot. Where did she learn to throw out a look like that? I could not have produced anything remotely familiar even if my life had depended on it.

The curbside situation comedy then admitted a new character. Another ragamuffin, the older, teenage version, raced toward us at breakneck speed. His bike wobbled wildly, but whatever control he lacked, he made up with the force of his thumb, which was pressing and releasing on the bike's little ringer for all it was worth. The American soldier grabbed the little girl's arm and swiftly drew her to the protected space between his knees, out of harm's way. The wild rider cackled with pleasure, enormously pleased that he could provoke fear.

The soldier smiled indulgently at the girl then used his index finger to draw air circles on his temple. "*Dien cai dau* (Crazy in the head)," he uttered the simple phrase widely used by American GIs in their interactions with Vietnamese nationals.

The little girl giggled and directed her slightly slanted, beautiful shining eyes at her hero, who presently pointed to his drink and asked, "Do you want a drink?" She shyly nodded.

All was quiet as we contemplated the drinks in our hands and, occasionally, one another. The sun had lifted its blanket of heat finally to allow a cooling breeze to come through. Suddenly, a preternatural stillness came over the din, almost reversing the natural order of things. I became aware of an ominous silence, a silence tense and profound, one that was felt rather than heard.

For the first time, I noticed the two men sitting at a small, wobbling table to the left of us. I could not detect any conversation from the table but sensed I had missed something important. As if she could hear my thoughts, the girl handed the drink to her brother and shifted her glance furtively from the table to the soldier then to me. She looked at me and pouted. When I bent down and asked, she whispered quickly, "Those men wait for Dung somebody. They want to take Mr. American's watch and wallet. You tell him."

The image that came to me then was immediate and horrific. I thought of the American who had gotten stabbed in Cowshed Alley and knew I could not let that happen here. I softly recounted to the American what the girl had said while keeping the moment inconspicuous by letting my eyes roam absently everywhere and settle nowhere. I suggested that he take the kids with him and go out to the main road, counting on the fact that those extra bodies, though small, would thwart any violent move against him.

I watched as they walked away. The girl jumped and skipped by the soldier's side, her little hand tucked in his, apparently ecstatic with her important mission, while her brother circled around them, hopping and chortling like a monkey. The men didn't follow.

I rode out of the alley moments later and found the trio still standing by the side of the road. The soldier ruffled the little girl's hair and said good-bye after fishing in his pocket for a packet of gum for her. She grinned and waved, while I sat on my scooter with both feet planted on the ground and the engine on idle, waiting for him to get into a taxi.

I never knew his name.

Just as American and Vietnamese blood soaked the hills and the countryside, war money continued to flood the economy. I believed there was some law of economics at play that was beyond the comprehension of the southern poor. One had to have money to make money. How did one get that first batch of money? It was not as if the funds needed were within the lowly sums attainable from a game of cards. How did the wily get their hands on so much money? Whatever, soon enough, the dealmakers were able to erect four- and five-story buildings all along our street to rent out to shopkeepers or American servicemen and contractors, or third-country nationals who worked at the base in nearby Tan Son Nhat.

The city looked like it had an overnight facelift. The change was so complete, pervasive, and quick it could have been realized only by an event of the magnitude of the Vietnam War. The streets teemed with humanity: American military vehicles intermingled with motor scooters newly imported from Japan, all jockeying for space on the now enlarged roadways.

Bars and hotels littered the path of progress. Every week hundreds of young girls joined the ranks of their sorority sisters to offer their tried and untried bodies to American, Allied, and Vietnamese soldiers. Their struggle for survival was no less desperate than the soldiers they serviced, even if it took place under somewhat saner circumstances in rooms seedy and fine encompassing all points south of the DMZ.

Many called them whores. Others viewed them as simply marginal women trying to earn a living as best they could with what they had. The more fortunate among them got selected to be regular bedmates to some foreigners for a spell. Most had a high sense of duty and responsibility and tendered love and respect to their benefactors in return for kindness and affection. Even without the ring on her finger and that ultimate ticket to Anytown, USA, the woman consort enjoyed the foray into the world of the "haves"—good food on the table, money to care for her parents—and intimacy with a liberal man for however long the relationship lasted.

Our women had given much for a lot less. There was one among them whose rise and fall, whose beauty and accomplishments completely captured my imagination at adolescence.

The top graduate of a class of agricultural engineers, she was transferred to the compound shortly after the new research lab came into existence. She was beautiful in a classic, elegant sort of way, much like Grace Kelly. With beauty and brains, she was sought after by the brightest of engineers who came through. She said no to all, only to become a mistress to one of the department heads, a rotund, married man of forty-some years her senior.

His wife found out eventually and hired a hoodlum to throw a bottle of acid at her. It destroyed her sight and her lovely face. She withdrew from society to return home to live with her parents in a house she had earned from her service to the old man. We later found out that she'd had to do what she did to keep her job.

That single act of cruelty almost destroyed her life, but love saved her. What she had done for love and duty—that of seeing to her parents' comfort by purchasing a home with an orchard for them to spend their old age in tranquility—ended up sustaining her. It was to that place of love and anonymity that she returned to live out her life.

She, and many others like her, were viewed with compassion, if not respect, among the poor in a culture that praised duty and sacrifice above all else. *"There's no greater love than these women who sell their bodies for the people they love…"*

Western observers ridiculed these affairs of the heart between local women and American men as tainted by the dollars. Derisively, they labeled the women mercenary, the label that, at certain times, could perhaps have applied to me. It was only years later, after much water had flowed under the bridge, that I would gain enough confidence in myself and know a little more about the world to wonder what those detractors would have done in our women's places.

Would they have had the courage to do as these women had, forsaking their own needs and wants for those of their families?

I willed myself to become used to the shame and the scorn, but the pressure was relentless. It seemed all the force was conspiring to make me pay the price for my promiscuity. Mr. Thao, my local supervisor and a wannabe womanizer, latched on to me after my disastrous love affair with Art. He bothered no other staff, for they were considered respectable and above reproach. He went after Diep and me, Diep to a lesser extent. Flirtatious as she was, she was properly married to a Vietnamese serviceman and thus earned herself a degree of respectability.

I received the brunt of his rejuvenated ardor. Barely eighteen, I had been despoiled by a westerner and was therefore seen as damaged goods. Stripped of honor, I became fair game for a lecherous old man. He brought in pornographic photos of men and women coupling in different positions and tried to get me to look at them, promising he could give sexual pleasure like no one else could.

I tolerated his crude innuendos to have peace on the job. However, I was not my mother's daughter for nothing; no one could make me do what I didn't want to do. I might have attained a veneer of sophistication from my exposure to Western cultures and my association with the Americans, but I was still that belligerent, independent child my mother had never managed to reform. He never gave up during the five years following my affair with Art, and neither did I. He did try to force a kiss once, on a weekend when the office was almost deserted. But I sidestepped so quickly, he ended up barely missing the wall.

Gradually, the distance of time helped me restore a calmness of mind to consider the cold reality of my ill-fated romance with Art and the promise that once was. *Marriage to a foreigner? Yes, that would work. My husband would be wealthy enough to take care of both me and my parents. And a foreigner would not care if I was still pure. At least, I didn't think so.*

But the revelation brought little comfort. I knew now which road to follow, but it was not entirely up to me. My future shimmered and shifted like a mirage before me, sometimes bathed in a glorious glow, other times swathed in twilight gray. To think that its color would be determined by a faceless man frustrated me so. But what could I do? I resolved to move forward and do what I could to influence the course of my life, all the while knowing my best might not be good enough, for the future was not mine to make.

TWENTY-FIVE

IN THE NEWS: 5/18/70 -
KENT STATE SHOOTINGS
SHOCK THE NATION.

American Embassy
Saigon, Vietnam, 1970

I met another man, one I had no right to
encourage. Joe was a high-level official in the
embassy, much older than Art, actually more
than twice my age, and married. The air did
not sizzle as it did with Art, but glistened with
the force of our attraction to each other. As tall
as Art with his over six-foot height, Joe had
those patrician looks of the poet Robert Frost
and the demeanor of an intellectual. His hazel
eyes could twinkle with amusement at some
insignificant thing I said one minute, only to
turn ponderous the next over a magazine article
on some abstract political theory. Most impor-

tantly, he spoke the language I loved. A noted linguist, he took to teaching me German as well as English.

With his being older and married, the gossip was brutal. Here was the case of a girl tempted by the American dollars and a man looking to buy sex and youth from a pretty young thing. The truth was, I was not seduced by wealth so much as by passion and what he represented—a liberal, educated mind, and especially a gloriously progressive homeland called America.

He could help me break away from the war and a society that was determined to keep me forever within the lowly confines of my station. I wanted to be free to make my destiny. I wanted to know what I could make of myself without barriers that were too high to cross, doors that were too tightly shut to pry.

As for him, the price of being with me was perhaps self-respect and the esteem of his colleagues. Our scandalous association placed him decisively in that category of married men who made good use of their unique status of being "geographically single" by engaging in romantic liaisons with local women during their unaccompanied tours in Vietnam.

Some of the men opted for the more stable, less-controversial relationships with older, more educated women. Others let their hearts rule and lived for the moment—*carpe diem* and damned the convention. They went ahead to set up house with the young and not-so-young ladies of the trade.

They would return to their wives after their tours of duty were over, closing up their bachelor pads and leaving those extramarital sojourns behind. Inevitably, some of the patched-up marriages fell apart shortly thereafter on the men's realization of the true loves they had left behind in Vietnam. Consequently, the disenchanted spouse but true lover returned to make a war bride of his Vietnamese sweetheart.

Vietnam, with all its danger and temptation, must have been a test of a man's moral fiber, his character, and his sense of honor. Some escaped the sexual snares that could not have been easy in the face of loneliness and disillusionment over the protracted and murderous war. I did not have the intellect or objectivity to judge these men. The practice was so pervasive that it became a feature of the war itself and I, part of it. Like the men, I yearned for forbidden passion. Like them, it was also a matter of survival. While they searched for distraction from the insane and the unfathomable, I sought that knight in shining armor to change my destiny.

My relationship with Joe was not without turmoil, for, hard as I tried, I could not change the fact that there seemed to be no promise and no expectation. But I kept on hoping. What else could I do? Like all others who got caught in this maelstrom of time, I clung on to the only thing I had—hope, illusive as it was.

Whenever Joe and I had one of those rare "talks" about us, which consisted mainly of long, pregnant silences, even that tiny ember of hope would be extinguished, leaving me with nothing but the dreaded certainty that I was wasting my reputation and time on someone who was in it only for the moment. Tears would threaten to come to my eyes, but in spite of youth and sentimentality, I had enough pride to remain silent rather than revealing to him that he was my only hope and my lifeline. Foolish as I was, I knew just enough about love and relationship to know my admission would not have changed anything. One could not force love or beg for it. I knew that. I was simply hoping I could earn it somehow, the way other women seemed to be able to do.

Following those enlightening moments, I would leave his house feeling utterly hopeless. *How can I not get this done? How can I not be able to find someone? Bar girls, prostitutes, peasant women turned orderlies at the base seem to find their benefactors with no problem. What is lacking in me that no one can love me well enough?*

Following one despairing incident, I stormed out the gate of his house, angry and determined. Without thinking, I flagged down a taxi.

"Where?" the driver asked. I replied with emphatic resolve, "Oh, any bar on Tu Do, near the river."

I walked into the most sedate-looking bar, one with no half-naked girls loitering at the entrance; they would have intimidated me too much. The interior was so dim I could hardly make out any of the faces. Laughter, conversations—comforting sound in English—flowed around. I was given a job then and there, even though I could claim no prior experience. My age, gender, and ability to speak English seemed to be the only qualifications required.

The richly made-up matron of the bar, who was as scantily clad as the girls, explained to me in ten short minutes the name of the game, that of getting GIs to buy me drinks. When I told her I could not drink and would therefore get drunk before too long, the girls who were hovering nearby let out squeals of raucous laughter. "You not get drunk; you drink tea or flavored water. We charge GI price of liquor and share with you."

Before she even finished giving me the rote, a GI separated from others at a table and came toward me. I was flattered. I really had nothing over other girls, nothing that counted in this place of the flesh. Compared to the lushness that was all around, I looked rather emaciated. I wondered if something was wrong with his eyesight. No matter. As far as I was concerned, he was everything that was right—tall, handsome … and American.

We talked as the house kept the "tea" coming. In educated, if not quite fluent, English, I told him about me—where I worked, why I was there, my hopes and my fears. I felt no shame and no inhibitions. After all, I would never see him again.

The small table lamp behind us cast his face in half shadow as we sat side by side at the counter, arms almost touching. He smiled from time to time. I started to explain about the "Saigon tea," but he raised a hand and winked. "I know, I know … no sweat." I told him about Quan, and Art, then Joe. He showed me a picture of his girlfriend back home. She was going to college and had promised to wait for him. He thought he was fortunate; some of his buddies were not so lucky—not all the girls wanted to wait for a guy who was in "Nam."

As I stared at the picture in his grip, I suddenly found myself choked with emotions just like he was, but for a different reason. I wanted to be that girl who undoubtedly had a good home in a wonderful, peaceful country, and a guy like this longing to go home to her.

Through the haze of smoke, the Beatles came though with "Let It

Be." Over the counter, our heads bent and touched. I breathed in the smell of sweat and dirt from a battlefield somewhere that still clung to his disheveled uniform and let myself imagine, for a moment, that all was well with him and me and the world, that he belonged to me, and I him, that we could walk out of the place and leave the craziness behind—the war, my hateful future. That he would love me...

Softened by the languid melody, I wondered if he was similarly affected by the melancholy of the moment and thinking of home and his girl. The faint smile on his lips told me he probably was. I told him to be careful, so he could live and go home. He shook his head resignedly. Our conversation shifted to the war, the frustration of not knowing who and where the enemy was. I admitted that even as a Vietnamese, I could not even tell which one of us was Viet Cong. Viet Cong did not have three heads, and the villager who did their bidding was exactly who she claimed to be—a villager—who was caught in the same madness we were. My ma said peasants had to do what they were told or die.

We laughed as I told him how my brother was going AWOL every few months. He said he would do the same thing if only he could, if his home were only a few hours away. We left the bar and walked three long blocks to the food corner at the intersection of Nguyen Hue and Pasteur. There, we found a table in front of the Chinese soup wagon and sat down among other couples, lovers, young girls; all had stopped in for a snack after a few hours of "*chay vong vong*," running around, or, in other words, "cruising."

I asked the vendor to put extra meat and wonton in his bowl of soup, knowing Americans liked more meat in their foods. We talked and laughed over the piping hot noodles and his repeat attempts to use the chopsticks. He raised his eyebrows over the loud slurping of soup all around us and shook his head resolutely against my offer to buy a paper-twist of roasted pig ears for him to try. The aromas of food drifted by... He lifted his face, breathed in deeply as if trying to identify the different smells, then looked at me and grinned sheepishly.

It did not take long for the whispers and scathing looks to come, even if I looked rather young and innocent and we did not appear the least bit amorous. "A prostitute … oh so young … what waste." As the comments turned more vulgar, and the vulgarity heated my face and chilled my blood, I urged him to finish up quickly then paid for the both of us with the money I had collected from the matron at the bar.

We returned via the same road we had come. Along Nguyen Hue, the shops had long been closed. Street urchins and beggars had settled down on their mats against the shutters. Several sat up at our approach, only to slump down again when I smiled and gently shook my head.

A few cyclo drivers pedaled along, hoping for a fare. When the reply was negative, pleas turned to jeers. "Let's go," I urged my companion. I wanted to send him on his way in a taxi, but he insisted on seeing me safely home first.

Inside the darkened cab, I listened to the thrumming engine of the taxi and felt strangely warm and light-headed. It was as if I had slipped into another world. To me, this soldier epitomized all the GIs I had seen. For him, I wanted all that was good, even though I wouldn't be part of it. Suddenly overcome with dread, I wanted him, specifically him, to survive. I didn't want his body to pass by the 3rd Field Hospital on the way home.

When the taxi stopped in front of my gate, he kissed me good-bye on my forehead. The kiss was unbearably sweet, warm, and soft. I held both of his hands in mine and reached up to teach him how to kiss Vietnamese style—by pressing my nose on his cheek and inhaling deeply, filling my lungs with his scent. He smiled and said, "Hey, take care of yourself, and be happy."

"You too," I whispered. "Don't die."

The heavens had started to weep. My heavy thoughts followed him as the taxi sped away in the drizzles. What was his name? Was it Rick, Bob, Dave, or Andrew? It could have been either. Or it could have been none. It didn't matter. Like the symbolic Unknown Soldier in Arlington National Cemetery, to me he was one and all.

TWENTY-SIX

IN THE NEWS: 7/1/71–PARIS–
VIET CONG AGREES TO TRADE
POWS FOR U.S. WITHDRAWAL
BEFORE END OF YEAR.

American Embassy
Saigon, Vietnam, 1970–1971

I became the lover of a married man, like thousands of other Vietnamese women. With my virginity gone, I thought I had nothing else to lose, least of all that intangible something called self-respect. I began to spend more time at Joe's house, a lavishly furnished villa on a secluded street in an affluent part of town. Silence was part of its exclusivity; the melody of cicadas and rustling of leaves from towering trees were the only disturbance to the stillness.

I knew this exalted place was not mine to

keep, but while it lasted I could imagine I had arrived to be among the ranks of the rich, the noble.

It was easier in thought than in practice. Joe's cook, A-Ping, a Chinese from the china town of Cholon, was part of the cruel world that intruded. Her disapproval of me was obvious. At dinnertime, she would set my plate down just a tad more forcefully than his. Any request from me for whatever—more water, an extra helping of food—was usually met with icy disdain.

She seemed to take upon herself to remind me that I did not belong, that I would never be. My face would heat up with humiliation at every scathing look she threw my way. My mother had taught me well. I was both perceptive and sensitive, both of which presently contributed to the shame I felt. What had I gone and done? In my haste to escape poverty, I'd foolishly taken on the additional burden of dishonor.

Away from prying eyes, I learned how the rich lived and what they thought. First, there were the swimming lessons. Joe registered both of us at a swimming club in town, not the *Cercle Sportif* where embassy people frequented, but a local club so we would not be seen by his colleagues. There I frolicked in the water like a child, hanging on to the ledge and kicking my legs, learning how to swim at last, a pursuit that was considered too *bourgeois* for poor city kids.

Next was a more subtle lesson on that hierarchy of needs. On the night of the August moon festival, Joe decided to treat a group of kids from the city orphanage to the timeless ritual of celebration. He bought store-made lanterns for each of the children and took them around the block. His colleagues participated in the good deed, helping to shepherd the line of children and their chaperone, an orphanage staff, from one road to another, with candlelit lanterns swinging from their hands. Afterwards, we returned to the house to enjoy a feast of sweet moon cakes and soft drinks.

I would never have thought of such a novel idea, of showing kids how to have fun as a gift. I would have simply given them food, unlike Joe, who, unburdened by mundane matters such as food and shelter, was able to think of the spirit and did what he could to give those orphans a moment of fun to lighten the heart. I would remember for years to come the hesitant smiles on the children's faces, as if enchanted by the kind, if odd, gesture.

As we moved through the quiet neighborhood where neither the children nor I belonged, I looked down at the well-made lantern dangling from my hand and thought of the simpler lanterns of my youth.

Before each August moon, Ma would find money to buy pieces of transparent, colorful paper, and Ba would spend an afternoon making bamboo shavings so we could bend them into different lantern shapes. He also gathered enough tree sap for us to use as glue. The boys, especially Big Rat, were more talented. They could create lanterns of all sorts of shapes. Year after year, mine was always a star, which was the easiest to make. Even in this, Ba had to help. I just did not have the artistic inclination or the patience to try anything else.

I saw Art passing by now and again as I walked from my office to the parking lot or while I was in Joe's car. His eyes would look sad or mocking, depending on where they found me. I hurt at the former and turned defiant at the latter. From his boss's girlfriend who was my workmate, I learned he had been divorced at last and was now going out with a secretary in his office. How would my life have turned out if I had stayed and waited, or if he had come back for me?

If I had thought more about the war, I would have behaved differently, settling for anyone who could produce that ticket out. If I had thought less about it, I would have been more cautious in matters of the heart, for I still must face the future that was to come. But I was ambivalent, remembering when I wanted to, forgetting when it suited me. This irresolution would lead me to a place of deepening uncertainty.

I enjoyed the temporary taste of affluence while hoping Joe would change his mind, that he would be my savior. Did he love me? I didn't think so. He was perhaps as infatuated with my youth as I was with his maturity, as enchanted by my *naiveté* as I was by his sophistication. From the far reaches of my mind, I knew our relationship would go no further than these passing moments, for he had been careful not to make promises he didn't plan to keep. He, like the others, would return to his orderly life, retaining only dim memories of this extramarital adventure. "What an experience," they could say with candor when asked about their part in the war.

However uncertain, for the moment he remained the answer to my hopes and dreams and my interim refuge. By his side, I learned all that was precious about knowledge. I was mesmerized by what a mind could absorb, what it could know, and the sheer enormity of what was out there for me to discover. I watched him ponder and choose his words with care as he described democratic processes and the psychology of man, all done in the language I loved. I did not comprehend all that his mind produced but understood enough to know that it was well articulated and brilliant. I took in his supposition, his sensitivity and decency, and came up with another wish—that one day I should become a thinker like he was.

I knew I had traded the engine oil scent of one man for the sophisticated cologne of another, the rough hands of a worker for the soft palms of an intellectual, love for presumed security, and became worse off for it. But I could not undo the past, hopeless as the present seemed to be. I clung to what I had, for there simply was nothing else.

The Vietnam War created a time warp that moved our lives in the most curious of ways. The young men who left civilization behind for the hellish war in Asia found their senses of value and morality shattered. Reality was incomprehensible, the future uncertain, they focused on the most basic of instincts—living and staying alive. Just as confused and scared, I, a teenager in their midst, felt too that time was running out. I answered the call of duty, as they had theirs. While death was not in the forefront of my consciousness, something else was—something equally final, something that prompted me to think only of the present, to live only for the moment. Alas, if only we had followed this dictate of the senses to serve our highest good in those supposed last moments of our lives instead of…

But there was no time to ponder. The threat to our very survival was so immense we were moved to pursue only the basest of needs. So I discarded caution and my family's honor, trampled on traditions, and sometimes lived like the young men who stole my heart, like there might not be a tomorrow for regrets.

They were giving up their lives for a country that didn't even know them. Even I, their steadfast supporter, betrayed them. I could no longer ease the weariness on their brows with bright, worshipping eyes. Whenever I caught sight of them while riding to work in Joe's car, my eyes would avert. I felt the accusation; they were on their way to God knows where, a nightmare from which some would not return, and there I was, safely sheltered in an air-conditioned car with a compatriot of theirs more than twice my age. Was that what they were fighting for?

It was such that I favored the independence atop my scooter. From its singular seat, I did not have to steel my heart against the jeers of passing drivers. And when a convoy of trucks carrying American soldiers rolled by, I did not have to look away or recoil from the assault of guilt. I could look my fill and try to throw a smile in that shy, coquettish manner young girls did. Then when the trucks were gone and the exhaust fume had blurred the lines of their faces, I would grind the engine furiously, as if in so doing I could pulverize that nameless ache in my heart.

I accepted a ride home from Art one late afternoon, which was to be our last time facing each other. He drove with the windows down, just as he had always done. A wayward wind came by and tousled his hair, which he raked back with his fingers just so. Everything about him was still so familiar. I stared at the gold-tipped hair on his arms and remembered how those arms used to feel around me once upon a time. I almost reached out to touch. Suddenly, I remembered. Even as I sat with the person I had once loved, and still did, I was pregnant with another man's child. However, I didn't think Art would have minded either my pregnancy or my touching him.

But I let the moment pass...just as Fate had intended. My journey was not to be over calm waters with bursts of sweet, mild wind at my back. Life with him could have been that.

Regardless of how confused the direction, how rocky the road, I could not tell my parents what I was searching for and why. They would have told me not to worry, that they would take care of things. But I knew better—not even Ma could fix this for me. Resourceful as she was, she could not have stemmed this yearning within me to find a path to the land where I felt my destiny awaited.

To atone for my sins, for the heaviness I had laid on my parents' hearts, I tried to be a good daughter in other ways. For Ba, I would stop by the Old Market now and again to buy a lump of butter for him to enjoy the refreshing, foreign taste. Without a refrigerator, the tropical heat melted the butter almost immediately, but it was of no consequence to my ba. He had gotten used to eating it that way, liquefied butter sprinkled on hot baguette. He handled the butter as if it were something precious, spooning every bit of it carefully into the little jar he had salvaged from my scrap heap.

For my mother, I handed over most of my pay and brought treats home on payday so she didn't have to cook dinner, so she would be proud of me when the cousins came to inquire about the package I had brought home.

Joe talked about the American dilemma. Having withdrawn almost two hundred thousand GIs due to domestic pressure, President Nixon was becoming increasingly frustrated with the Communist's unyielding stand on the war. The experts debated on opportunities lost, but subsequent events would prove what the northern refugees had always known—that regardless of any promise or apparent overture at peace, the Communists did not plan to stop until they had fully subjugated the south.

The view had always been clear from the streets. American resolve was being worn down, corpse by corpse of young American men. Over coffee, the wizened mused on ways to salvage the South. Perhaps President Nixon would send troops to Hanoi. Or better yet, would he drop an atomic bomb on the North? Only then would we be safe from the Communists.

While I had a dilemma of my own. Joe's tour had been shortened, supposedly because of our affair. A colleague of his revealed to me that Joe's indiscretion had caused displeasure among the higher-ups in the embassy. It was not that the practice was not prevalent; we were just more careless and ended up paying the price for that imprudence. I didn't know this then, but as far as Joe's superiors were concerned, there was also the unpleasant possibility that our relationship had made Joe more susceptible to hostile intelligence.

My pregnancy didn't change Joe's mind about our relationship. Despite the fact that he was an honorable man, or perhaps because of it, I had to accept I would be left alone with the responsibility of caring for my child. He did not know that the Communist threat had become personal to us. He could not have known that the danger had become dire because of the American child yet to be born. Suddenly, the responsibility of caring for my parents had become trivial. It was no longer about poverty, no longer about us. The Communists would not overlook so blatant an American association. As I watched Joe pack for his departure, I cried, though not for the loss of him, for he was never mine to keep. The tears were for me and my family. *There was only one thing left to do: I would have to double my effort to find that someone to save us all.*

I spent my last night in the villa of the cicadas. Dawn was still a distance away when I walked out of its gate for the last time as the embassy car bore Joe away toward the airport. I started down the still darkened, deserted road, with tears seeping from my eyes and misery bearing down on my every step. I touched my stomach, which was still flat, and cringed … "Now how will I tell Ma?"

Ma was puzzled but delighted that I was taking the day off, fluttering about to see if there was anything special I wanted to eat. When the evening meal was over, I asked her to take a walk to the gate with me.

We followed the narrow, well-worn dirt path through the orchard. Among the shifting sea of change, some things in the compound had remained the same—this trail was one such link to the past, a past of comfort and familiarity that had the power to soothe even as it shamed.

I halted just before the gate. In the thickening twilight, I felt my girlhood and innocence slip away as I struggled to find the words to tell Ma. She did not rant or rave, shout or curse, or even look disappointed. She just looked sad, utterly, impossibly sad. She rubbed her eyes, blinked, then focused those tired, old eyes on my face. "You are healthy? When you give birth? Baby's father help you?"

As I moved into the world beyond the orchard, I often felt nothing but scorn for our poverty, for the dilapidated tin-roofed house my father had built with his own hands, and for my mother's simple, country ways. Unsophisticated as she was, and poor as a church mouse, she would prove to be richer in love and compassion than anyone I would ever know.

More astute than a trained psychologist of my future, she did not ask if the baby's father would return to marry me. I volunteered that information on the walk back, for which I, yes, I, was praised profusely. "Good daughter. He has family. Let him take care of his family. Not make him leave his family for you. You not want to incur karmic debt that way." Her words shamed me, for I would have asked him to leave his family, if I'd thought I would succeed. She added, "He send money to help? *Khong sao*. No matter. Baby not eat much. Have money, we eat meat, eat fish. No money, ah ... eat rice with salt."

I had to ask the question even if I dreaded her answer, "You want me to leave, to rent a room somewhere so they not laugh at you and Ba?"

"Nonsense. You not go anywhere. Let them talk." With a defiant tilt of the head, she preceded me back to the house.

My father didn't say a word about any of that to me, nor looked at me differently. The only indication of his knowledge was his asking me to save money from my next paycheck so he could buy enough wood to make a crib for the baby. Ma was taken aback by the request. "A crib? What for? Baby sleep in hammock."

"Ah, no, hammocks are for Vietnamese children. American child has to have something finer. I go to shop and copy what they have. Just buy the wood."

Two months before the baby was born, the finished product was presented to us. The shiny new crib looked out of place next to Ma's bed and mine in the squalid lean-to.

"See if you like. Something you not like, I fix. You like that dark color wood varnish? Not like, I scrape off and use lighter color."

The following week he brought home a stained, frayed cotton mattress. He had asked Mr. Engineer, his benefactor, for the mattress, which had long been relegated by the latter to the shed near the henhouse. He and Ma spent that day beating on the mattress, ridding it of dust and chicken fleas, stitching up every little tear, then airing it out in the sun. When it was as perfect as they could make it, he carried it in and proudly placed it on top of my straw mat. "When you get bigger, your back hurt. This help."

It was scandalous enough for a young girl to bear a child out of wedlock. To so bear an American child was considered the worst sort of dishonor. Away from the protective shield of my parents' passionate defense, I faced a public judgment that was both audacious and brutal. The inquisitors did not bother to veil their looks or reduce their vicious comments to whispers, so firm was their conviction of the right to condemn.

Among the three once dreamy-eyed young girls, my life was the only one that had taken an unexpected turn. Diep had survived an affair with a pilot with her marriage fortunately still intact and since settled back in the roles of wife and mother and dutiful daughter-in-law. Ngan was married now, to an officer in the army. She had the luck of the draw as far as mothers-in-law went; hers treated like a daughter rather than a bonded servant.

We no longer looked for fortune-tellers, for the future now lay open before us.

I recalled our first years at the embassy when there was so much hope for our respective lots as well as for our country—that the South would emerge victorious, that the aggressors would be pushed back North. But hopes went where hopes go in a hopeless war, to that void where so many had gone ... For a time, the war was kept at bay while we adjusted our lifestyle to accommodate the sometimes danger on the one hand, and to enjoy the relative material abundance on the other. Except for the news on war dead, life was good on the home front. Everyone was busy working, making money, and eating well.

As the fighting ebbed and flowed, so we accepted that changes would come and go. However, when the change of all changes came, the Americans' decision to withdraw, we could not accept it as an inevitable turn of events but rather chose to believe it was a clever political or military strategy of some kind.

But as a strategy, it failed miserably.

It was called Vietnamization—Vietnamization of the war efforts, which began with the Vietnamese-led incursions into Laos to disrupt the Ho Chi Minh trail supply lines. The operations foretold a perilous time for our troops. Used to following American lead and relying on the massive American firepower support from the air and on the ground, our men had become complacent. To them, the American disengagement not only meant losing the better half of the fighting force; it also meant the loss of hope for American assistance, which would likely translate to an eventual Communist victory. Among the three warring parties, our men were the least advantaged. The Communists had their ideology and the heat of aggression to empower them. The Americans had their moral conviction. We, the apolitical defenders, had no such powerful motivation. For that complacency, our men paid with their lives.

News of the casualties hit Saigon hard. Almost everyone knew of someone who had perished in what was to be the turning point of the war. Regardless, the mood around town was still one of controlled pessimism. As the students took their protests to the street, this time against American abandonment rather than involvement, talks in the coffee shops remained upbeat as veteran observers of the war boasted of their understanding of America, of its aversion to defeat, which aversion would likely mean a decisive and last-minute blow to stop the Communists' advance.

For the many who remembered the bloody specters of the purge of 1954 and the massacre in Hue in 1968 by the Communists, there were talks about how better things were with the French. Given the Communist cruelty we had seen to date, some thought that even having the French back was preferable to the Communists.

Like the death tolls, which climbed steadily upward, and the pessimism that refused to let up, my pregnancy dragged on. I had the kind of morning sickness that lasted all day every day for the entire pregnancy. Eyes followed when I rushed to the bathroom; tongues clucked and heads shook on my return to the desk. Sometimes the shame was so unbearable that I wanted to crouch in a hole somewhere until my child was born when the stigma of shame was no longer evident.

Courage came from the strangest of places. I finally became tired of being the butt of ridicule and decided to be brazen about it all. Let them wonder if something was afoot. My playacting was so convincing, even I eventually bought into the deception. I walked around with my head held high and my nose turned up, as if I had a plan of some kind to salvage the future that at times seemed as foregone as the war.

You could say that my confidence came from knowing that I had a plan. I actually didn't; I simply knew I had to, which resolution was apparently enough.

I could not accept the alternative of seeing my innocent baby living a life of rejection, a life worse than any in our family had ever known. The stigma, which would no longer be visible on my body, would be transferred to hers until death. She would carry the sins of her mother on those prominent occidental features for a lifetime, attracting the worst sort of bigotry this closed, traditional society could dish out to a half-breed.

November came, bringing with it the cool night air to ease the sweats from the backs of the poor. At our home, preparation began to bring another to join our ranks. Ba removed the mattress and cut a square hole in the middle of my wooden bed. Following the birth, a tray of coal would be placed squarely under this opening, to be lit and stoked twice daily to accelerate the recovery of my reproductive organs. I wouldn't get my mattress back until the coal tray was removed a month after the birth, when we would celebrate the event with offerings to the gods for their protection of the baby. At one month of age, babies were thought to be beyond the stage where their souls could be easily snatched by evil spirits—certainly a milestone in a person's life.

When the doctor made a wrong diagnosis at the eight-month mark, telling me and Ma the birth would likely be a breached birth, Ma went into panic mode. She sounded the gong every morning, every night, even midday, and searched far and wide for this herb and that herb to help me get stronger so the baby could turn to the correct position before delivery. Walking, yes, definitely a lot of walking was among the recommended remedies. From work, I would walk to the three-wheeler stand at the Central Market rather than taking a cyclo from outside the office. Each time I did so, the same thing happened—the savings I thought could go toward delivery and baby expenses ended up on the palms of the multitude of beggars lining the road from the Old Market to *Ben Thanh* or Central Market. I retained the health benefits of the walk, if not the money.

After supper, I walked around our little dirt yard since the main gravel path had become the domain of others. Through the leaves of the shrinking orchard, I could see daughters of Mr. Engineer taking their after-dinner stroll, looking elegant and refined in their flowing silk pajamas. The pajamas were always white, the color of purity, which surely was their essence in body and spirit. Certainly, they had never known, and would never know, any shame or debasement.

Meanwhile, in Paris, the American delegation headed by Henry Kissinger continued the peace talks with North Vietnam, South Vietnam, and representatives of the Viet Cong. The wizened men thought they knew how the end would be just by looking at the composition of participants at the talks. The Viet Cong was the local militia arm of the North Vietnamese Communists. To us, by giving both a say as if they were two different entities did not bode well. The accommodation seemed an appeasement and a defeat.

The wizened reminisced now about President Diem. They thought he was the South's first and last hope to defeat the Communists and remembered with nostalgia his honesty and nationalism. It was said that his fatal flaw was his filial loyalty. Ironic, that, for such was and always will be the most valued trait in our culture.

Even as a devout Catholic in a country where Buddhists held the majority, President Diem would have fared well enough if he had not been saddled with egotistical brothers the likes of the Catholic bishop, who was so fanatical in his own religious belief that he could not consider the accommodation of none others, and a powermonger to boot. Or the weak-willed younger brother who let his contemptible wife ruin the fragile balance between what could have been benevolent authoritarian and oppressive totalitarian.

I went into labor at ten p.m. in the evening of December 1, 1971. Ma and Older Sister Phuong took me to the maternity clinic, one of the upscale ones with a doctor in residence. At five o'clock the next morning, my daughter was born, a nine-pound bundle of red with a thick fluff of dark hair. After three days at the clinic, we arrived home to a welcoming crowd, or, more accurately, a curious crowd. The busybody relatives wanted to see the baby. What was she? They wanted to know. Was she American, or Korean, or God-knows-what?

Van did not disappoint. Opening her eyes wide to show them the "round eyes" of an American, she fluttered her extra long lashes so as to leave no doubt about her Western parentage.

In the weeks that followed, a routine was set. Ba would help care for the baby, holding her while I ate and Ma tended to the pigs. He held her firmly in his bony hands and bathed her from the little tin bucket like an experienced father he was. We gave her formula from the bottle, because she was an American. Inasmuch as baby formula was used only by the middle class who could afford it, it became a status symbol fitting for an American baby.

TWENTY-SEVEN

IN THE NEWS: 8/11/72–U.S.
COMBAT ROLE ENDED WHEN
THE MARINES EVACUATED
DA NANG. ON THE SAME
DAY, LAST U.S. GROUND
UNIT DEACTIVATED.

American Embassy
Saigon, Vietnam, 1971–1973

American bases had started to shrink. At the height of the American force buildup, the bases in Long Binh and Bien Hoa and MACV at Tan Son Nhat must have employed hundreds of thousands of Vietnamese, mainly women, since most men in employable age were in the military. On losing their jobs, most of the women found it hard to go home again. They could no longer return to be costermongers or fishmongers or servants in middle class and affluent households, having had a taste of equality—good pay and an absence of social distinction—accorded them by the classless Americans. While it was true that war was the greatest social equalizer, it did take more than a war to knock down some of our class barriers. It took the Americans' fine sense of equality. American employers didn't discriminate between the rich, the poor, or the socially connected as they selected applicants for employment. Nor did American men choose their romantic interests on the basis of wealth or class.

Amid this societal upheaval and economic meltdown, we found delights in Van, who was the apple of my parents' eyes. She waddled after Ba as he did his chores, helping him call out to the chickens at feeding times. By the time she was two, she'd already had the demeanor of an adult, pensive and solemn. Her big, beautiful eyes and thick brows and full lips were her father's. Even her serious expressions lent a scholarly look that was clearly his. I would look at her and see him and wonder how he could not want to know her.

For her part, Van didn't know she had no father. The love we showered on her more than made up for any lack of fatherly affection. When Ma and I were at work, her grandfather cared for her, watching her play in the mud, or carting her to the warehouse and picking vegetables on the way. They were inseparable; the wiry old man whose eyes had become so filmy with cataracts that he could no longer see so well, whose skin had turned leather tough, whose back had bent so from hard labor and bad nutrition, and the vibrant child on his hip who was a picture of health and beauty, with that light complexion of the rich and hair the burnished color of autumn leaves.

Neither the man nor the child knew how much the poignant image they cast lightened my heart even as it embittered. If I had chosen well, my husband would have been by my side to watch these endearing moments between our daughter and her grandfather rather than me standing alone, feeling strangely hollow one minute and full of resolve the next as I tried to figure out how to keep us safe.

The policy of keeping dependents away must have been changed.

One of my new American bosses brought his wife and two small children to post with him. Every time I saw him coddling or hovering over them in the pool or at the poolside restaurant, I felt the yearnings coming back in full force, again for something I couldn't have.

Every bout of regrets renewed my determination to correct my past errors, to salvage what I could. I had to get my daughter out of harm's way, to the land of her father's birth. I no longer considered sending her to Joe. He had never offered anyhow. That gesture would have given us so much comfort in those days of confusion and desperation. Somehow she was less his child because she was born to me rather than to his wife. Such was the question that plagued my mind whenever I felt defiant enough to ponder the imponderable.

In this matter, if no others, I felt American men could have taken lessons from those faithless Vietnamese men. I would not have gone so far as to condone the cheating or advocate the setting up of supplemental households in tidy little houses across the city but had to admire these wayward fathers' attempts to look out for their children, all their children. The Asian machismo perhaps had its uses. The children, the fruits of their loins, were equally loved and cared for.

Because of my recklessness, now it was up to me to find ways to care for the daughter her father didn't want.

The danger became more intense, and the war closer, with each funeral on our streets. It seemed that only young men died any more. A close-up look at the photo on any funeral procession would show a man in uniform. The world had gone mad. Ma clucked her tongue and sighed deeply. Deep lines of worry now etched her face. She found comfort only when my brother was in prison for AWOL. It meant he was not on a battlefield waiting to be killed. Thankful that he was alive, she scrimped and saved to make his favorite food to take to the prison once a week. As she set off with laden bundles on the crooks of her arms and bright, shining eyes, an unknowing bystander could have easily assumed she was en route to visit a heroic son away on an important mission. It didn't matter to her what others thought. She was simply a mother celebrating her son's life.

MPs and QCs (*Quan Canh*, or Vietnamese military police) continued their patrols on the streets of Saigon. It was an easy job for the QC; anyone who was not too old or too young was presumed to be within the drafting age. There were not so many MPs any more because more than half of the American servicemen had gone home. But the QCs stayed busy, grabbing AWOL and draft dodgers and throwing them in jail. But such was not meant to be their punishment. The ultimate sentence would take place on the battlefield, where they would be sent back after a token period in jail.

The Americans intensified bombing raids over Hanoi and Haiphong, but the ferocity of the actions did not reassure. From what we knew of Communist resolve and following the disappointing direction of the peace talks, the rich began to convert their wealth to dollars and gold, even though there were still hopes of a final American solution.

The climate in the office had changed. We no longer basked in the good fortune of our lot, that privilege of working for the Americans at the embassy. The label that was once our badge of pride now looked increasingly like a liability, almost a death warrant.

The Vietnamese-Chinese men who were the most senior in the office and therefore had the most money saved up were considering buying passports and going to Hong Kong. The few women who had American boyfriends were close-mouthed about their prospects. Some were thought to be setting up new households in different parts of town where no one would know of their American connections when the Communists arrived and fingers started pointing. Those who had country roots were planning to return there, to put distance between them and their once-celebrated place of employment—the embassy— that ultimate symbol of imperialism according to the Communists.

I was still on a determined search for salvation, embarking on one fruitless date after another. I returned from each outing more dejected than the last. I could not understand the possible reason for my failure until years later. I was neither innocent nor sweet and bright-eyed like a typical Vietnamese girl from a respectable family. Neither was I a practiced courtesan with generous physical attributes and expertise in the arts of seduction. Neither was I simple in my needs or wants. Under this ambivalence lay a restlessness of spirit and an obvious desperation that must have affected my words and demeanor, effectively discouraging all would-be prospects.

Or it could simply have been Fate.

Each day that passed, each date that came to nothing, reduced me a little bit more. My mind twirled in confusion like a woman crazed. My heart would lighten when I left the house, only to sink again on returning. I watched my parents coddle their precious granddaughter and knew I could not give in to despair. Everyone I loved was depending on me.

The South China Sea, 1973

Salvation of a sort finally came in the form of another married man. Steve, an official at the Consulate, was even older than Joe was. It was only by the remotest of chances that we met, for his workstation was in the highlands.

I began traveling to Da Nang to see him every two weeks, courtesy of his influence with Air America. I was immediately in awe of him, this wiry man who spoke plainly and decisively, whose forceful steps bespoke his confidence and steely determination, and who was as different from Art and Joe as the sun from the moon. A high-level official with authority over aid disbursement, he carried a lot of clout with the provincial government. He was perhaps popular for another reason. An old hand in Asia, he knew how things worked and did not mind greasing a few palms along the way to get the results he wanted.

He was not polished as Joe, but resolute and straightforward. He despised Joe for the latter's lack of backbone and for being unprincipled, for not looking after me and Van better. Not caring much about what others thought of him, Steve openly escorted me to casual dinners and social gatherings hosted by his colleagues at the Consulate.

I would listen to him and his friends, some of whom were CIA officers, expounding on the direction of the war. They talked of the Communists' steady progress and suspected the latter would soon gobble up South Vietnam. They concurred that the peace agreement was not worth the paper it was written on. Those get-togethers sometimes included officials of the multinational International Commission for Control and Supervision (ICCS), who, in spite of their personal opinions, dutifully carried out those perfunctory, thankless tasks of verifying armed violations and naming the aggressor.

These political analysts debated on Communist intentions and, like the wizened men of my hamlet, didn't think there ever was a chance for peace unless it was total surrender by the South. With the Americans gone and the South Vietnamese government weakened by corrupt and inept leaders, the end seemed obvious.

I sat in wonderment and awe while they paid me little mind. To them, I was just another girl one of them had picked up as a temporary companion. On introduction to me, almost invariably they would spare but a short exchange of pleasantries. Not that they were snobbish; it was just the way things were. I was a Vietnamese, in a country full of them, at a time when some of us were more frantic than others in our search for American men, foreign men, to deliver us from war and poverty.

Many of us could be had for that ticket to another life. Any life, as long as it was away from here, was presumed to be better. Some of us risked the better part of who we were simply for a ghost of a promise. In those desperate times, we were a dime a dozen.

For hours I would sit, listening to every word they uttered, beautiful strings of words I barely understood, let alone emulated. Often a humorous message would dawn on me long after the repartee had been made, the laughter died, and the group moved on to another subject. These people knew so much. They had thoughts, thoughts that were their own, thoughts expressed so eloquently they made my heart ache for the depths and brilliance of the discourse. I had heard politics discussed before, of course, from the canvas cot of my home and from the coffee shop on that dusty street, but never did I know such well-formed, elaborate thoughts. I began to see the war, and the world, through the eyes of learned men, men who were knowledgeable and objective, men who had the curiosity to pore long and hard into our history and the intellect to make reasonable deductions on what was to come. Most of them were men with kindness and compassion. I wondered if I could ever get enough education to have thoughts as such for my very own. I was too ignorant. My mind was not fully developed. I consisted of only the basest of emotions, the most rudimentary of thoughts. I was simply a ball of anger and desire, rebellion and inhibition, fear and passion.

Steve's authority and decisiveness did lend the comfort I needed. It convinced me that he would see to our safety. He was a man of action with the know-how to make things happen. I might not be en route to America with a loving husband and a caring father for my daughter, but at least we would be en route.

I accompanied him to parties at the beach house leased by the Consulate for use by its employees on a space-available basis. There was also a good-sized powerboat provided for their use. A few of his friends, especially the women, seemed as judgmental as my countrymen. They must have thought I was no better than a prostitute, trading my body for whatever luxury or for that ticket out. By this time, I had learned how to brace myself against public censor, but what I gleaned from their gazes still made my face hot and caused my stomach to clench. I had come to forget my circumstances, to pretend I belonged, only to be shown exactly who I was. I should have known that the price would be high, no matter how short a reprieve.

This public scorn produced a self-loathing that was impossible to banish. I faced the accusing eyes from Vietnamese and American alike and turned indignant. *What am I supposed to do? Sit helplessly and wait for the end?* But however I justified to myself, the more accusatory their glances, the less I felt. I could share with no one. In all my life, my dreams and fears had always been so outlandish I could share with none others. It was no different now. Any despair, any shame that steadily reduced me to nothingness, I bore alone.

I watched the fortunate Americans frolicking on the sand and in the water on thin, long boards called skis, which barely skimmed the blue-green water of the South China Sea, and silently questioned Fate. So this was how they lived in that faraway place. I wanted to know how to do that. Worse, I wanted to know how to do it well... as if I had done it all my life.

On the rock I sat, alone and despondent. My mind saw the gap between my world and that of the merrymakers, and my heart sank. Oh, how they could use the sea for pleasures, playing in that which we depended on for survival, that which I had seen only once, had never really known except by the poetry and novels I had read, and through the fish that made it to our table and Ma pointing out, "Long-ne, this's sea fish; that's river fish. When constitution not so strong, not eat sea fish. River fish easier to digest."

It was enlightening to find that what we had known only as a provider of food could be used to bring joy to the spirit. Unbidden, the phantom of self-pity rose from the very depths of my heart, clawing its way to the surface in spite of my willful suppression. I did not want the tears to come. But they did. A drop fell, then another, and still another. I put up a hand as if shading my traitorous, foolish, disobedient eyes from the sun and discreetly brushed my fingers over the trails of tears. If someone had seen my bright eyes and asked, I would have said, "Oh, the water... the salty water, it got in my eyes."

TWENTY-EIGHT

IN THE NEWS: 4/4/75–100
VIETNAMESE ORPHANS
ARE KILLED IN CRASH.

American Embassy, Saigon
1974–1975

We moved to a new office building in the compound behind the new Embassy Chancery on Thong Nhat Street. The move effectively took me away from the scenes of my youthful follies; I could no longer see the river where I had sat with Quan, the bridge where I used to watch for the sight of Art, or the Old Embassy entrance where I loitered about to wait for Joe to come down from his office.

Big Rat finally returned after almost two years at the various air bases in Texas for pilot training. He brought back several pullover sweaters for me, along with several lipsticks bearing American name brands. I wore the lipstick and sweaters proudly for days on end regardless that the sweaters often proved to be too warm in the tropical heat. But they were not what I ended up treasuring most. What really captured my imagination was a photo of him in a park somewhere in that mystical land. There were stone benches that beckoned many a weary wayfarer and tall trees that stood in perfect symmetry, proudly sporting leaves of every color of the sunset.

Ma was enormously proud of him for bringing honor to the family. His exalted accomplishments made her feel she had done right by her sister's memory, by raising the latter's son to adulthood to become a man who commanded such adoration and respect. Besides his training in the United States, which brought with it exceptional honor and prestige, Big Rat was also a graduate of the Da Lat National Military Academy, similar to West Point, and generally considered to be among the best and the brightest.

Almost immediately on his return, he began flying sorties on F-5 to support ground troops. He and Bong would trade war stories whenever they happened to be home at the same time. An artillery officer, Bong regaled him with tales of battle from the ground, especially the euphoria that ignited among the troops whenever they heard jets thundering overhead, to which Eighth Uncle once noted sardonically, "Happy? What for? To die another day?"

Even as rumors flew all around the city on an imminent Communist takeover, there seemed to be business as usual inside the embassy; there was no obvious preparation for emergency departure or anything of the sort. The semblance of normality fooled those of us who wanted to believe that all would be well, that America indeed had something up its sleeve.

But the illusion faded as time wore on. I clung to my connection with Steve, committing my all, believing that if I did my best to sustain the relationship, I would save those I loved.

The state of the country was uncertain. Even more so was our escape from annihilation. Yet I might have known how it would be had I recognized a rather prophetic incident. On leaving work one afternoon,

I drove by a peddler whose burlap-wrapped plants on the backseat of his bicycle beckoned a closer look. As I slowed down to a near stop, the peddler called out, "Jasmines, jasmines, *Co, mua cho toi Co* (Miss, jasmine, Miss, buy for me)," while showing a big smile he hoped would make a sale. It did. His missing teeth and the gnarled, bony fingers helped me make the decision.

I took both plants home to my ba and told him in a voice of a stranger, for I had no idea why I said what I did, "Ba, plant this for me? When I am gone, you smell flowers and think of me." Ba smiled, not really hearing what I said, but on catching the alluring scent of jasmine, the flowers that had eluded us for so long. He sniffed a little bud and was still smiling when he looked up. "I know just the place for it."

I do too.

He planted the two plants beside the jackfruit tree, five feet away from the pomegranate tree, about ten feet away from the *vu sua* tree, and a good seven feet away from a singular, shriveling vine of green grapes on a barbed-wire trellis. All of these trees he had planted at one time or another for me.

They were the fruits I loved but could not get enough of because we did not have money to buy. When acquaintances asked if he could think of something they could do in return for his help in some thing or other, he would remember that this person had a garden of jackfruits, or that person had a dozen odd pomegranate trees in his yard, and ask if he could have a sapling to plant in the yard for his little daughter. "My poor child, she like it so much."

The little patch of my favorite trees, this circle of love, was all the payment he got for decades of helping others. That was all he wanted. Love extended to his fellow men; love returned to his child. As far as he was concerned, the karmic circle was complete.

And it was, except for my part. As the recipient of the generous, unconditional love that was my father's, I was forever delinquent in returning that love. It was only by accident that I made him the happiest of men in the winter of his life.

Van brightened my parents' lives in ways I had never imagined. They laughed more and even learned how to play. The adorable child captured their hearts as nothing ever had. They seemed in awe of her foreign looks, as if wondering how those looks could have come from me, from them. The act of conceiving her may have been a result of my foolishness, but the child, the fruit of that impetuousness, became the best gift I could have ever given my parents.

Their world revolved around her. Ba would sit her atop his shoulders as they made their way to her pre-school, stopping without fail on her plea to let her play with tadpoles in the rain puddles in the orchard.

As dark clouds moved relentlessly toward the sun, Van became that last bit of sunshine to warm us before calamity descended. Instead of feeling shame for her American looks and hiding her away, my parents delighted in her uniqueness. We enjoyed those moments of tranquility, blissfully unaware that the wind had shifted to make way for the coming of death and destruction. The sun flared brightly … as if for the last time.

While others plotted and planned, my parents stayed focused on their little piece of the sun. When Van began to get festering boils all over her head, it was duly blamed on the hot climate. "An American child, how can she live here? Too hot … too hot. Oh, now I know. Those poor Americans! How they suffered … "

They shaved her head again and again to allow her internal temperature to "cool off." The little they had learned about America from Eighth Uncle, they knew it as a place of cooler climates. Whenever Van suffered from a cold or flu, they agonized and worried about her body's failure to adjust to our ghastly heat. In their grandchild, they thought they finally understood what those poor American soldiers had gone through.

Tried-and-true home remedies were never good enough for Van. She had to be taken to a doctor, and naturally, it was not the eastern medicine doctor. "He not know how to treat an American." Only the western doctor was good enough for a child with American blood. Going to the doctor's office on the back of Ba's bicycle was most definitely not fitting for an American. Ma had to find money for a cyclo ride. "American child, she is used to better things..." There was no doubt in their minds that Americans were used to finer things, and therefore Van was entitled to the same.

They didn't know how frustrated I was on that notion. They accepted without question the misfortune of our country, of our lot, readily surrendering loftier expectations to others, to their betters. That was, I thought, how we got the leaders we had, because poor peasants like my parents conferred on them providential powers they by no means earned or deserved. That the rich were meant to lead, to take and enjoy the best of what was available, while the poor and illiterate merely subsisted in life and died serving them and those noble causes sprouted from their superior minds.

I used to resent watching them kowtowing to others—those with authority or wealth and even those without. I thought that reduced us further. *How low can we sink?* What I didn't know was that the humility did not diminish them. Rather, their respect for others, whether they were better or worse off, showed a sure sense of themselves. They knew no envy or hatred but had only an unreserved acceptance of their lot and a generosity to allow others enjoyment of theirs.

When, on moonlit nights, silver beams lifted our flagging spirits and soothed our tired bodies, my parents would take turns holding the littlest American on their laps, reflecting all the while on the Americans of yesterday, their granddaughter's "people." They clucked their tongues on the horrific conditions under which those Americans had to fight— the traps, the mines..."*Toi nghiep qua*, how they endure it? Too gullible, can't win with Viet Cong. Viet Cong too cunning, too deceitful. American soldiers, such young, innocent faces. They are scared. Oh, karmic debt...Toi nghiep qua! Why they come? Stay at home to enjoy good life. Gentle, always smile."

Ma talked about her American name, Mamasan. She would chortle as she recalled the times passing soldiers called out to her in Vietnamese. To demonstrate Van's Americanism, Ma would ask her to smile. As Van complied, she and Ba would clap their hands and laugh, saying how she looked just like her "people," with shining eyes and a happy, endearing face. How did my parents manage to turn my shame into a blessing?

Love.

When Van's little cousins—there were three of them born around the same time she was—called her names, "American mixed breed or mixed breed," a reflection no doubt on what they had heard from their parents at home, Ma and Ba would teach Van to fight back. "I am American and beautiful. What are you, ugly savages?"

Did Ba and Ma think we were savages compared to the Americans? Yes, I believe they did. Not in the negative way that word might be interpreted, only that the Americans were rich and advanced, while we were poor and rather backward, simply a little bit behind. They bore no embarrassment for being who they were.

I wish I had learned that lesson well. I would not have been saddled with shame for being poor during what was the best part of my life.

龙

The once-valiant war had been reduced to a grim spectacle, foretelling a murderous finale. Americans were coming back to save their loved ones. Two of the older ladies in the office were preparing their paperwork to depart for the United States, and I didn't even know they had ever associated with Americans. Apparently, the relationships went back many years, long before my time, and now, as the end drew near, the men from the past thought again of their one-time paramours and returned to lift them to safety.

The lines outside the consular section got longer and longer every day as American servicemen, contractors, and government employees applied for paperwork to marry their Vietnamese sweethearts. I watched the well-dressed women and children and their eager, happy faces, and had to suppress the tears lest they come to my eyes for all to see.

In the office, at last we had orders to begin packing personnel and financial records for shipment to the State Department in Washington.

The end seemed obvious even if I was still hoping for that last-minute solution, until Steve came south for a weekend. With Ban Me Thuot gone, he didn't think it would be long before the Communists came south. We went to our favorite garden restaurant, dining al fresco. I bought two extra entrees, one of grilled pork and the other, crabs steamed in beer, to take home to Ma and Ba and Van. Steve didn't even raise an eyebrow at my extra orders, for which I was grateful. I could only do this when dining out with him. While he was not a sensitive man, he was gallant and generous to a fault.

As I took in the depressing news, Steve confirmed a rumor I'd heard from my workmates that the U.S. Mission had plans to evacuate all of its employees and their immediately family members. By the time dinner ended, he had convinced me he would take care of my family.

Over the late-night treats, I told my parents what Steve had said. We agreed quickly on the composition of "our family." Ma, Ba, Brother Bong, me, Van, and Cousin Mai. The boys, Ngau, Big Rat, and Little Rat, could come if they were allowed. Otherwise, they could hide out somewhere until we came back for them.

Ba looked up at me as he dug out the last bit of meat from a crab claw for Van. In his eyes, I saw my own fears and doubts. He asked hesitantly, wistfully, "We come back later?"

"Yes, Ba, we come back when Communists gone," I responded brusquely. Even to my ears, the tone was one of defiance rather than conviction.

A shocking option came, seemingly from thin air. One of my American bosses, Roy Young, called me into his office one day and, with the door closed, asked if I would be willing to give Van up for adoption to an American family.

Ma could not consider the prospect of surrendering Van to strangers. The idea of giving Van up and never knowing what would become of her left us cold. Ma told Ba to collect a bottle of DDT so we would have another option if all else failed. When the Communists arrived, we would kill ourselves together, so that not any one of us would have to live on and suffer alone.

When I told my boss that we couldn't bear to give up Van, he under-stood. To calm my fears, he confirmed what Steve had said, that we would be evacuated if the worst were to happen, that by having worked for the American government, we belonged in the high-risk category. To save us from a massacre, America would give us sanctuary. He had no idea how things would unfold at the end but would do his best to ensure that my daughter and I would be safe.

Had we given Van up, she might have perished. The plane that evacuated orphans to the United States for adoption, the one she could have been on, crashed on takeoff outside of Tan Son Nhat Airbase. Ma prayed for the lost children and thanked Buddha for saving Van.

The increasing threat to Van spurred my parents to action. They could not be passive any longer—the price had gotten too high. They could not subject their granddaughter to death or, if she should survive without us, to a life on the street.

I came home one day from work to find Ba gone. Apparently, he had left for his home province of *Tra Vinh*, a town close to the Cambodian border, his first trip back there since leaving it as a teenager. I suspected he had joined the rush to find a place for us to resettle. He did not return until four days later.

It turned out Ba didn't spend those days searching for long-lost rela-tives or a place for us to settle. He was looking for an escape route to Cambodia. From there we would find a way to Hong Kong, where Van's father was. Maybe he could help us with some money and the means to get to America; or we could simply find a patch of land across the border to farm until things got better on this side. I didn't know how he had learned about the geography of other countries and how to cross borders and presumed it had come from Eighth Uncle.

As we contemplated Ba's plan, a look of sorrow came to my mother's eyes. She lifted her rough hands to stroke Van's hair. The unconscious gesture reminded me, and them, why we had to do something, why we had to leave. We knew the end of war did not mean peace, at least not until the Communists had leveled all they thought were American and

South Vietnamese legacies, killing all things associated with such. We didn't bother to read the peace agreement; we already knew what the end would bring. Vengeance—that was what.

Across the city, there was still that hope for a nuclear strike, or else the landing of American, Vietnamese, and Allied soldiers in Hanoi. We didn't have any right to demand intervention or salvation from America. But we didn't know that. They had been a part of us for so long; we felt the two had become integral. So many Americans had died defending us. It was incomprehensible that they would not want to ensure all would be well at the end.

TWENTY-NINE

IN THE NEWS:
3/25/75–VIETNAM - HUE LOST; DA NANG IMPERILED; U.S. ORDERS REFUGEE AIRLIFT.

American Embassy, Saigon
April 1975

Steve came south, fleeing the city of Danang, which had fallen on the heels of Hue. He settled in the hastily established refugee task force office on the ground floor of the main Chancery, rushing from there to the airport and the port to locate friends and colleagues who had successfully made their way south. To ensure my departure when the end came, he volunteered me for after-hour duties with the task force.

One of our tasks was to catalogue those U.S. government employees, both American and Vietnamese, who had started to pour in from the highlands. By land, by air, and by sea they came. The phones rang continuously—welfare-and-whereabouts calls from families and friends in the United States.

I was at the embassy up to eighteen hours a day now, working the task force and then returning to my own office, only to find that the number of colleagues had dwindled. Several of the women had received timely marriage offers from Americans. Others had simply disappeared.

Ma didn't want to leave anything to chance. She had already destroyed all of our (South) Vietnamese ID cards and was prepared to burn my Western-style clothing and embassy ID card to sever our American connection. To hide Van's occidental features, Ma planned to rub coal dust on her face and hair as we traveled through the countryside and the jungle toward the border of Cambodia.

Meanwhile, a marriage of convenience had been made for my brother. Our neighbor, the greedy northerner who had moved in the compound with the new office buildings and thereafter plundered the warehouse contents like there was no tomorrow, had introduced Ma to a family from the countryside. For my brother to deny his military background, he needed the anonymity of the rice field. His intended, who came from a well-to-do merchant family from a province not far from my ba's hometown of Tra Vinh, offered the best chance for that. Brother Bong had been desperately in love with someone else but agreed to the match to save himself and us.

I had begun saving money for some time. In the preceding months, every time I visited Steve at the U.S. Mission lodging house, I would take a three-wheeler there and, at some time during the course of the evening, would casually mention that I had taken a taxi. He would give me some money for that and also the fare home. Again, I would take the three-wheeler home to save what little bit I could. Once, he insisted on waiting and putting me in a taxi. Not to be deterred in my quest, I asked the driver to let me out a block away. There I stood on the almost-deserted street to wait for a lonely three-wheeler to come by so I could save the money for our escape.

The race was on. There was a rumor that American ships from the

7th Fleet would be anchored in international waters of the South China Sea when the end came. Already, those who had the wherewithal, either boat or money, had arranged for space on one of the fishing boats that would take them and their families out to meet the fleet.

My chance came on the morning of April 23. Steve had just returned to the task force office from a meeting when, without preamble, he told me to go home to get my daughter and a bag no larger than a carry-on flight bag. We were to leave. Yes, there was a plan, but everything had become so disorganized that he didn't think he could get me on a plane if we waited any longer. On these early flights, he said, no one other than children and spouses were allowed to come with the employees.

I would find out later that this was not entirely true.

Steve perhaps didn't know what my parents meant to me. Not a sentimental person, I suspect he thought he was giving me a chance to start alone, that I would likely succeed with fewer family encumbrances. He had no idea my family was not my burden but rather my strength and my motivation. He didn't know how much of a handicap I would be without them.

He sat in the car while I ran into the house to grab Van and, as instructed, only a few items of clothing for us. If I had only had more time to ponder, I might not have left my parents. I might have brought them along, regardless of Steve's explicit instructions. But I was frightened, too frightened by the stark danger that was to come to Van and me if we were to delay and risk jeopardizing our escape.

So I relied on another to fulfill my duty. Steve's casual assurance had seemed adequate because I wanted it to be. He said it was possible that I would have time on arrival in the United States to find a job, a place to stay, and then return to fetch my parents. He promised that if a Communist takeover were to happen before I could return, he would get my parents to safety and help them find me.

Perhaps I did hear the emptiness behind the words, words that were meant only to ease a child's concern for her parents, words not meant to be kept, but I chose not to acknowledge it.

When my parents asked to come along to help with Van, I had to say they could not just as yet, that I would return as soon as I could. "Not worry, I make some money quick and come back for you."

It was the first and last time I saw my father cry. He stood there and sobbed. His arms turned lifeless alongside of his skeletal body; his hand loosened to dislodge a fistful of chicken feed. A chorus of hens *cuc… cuccing* rose. My mother wailed as I put Van on my hip, slung the canvas bag on the opposite shoulder, and ran down the path to the gate and the waiting car. The dawn had deepened and the day grown hard to witness the end of my childhood.

I rushed at the future … to the heartbreaking sound of my parents' sorrow.

Ma told me, years later, that during that week, the week before his death, Ba had sat on the verandah and pointed to the newly blooming jasmines, lamenting aloud how I would enjoy the blooms if I were still home. "Finally, we have jasmines, and she not here," he had said as tears streamed down his face. He would cry off and on throughout the week, missing Van and me, burdened with a premonition that he would never see us again. As words of the chaotic escapes going on all over the city reached him, he didn't think once of joining the exodus. He was going to wait for me. He was afraid I would not be able to find him and Ma otherwise.

He was worried about Van and me. I didn't even know how to cook. How was I going to work, take care of both of us, and still be able to save money to come back for them?

It was the last week of his life. A stray mortar landed in the house as the Communists peppered the city with them in advance of the invasion. It decimated the lean-to, where I would have been sleeping had I remained, and the washstand, where my ba was washing his face after having been awakened by the sound of mortar. Ma was in her usual position when danger was near—praying. She fell from that wobbling high chair, suffering a broken hip and absorbing dozens of metal fragments inside her body, but she lived … to bury my father.

THIRTY

Saigon, Vietnam
1975, The End

By the time the war ended, millions had perished. Communist leaders years hence would speak grimly of the loss of human life while decrying the imperialism of America and the corruption of its puppet regime—the South Vietnamese government, and condemning the atrocities committed by both. Even with glaring historical facts that put them at the scene as one of the perpetrators in this crime against humanity, the Communists still maintained the rightness of their struggle, just as they had at the dawn of the revolution. For some, it was simple.

Comfortable with their lots in life, they became restless and dabbled in idealism. A little education is a dangerous thing, so it has been said. Idealism without virtue is even more so. It was easy for them to rouse the simple peasant hearts. I remember feeling intensely patriotic at six years old on first learning about the history of armed struggles by our people against foreign invaders. Standing at the flagpole every Monday morning for the ceremonial raising of the South Vietnamese flag, I balled my fists as I sang loudly the words of our national anthem. I was quite ready to march against the present enemy, the Communist aggressors.

What chance did peasants and fervent young men have? In the countryside, the Communists mixed and mingled, cajoled and threatened. In the city, the mandarins turned revolutionaries played a heady game of spy and treason. They must have felt quite smug ensconcing in material comfort—traveling in their Mercedes, eating high-priced abalone, sipping jasmine tea—while playing a game of chess with lives and calling it idealism, the crowning of the mind.

Their arrogance knew no bounds. Even after the guns had stopped, they persisted with vengeance and continued the violence, this time targeting the hapless South Vietnamese troops and their families, especially those who were occupying precious city space, evicting them to make room for northern communist faithful. As the killing fields began to fill up in neighboring Cambodia, southerners were swiftly and involuntarily resettled in parts hitherto unknown, forced to make farmland out of virgin forests. What did those city folks know of farming or of clearing land? Sure enough, most of them succumbed to hardship and disease, a fitting end for enemies of the state. What had the inhabitants of the gentle land of the south done but tried to survive a senseless war not of their making? I suppose I could understand the need for vengeance. Once, we had felt the same about the northerners.

A pacifist now and an eternal optimist, I could explain and justify a great many things. But I had difficulty absolving the actions of those arrogant, restless beings who had the gall to test this idea and that theory on the lives of their fellow men, men equal to them in the eyes of God, men whose lives were no less precious than theirs, men who were blessed with the same endowments as they, of love, hate, pain, and comfort.

Most of the principal perpetrators of one of the worst monstrosities the world had ever known were gone now. But their demise failed to erase the legacy of their shameful conduct. It lives on in dreams forever lost, lives forever altered. How incomprehensible is it that a dozen misguided men could cause destruction of such magnitude?

Only now could I presume to understand the biblical verse of "the meek shall inherit." In this busy universe, who are the meek if not those enlightened spirits who cherish life and who live honorably, peacefully, and lovingly, and without a shed of avarice or judgment? There simply have been too many misdeeds by the movers and shakers of our times. The meek should indeed inherit, so as to change the violent face of human legacy.

Another Beginning

On that spring morning in 1975, Van and I settled on a C-130 en route to Guam. Our fellow countrymen settled around us on slung canvas seats lining both sides of the plane. As the plane accelerated down the runway, the heart-wrenching sobs peaked. Van whimpered softly, wanting to know where *Ong Ngoai* and *Ba Ngoai* were. I held her tightly to my side, pressed my face on top of her head, and closed my eyes. I didn't even know how to be a parent. My parents had raised Van like their own child. What was I going to do?

As the plane lifted into the air, the wailings rose. The soldiers on the flight looked grim as they walked down the aisle to ensure we were all properly harnessed. By their solemn demeanor, I felt empathy and commiseration.

I could not believe my long-time wish of getting away from this dirt-poor country was being realized. It was shocking to see how it was being done. Through all the days of wishing, in all the dreams, I never thought I would be flying toward my future. Wasn't the future time and not space, to which one advanced slowly, one day at a time? Who had ever heard of flying toward one's future? But that was what seemed to be happening. Did I wish so hard to get away, and that was why I had to pay this terrible price of having to live on without my parents?

I would have to continue without them, the people who had been my life, who had lived for me, and for whom I had lived, worked, and dreamed. What good was anything if I did not have them there to tell me how good I had done?

Now it would be just me. My dream of making it alone was just that—a dream. My idea of aloneness meant without a husband provider, not alone as without my parents.

Even as a dream, it was born out of resignation rather than desire. I had given up hoping that I would ever meet someone who would provide and care for me, so I set out to dream of making it alone. The idea seemed outlandish for my time and my circumstances, which made it even more appealing to me. However, more often than not, I had hoped to submit myself to some man, giving respect and affection in return for being "taken care" of.

I didn't know anything about individual autonomy or independence, let alone planning for such.

At the end, it didn't matter what I wanted, what I did or didn't know. Fate had decreed that I was to make my own way; the dream was perhaps my soul's way of telling me how things were going to be. I was to know hardships external to my family as well as within. I was to carry the responsibility for my family, just as my ma did, just as she had prepared me.

I did not know it at the time, but this was to be the pattern of my charmed life. Sudden, drastic bursts to the future and beyond, ending one life, beginning another, and so it goes, all in one single lifetime.

THIRTY-ONE

IN THE NEWS: 4/03–RUMSFELD OK'D DOGS FOR INTERROGATION.

From Colombo, Sri Lanka, to Virginia, 2003
The Fall of the Dragon

This can't be. Ma... what do I do? You know how... Take care of the kids for me, Ma. Yes, I remember the cycle of life, the drought and the rain... the joy and the sorrow. I know I have to do this... but I am so cold. I am so scared... help me... Please... please, Ma, come...

I wished so hard for my mother. I screamed hysterically, endlessly, and silently.

The diplomatic service (DS) agent had taunted me during that brief interrogation at the small conference room at the embassy in Colombo that my kids—Zu and Tyler—those helpless, innocent little children of my heart, were going to be picked up by Child Protective Services. "They will probably go to foster homes." He seemed to spit out the words.

As the interrogation heated up, a cold materialized seemingly out of nowhere. *It could not be from the air conditioner in the room.* I had been in this room before, when it was a benign little spot used by the general services officer for his weekly staff meeting, but never felt so cold as I did now. From wherever, the cold intensified as minutes stretched to infinity and immobilized all sensations save for dread and fear. My mind was so numb it could not infer that the cold actually came from within—from the fear that had spread and taken over my entire being.

Finally, our misdeeds have caught up with us. For many months now, we have been giving entry visas to the U.S. to friends and relatives, some of whom later turned brokers for others in similar circumstances as they—poor and ineligible—all of whom entered as tourists but remained to live and work illegally. Now, in the eyes of the Department, it was a case of abuse of power and fraud of the worst sort. It was good that I didn't know at the time, but for the offense and for betraying the public trust, Acey and I would receive a prison sentence of five long years each—his for issuing the visas, mine for being a conspirator.

The agent went on about arrangements with Child Protective Services, perhaps as part of his discovery tactics to intimidate and elicit cooperation even as I refused to accept it was over, that all precious to me, including the control over my children's welfare, had been lost. But the waves of pain that roiled in the depths of my heart told me differently. That it was true ...

No ... not my children. Zu is so difficult to care for. They will abuse her ... they will hurt her. She will not know what has happened ... why she has been abandoned ... Where is Mommy? Where is Daddy? *She will wonder ... She will not stop crying ... Not my kids ... n-not ... Zu ...*

"Ma, help me ... help them!" I called out again, soundlessly, desperately, just as I did when I was eight, when the kettle of boiling water slipped from my hand and sluiced scalding liquid over my legs. I remembered the mind-numbing pain, the terror, the reasons that fled, and the screams that went on and on as pockets of water got stuck in the elastic gathers of my shorts and continued to burn the flesh on my thighs. And the love that followed. How my ma managed to stay awake all night to *tap … tap … tap …* ever so gently on the injured area where the new skin was still red and tender so as to relieve the itch but not disturb the healing. Even in half-slumber stage, she retained the presence of mind to whisper gentle words of assurance every time I whimpered in discomfort and pain.

Was Ma looking down now, in disappointment? Even as I asked, I knew she wasn't. She had her own set of rules, of God, not of man. She would look at the other side of the equation and see some of the goodness that had been. However, she would not judge. In her eyes would be that love, the unconditional love that was there no matter what, and the sorrow for the trials that were lying in wait for me.

Blessedly, the shock began to numb parts of my mind and my heart, easing the pain. I was not handcuffed on the long plane trip home, but even without that public debacle, I felt the pain of humiliation. At the layovers in Zurich and Frankfurt, the resident regional security officer (RSO) from the U.S. Embassy at each location came out with a police escort to lend support to his colleagues for this pseudo-extradition. I vaguely remember walking in the middle of the entourage, down one corridor to another, moving and yet not moving, seeing but not seeing. The surrealism of the situation helped me retain a sanity that seemed poised to take flight. As the plane crept closer to the United States, to home, the shock deepened, further protecting me in its sweeping devastation.

Each time I had to use the restroom, the female DS agent came in the room with me, giving me barely enough privacy. She wanted to make sure I would not hurt myself in some way … *Ahh … that was why they required that I take off those small laces from my leather shoes before taking me to the Colombo airport for the final departure.* They should have known. There was nothing that could make me seek that sort of escape, thus leaving my children to the mercy of others. True, the thought did flit through my mind at the onset, but even then, I did not think of self-annihilation, but rather a divinely orchestrated oblivion. Surrendering had never been part of my makeup. My soul remembered that even as I felt a pain so raw and grief so deep, I begged for relief in whatever form.

The lead DS agent was cold and condescending, becoming even more so on my refusal to disclose any details of substance, to affirm anything beyond the obvious. There was an air of importance about him, a knowing that victory was at hand, like a hound at the smell of blood. Viewing him distantly, I thought I was able to tell when each frisson of pride coursed through his vein. No doubt this would go into his performance evaluation and lead to a promotion and eventually to that cushy posting in Paris or Lisbon or an enchanting third-world capital. At this mid-level point in his career, this should really help pave the way to the top ranks.

I could not eat, even in the first-class section where the food was definitely edible. I did not want food. There was no thirst, no hunger, no need for sleep, only a weariness of the soul. I thought of the career that I was once convinced had been especially fashioned for me and felt increasingly tortured by the loss.

I evaded the pain by shifting to thoughts of my children, but instead of comfort, I found again a throbbing panic. Zu! Again, my mind raced frantically. *Oh my God, not Zu. What is to become of her? And Tyler? Shen will probably take over. How will she do this, and for how long? Will Van step in and help? She and Shen are not even on speaking terms. How will they get this done? Thuy can help … Will this bring the three of them together at last? For me?*

Whatever uncertainty plagued my then-insensible mind, I was sure of one thing: my children would not judge me. Like me, like my ma, they were stubborn creatures with extremely independent thoughts. They would use compassion as a guide in how they thought, what they did, just as I had shown them. Not that I needed any further reproach. In the space of hours, I had developed enough self-hatred to last several lifetimes. How could I have behaved so irresponsibly as to place my children's well-being at risk?

When at last the plane landed at Dulles Airport, the two agents who'd escorted me home jumped up from their seats and put on their dark windbreakers, the backs of which were emblazoned with wordings identifying them as federal officers. It was a move meant to comply with procedures perhaps, but I was sure it also provided a soothing touch for the ego.

We disembarked by way of a mobile stairway, separate from normal traffic. The flight attendants held other passengers back; all eyes focused on us as we made our way through the portal. With the horrific specter of 9/11 still looming, the scene cast a rather dramatic scene. Those bystanders perhaps wondered if I was a terrorist who had been apprehended by these courageous officers from overseas. The likelihood of that probably enlivened a flight that had been altogether too ordinary.

From the bottom of the steps, a DS employee started snapping photos of us descending. The photos would undoubtedly be immortalized in some training programs for DS and State officers, possibly captioned: How DS agents captured a wayward FSO.

We proceeded to an office where I was fingerprinted and photographed for the Department's version of the "mug" shots. When we were ready to leave for the county jail, the handcuffs were produced. The cold steel encircled my wrists then snapped shut, the sound deafening and final, like the proverbial nail on the coffin.

I cringed and felt tears welling. *Flash.* The whirring of shutter told me the camera had caught that emotional moment. Anger stirred, for I hated the tears, the show of weakness in front of colleagues turned adversaries. But the cuffs had caught me by surprise, lending weight and substance to a reality that was moving in and out of focus, like my consciousness.

The agents escorted me back outside, to the parking lot at the edge of the tarmac. As we drove off, one explained that he had made a mistake previously, that I was being taken to the county jail in Alexandria rather than Arlington. *What difference does it make anyhow whether it is Alexandria or Arlington?* I wondered dully.

I stared out the windows at the passing sights, the highways, the woods that looked all too familiar, and thought absently of other trips. The agents started talking; one asked the other if the trip was tiring. I listened to the banal conversation, the tone and content of which were so familiar.

How often had I heard that on arriving at past seminars and workshops overseas? The reflection brought a fresh wave of pain that, mercifully, did not last as I again slipped into the welcome arms of insensibility.

At last, we arrived. I remember walking with the agents through some sort of door or, perhaps, doors. Whatever, I would have no recollection of what the jail looked like from the outside.

I stood motionless, a shell without thoughts or substance, while the agent conducted the transfer of custody to the sheriff's office. Afterwards, he turned to tell me he would be back in the morning to take me to court for the arraignment. His voice sounded as if it were coming through a tunnel or even from another time zone. I understood the message but could not recall clearly what was said.

My senses, however, were engaged enough to register the moment he left, for the void was absolute and immediate. With his departure, he took that link to the life I had known. A new life had begun, and I was going to start alone, with no witnesses from the past to bridge the transition.

A portentous beginning, that, for my body was cold, my mind had emptied, and my soul watched in somber silence. One deputy gave me a square remnant of a wool blanket; another took my arm and escorted me down the hall. A door opened, and I was thrust inside. The steel door slammed shut.

I looked vaguely around me. The dim light showed two slumberous bodies on the floor, another on a concrete bench along the wall, and two empty mats. I stepped hesitantly toward a mat, gently unfurling my blanket to cover it. There was an odd mix of odor in the cell—alcohol, unwashed bodies, and urine. I sat down cautiously, not knowing how much of the odor came from the mat.

The woman on the bench snored loudly; the other two opened their eyes to peer at me. The one closest to me groaned, wiped her drool with the back of her hand, then turned away.

I lay down and gently draped the other half of the blanket over my body. Feeling the cold seep in, I crunched into a ball to find warmth. Thoughts of my children filled my mind as I buried my head between my arms and wept into the sleeve of my sweater. The pain swept me onward. Mindlessly, I bent into the fall, into that interminable descent toward darkness. In the last moment, a wave of terror seized me. I prayed. I had never prayed so hard; God must have been wearied of my supplications— "God, take care of my kids, pl-please…please…God, protect them."

And he was. Through a phone call from our house in Colombo prior to departing for the airport, I found out that Shen had arrived at the house in time to assume custody of the kids. She had arrived on the scene. Now I didn't have to worry about them getting caught in the foster care nightmare. The thought that my children could have been subject to abuse filled me with dread and vengeance.

The clanging sound of keys approached. The door opened, and a woman stumbled in. She wobbled slightly in the dimness then bent over to drag the remaining mat to an empty spot at the farthest wall, even if half of the space was under the toilet. She responded to this discovery by kicking the toilet, cursing it and the government and the police. The ruckus roused her compatriots on the floor, who promptly spat out a few expletives of their own.

She plopped down finally and draped her legs over the toilet. She heard my stifled moans and lifted her head. "Don't cry, baby, you be okay. You go home in the morning. These filthy pigs, this good-for-nothing government, they have nothing else to do." She started mumbling about her nephew calling the cops on her. "Disturbance? The liar…I will give him disturb. When I get home, I am going to kick his teeth in, the stupid…"

She belched once, shifted on the mat, and, after a few moments, started snoring. I drew my knees up still closer to my body and closed my eyes. The sound of police bantering from the counter outside came through. It spoke of the mundane, of life, of that which I used to know. I studiously blocked out the sound and searched for those happy memories of my children, holding on to mental snapshots of them blowing candles on their birthdays, frolicking on Nukulau Island, playing along the windswept shorelines of Iceland as if they were my lifeline.

From somewhere down the corridor came a shout then a series of horrendous banging. "Hey, old man, go to sleep," a deputy responded to the sound.

"You pigs, you want to take me on ... right here ... right now. I am ready for you, pig ... Come on ... come on ..."

A good-natured laugh came from one of the sheriff's finest. "I don't think you are up to taking me on tonight, Pop. Go to sleep." From the cell, "Pop" kicked the door again and again, until eventually he ran out of steam. A wild, fiendish laughter issued from one of the other cells. Then a heavy silence settled on us.

The cell had gotten colder. Despair had wrapped itself about me and was now fanning my face with foul, frigid breaths. My heart worked feverishly to pump warmth through my body, but the cold was relentless. A tortured sound of a sob broke from among the shards of my shattered spirit. From the general direction of the wall and the toilet, a voice came, "Don't you worry, baby! You go home early in the morning. Get some sleep now." The promise in that remark stirred me, even if it did not reassure. I doubted it would be as simple as that to go home again.

I opened my eyes and peered at the source of comfort, feeling my heart warmed to the stranger. Her familiarity with this place of detention told me of her background, of her difficult journey. Whatever, she did not presume to judge me, caring little for what I had supposedly done. She knew only the terrors of the cell and simply wished me gone. The simple words, the casually dispensed sentiment, bridged my world and hers and gave rise within me an affinity with the persecuted.

Just as well, for I was now one of them. Even as that realization dawned, I knew I was different, that my spectacular rise to the top and the privileged life I had known now gave me the self-assurance that separated me from these men and women.

Through these sad corridors they were marched to cold, dark cells. There they would sit, awaiting judgment and eventual return to the same merciless world from which they had come. It would be no better than what they had known before. In fact, it would be worse. For each time they came through, there would be another label attached to them to let their fellow men know how flawed they were. The more labels … the more hopeless, or so they would be judged.

Perhaps the same bias would reduce me to the ranks of the permanently dispossessed, but I had done much and seen more, and those experiences convinced me differently. I would triumph over this latest obstacle, just as I had all others.

Hope stole into my body, soothing my mind and lulling me into the familiar landscape of daydreams, where I imagined I had stumbled down a rabbit hole of a dream. I waited, then, for the dream to recede and reality, that reality I knew, to be restored. It didn't come; there was no magical phone call from the President of the United States to the station to demand that I be released immediately. So I negotiated with God. If only God would save me from this, I would devote myself to doing good deeds for the rest of my life.

Time crawled forward. I knew dawn must have arrived, or was fast approaching, but could not tell from the interior of the cell. There was still the sameness of sound, of lighting. Long moments passed. A screeching of wheels, a rattle of keys, then doors opened and shut from down the corridor. Our door opened at last to the looming shadow of a deputy. He didn't enter, just lifted a tray from the cart, placed it on the floor, and gave it a shove with the tip of his boot. One tray after another stopped at the edge of my mat, which was closest to the door. I looked at the tray. There was a glob of something resembling oatmeal in the largest compartment of the tray, along with a piece of cake and some bread. The trays looked foul even in the dimness of the cell. They really looked like dog bowls that had been chewed on savagely by many angry dogs over an extended period of time. The pitiful-looking trays and their place on the floor turned my stomach. I had been reduced to this!

The women got up and reached for their trays. I pushed mine to the side, where it was eventually picked up and the contents polished off by one of my cellmates.

The cell did not warm with the arrival of a new day. Nor did the day bring any good tidings. The appearance in court was devastating. Even in my darkest nightmare, I could've never imagined that I would be found at the table of the accused in a formal courtroom.

However, since the dawning of this odyssey, I had thought long and hard about the life I had led and thought I knew why God had taken me away from the superficiality of such a life. Within the past hours, I had dissected my life numerous times in a multitude of ways and found it significant that I remembered less of the accolades for the job well done but more of those random acts of kindness I had dispensed over the years.

Slowly, I found comfort in the growing conviction that this monstrous experience was what had to be. I had no idea how it would serve my highest good; I simply believed with all my heart and soul that it would. Even as faith calmed my heart and softened some of the pain, the encroaching shadows kept threatening to devour me.

In the haze of terror, I actually felt my mother's rough, gnarled hand as she smoothed back my hair. I heard her whispers. *"Long-ne, suffering, no matter. Not kill you. Pay all your karmic debt, then joy come. Sad, happy... only life. Not scared. Endure. It will pass."*

The echo of her words conjured up wondrous remembrances of that earlier lifetime when she was by my side, time that was sometimes hard, sometimes tormented, but always full of love. I thought I could see her face, the face of my determined, indefatigable mother, on the dim gray wall, and knew I could not give up. I had to keep well. I had to stay healthy so I could go home again.

The memory of her love produced the magic I needed. At the end, there were two things that saved me from tumbling over the abyss: her love for me and my love for my children.

Her love knew no boundary, reaching for me even from that unfathomable chasm of time. Even though my reality with her had receded to bands of memory, I could still feel the love that was as vibrant presently as it had been in the days when I ran circles around her and vexed her so. It empowered me now, as I remembered how fine and worthy I was in my mother's eyes. As she'd believed, so I was.

Just as her love, undiminished by time and mortality, confirmed my worth, my love for my children reminded me of a promise unfulfilled. I had the responsibility to see them to adulthood, to self-sufficiency. I had to make sure they would have my love to carry them through the pain that was part of life—except for this. God help us, I never wanted them to feel even a tendril of this sort of despair.

I thought of how fiercely I had wanted to protect my children. If only I had prepared them better for life, coaching them through the difficulties while I was around to wipe off the tears… If only I could stop regretting all that I had failed to do… If only I had been more merciful and less judgmental… If only it were not necessary for me to walk a mile in the shoes of the most miserable of men… If only…

Thirty-two

IN THE NEWS: 4/03
- GUANTANAMO BAY–
TRANSLATOR TELLS OF
SEXUAL TACTICS USED TO
BREAK PRISONERS.

Harrisburg, Pennsylvania
Oklahoma, April 2003

Con Air awaited its charges on the tarmac. The sun ruthlessly bore down on the hard cement surface as if in anger. The handcuffs, the waist chains, and the leg shackles forced the prisoners to shuffle clumsily onward.

The sharp shackles cut into my ankles with every step, making each move tortuous. My soul recoiled even as my body moved forward to the prompt of the U.S. marshals. Myriad sensations cut through me in this moment of infamy, all born of shame.

Suddenly, the sight of all of us moving to the shouts like cattle stirred something within me. *I am a good person. I have done a lot of good things in my life. I will not cower like an animal.* I lifted my head high, held my back straight, and walked toward the plane with determined steps. The shackles shifted and tightened. The pain told me my ankles were probably bleeding.

A middle-aged woman, a fellow prisoner, dropped her head and wept as the plane accelerated down the runway. I felt tears brimming in my own eyes. The flight, the cry, the despair … that other journey …

It had been said that God would not give more than we could handle. How did God think I could take this? And why?

By the time I arrived at the Oklahoma Federal Transit Center, I had mastered the art of walking with restraints. When the shackles came off, I learned, truly learned at last, the wisdom of paradoxes. If it had not been for the pain, I would never have known the indescribable bliss of being able to walk unhindered.

As I stood in line for chow, I remembered the refugee chow lines at Andersen Air Force Base in Guam and Camp Pendleton in California, which were filled with eager faces and hopeful eyes, and cringed at the dissimilarity. Here the faces were either resigned or defiant, eyes despaired. Their very misery touched my heart, but my own sorrow had so reduced me that I was incapable of nothing else but hanging on for survival.

Day after day, in a large pod of about sixty two-person cells on two tiers, I sat alone at the table in front of my cell and faithfully, woodenly, recorded impressions and images of my new surroundings. I kept my mind fixed on my writing so the pain and the hurt could not seep in. It came nevertheless, especially during my phone conversations with Shen and Thuy, my remaining links to that past life. Sounding like little mothers now instead of the spoiled, coddled daughters they had been, they reminded me of the worthy life I had. They affirmed to me how good I was, telling me repeatedly that I was the most tenderhearted, the kindest person they had ever known, and they were proud of me no matter what.

Shen said she had found one of the best lawyers in the business for me, that I would be all right. In between those words of encouragement, I could sense her shock and bewilderment and felt the pain in me deepen for bringing this despair on her, on all of my children. I didn't know how I was going to do it but was determined to make it right again, for me and for them.

I clung to that resolve, trudging along one step at a time. I smiled and nodded to all in passing but rarely spoke for any length of time to anyone, except for a one-night cellmate who painstakingly ministered to me in spite of my withdrawal. She cited a verse in the Scripture and spent hours that night using the strength of her faith to convince me how special I was, how Christ had a plan for me. I let the words surround me and that night fell asleep at peace for the first time since the journey had started.

Over the course of that week, my heart opened and engaged my mind, convincing me that it was not yet over, that I had a life left to live. Reduced still to the bare minimum of instincts, I however realized I had everything I needed to survive—the fighting spirit from a mother who didn't know how to quit, the fortitude from having known hardships, and a job so exalted it enabled me to see possibilities in the most abject of conditions.

In between reflections, I yielded to the shocks and aftershocks, feeling pain then insensibility then pain again. As I drifted in and out of awareness, Fate was busy paving the way; I would have plenty of time to acclimate to my new lot. Any debasement or cruelty would come in small doses until I was ready. My fear of physical aggression from other inmates, jailers, would prove to be baseless. I was to know only the pain of the heart and the mind, so I would understand the suffering of others, so I would not judge.

Alexandria, Virginia
April 2003

After thirty-six hours in the holding cell in Alexandria, I was transferred to general population. "General" in this instance meant a small pod consisting of four two-person cells, but which at the time housed only five women. A female deputy unlocked and pushed the steel door open. "I believe this is the place for you. You will be happy here." I stared into four pairs of bright Asian eyes and expectant, curious faces. It was a good thing they didn't understand me when I said, somewhat pompously, "I am an American. I would be more at ease among the American women actually." What I really wanted to say was, *"I can't deal with that infamous Asian inquisitiveness and judgment right now."*

The deputy simply smiled and gestured with a sweep of the arm to my roommates. "That's okay. These nice ladies here will take good care of you." She pointed to my cell, the first one on the right of the door, and instructed me on the routine of count times and meals. The inmates of the room stared and waited.

The officer was civil and kind. In words and demeanor, she behaved no differently than those in that other world I had just left. Not that I expected her to. This was my first brush with the law, after all, hence my naïve outlook on the "justice" system and the ego-ridden souls who populated its ranks.

Three correctional institutions later, I would know that the police officers I encountered in Alexandria were the exception rather than the rule. I would not find many such as them along the path to purgatory and back, who had such a sure sense of self they didn't need to flaunt power over the helpless to show their worth. Blessed are they whose humanity was so refined they saw us as people and not a subhuman species.

The inmates in this little pod were illegal aliens who were accused or guilty of possessing fraudulent passports or visas for the purpose of entering the United States. Two were from Nepal, one from China, and the other was from the affluent country of Singapore. Among them, the Singaporean woman was the only one who spoke English with any degree of competency. There was another inmate with us, a black American, but she was under discipline and on "lockdown" status, another term for solitary confinement. She was allowed to come out of her cell to watch TV and showers only after we had been locked in our cells for the night.

It was ironic that I was lodged among them. If only they knew that my crime was for the same thing, at the opposite end. These aliens had not seen much of America—only what was around the airport at arrival and along the roadways during transfer from one detention center to another.

Naturally, they craved for any nugget of information about the land for which they had risked their freedom. And so it was in the days that followed, whenever I was not weighed down with desolation and grief, I was called on to regale them with the wonders of America.

On those occasions, I had to look past the presently lifeless land-scape of my soul to the past where once America represented a promise so vibrant it guided my entire life and blinded me to all else. Only in that frame of mind was I able to tell them about the land and its riches, the land that was as varied and beautiful as its people were generous. My troubled thoughts would be momentarily allayed, and I became animated as the tale wore on. The audience's wide-eyed fascination kept me busy spinning tales rather than dwelling on my wretched reality.

To them, I must have been a celebrity of sort—a hyphenated American—the dream they had sought to realize. In me, they envisioned what could be. Instead of becoming bitter because their dreams had turned into nightmares, they saw me as a glorious manifestation of those dreams and felt vindicated in the risks they had taken. Even though all they had now were years of incarceration followed by deportation, already they talked about returning, legally this time, to find a good life here for their children. They held on to their dreams and, by that courage, helped me find my own strength. If they could still hope under those miserable circumstances, how could I not?

My anecdote on the kindness of Americans was soon validated. A good-hearted federal defender, the designated attorney for one of the Nepalese women, used twenty dollars of his own money to buy a phone card for his client so she could call her parents and children in Nepal.

The inmates looked after me as if I were a foreign visitor who was ignorant of indigenous rules and the lay of the land. They rushed me to my cell when it was count time, closing my door shut before heading to their own cells, and came for me when the P.A. chimed, "Count clear," to let me know that it was all right to come out. They included me in their evening snacks and showed me one way to cope with prison life—hoarding food. We saved morning coffee, a cross between tea and coffee, tasting like neither, so that at night we could have a steaming cup of the day-old brown water, to be enjoyed with slices of bread toast-hardened in the microwave oven. I took little bites, taking my time to contemplate the new taste, while they inhaled theirs. Obviously, my palate had not reconciled to the fact that life had changed, that until the next transformation, this was all there would ever be.

Gradually, I became used to the dented, dirty-looking trays and the unappetizing food. I focused on surviving. Oatmeal was nutritious; I remembered that from the days when my children were young and I, as a newly transplanted American, had tried to learn about the strange American fare to ensure they had nourishing meals. So I ate up the gooey mush. There was no sugar, so I crumbled the cake that came with every meal into the oatmeal to sweeten it to taste.

There was hardly any meat, but the inmates enthused, "We get a chicken drumstick with dinner once a week." They planned on it and talked about it especially at dinnertime, as if the image of tasty chicken drumsticks could help us swallow the pitiful choice of the day. The anticipation was heady. It was almost like waiting for the president's arrival during a POTUS visit. In a light moment, I shared that analogy at which they laughed uncertainly, not sure if I was jesting or if they had missed something in the translation. On the day of the chicken drumsticks, they collected half the meat from everyone's trays but mine to save for a special meal later that evening.

"Eat, eat all, you eat," they urged, and indulgently watched me devour the piece of chicken clean to the marrow. After a week of subsisting on a diet of oatmeal and cake, I found the meat indeed as delicious as my pod mates had promised.

On Saturday, we were taken up to the enclosed rooftop for an hour of recreation. I looked over the blossoming treetops and thought I could see the Kennedy Center. I remembered the many times I had passed it on the way to and from the State Department and felt my heart tighten. I jogged around the small, enclosed area, and for a few short moments, I felt a pain so wrenching that I wished my memory were gone, that I were dead. The birds pecked noisily from atop the mesh that imprisoned. I looked at the birds, the sky, and the vastness between them and longed to know again that infinite freedom of space. The sun had begun its descent to the other side of the world, just as I had, on a journey to the fathomless beyond.

The women seemed to know the transfer schedule, anticipating that I would be moved to Oklahoma the following Monday, since they themselves had arrived here from Oklahoma on a Monday. On my last night, they prepared a special dinner that consisted of a dozen pieces of canned green beans they had saved from our dinner trays and three cups-of-noodles soups.

As we ate, they gave me details on the upcoming Con Air flight. If their disclosure meant to reassure, it did not. Between the Asian propensity for drama and the incidental showing of the movie *Con Air* on TV that night, which my pod mates swore quite depicted the real flight, my nerves revved to new intensity as terror mounted.

However, there was a positive side to the impending "doomsday" flight if only I would survive it—the good food in Oklahoma.

The storytellers' eyes brightened perceptibly as they debated their individual preferences—the fresh dry cereal, the muffin or bagel with cream cheese at breakfast, the fresh fruits and salads that came with every meal. And yes, there was meat, real meat, every day.

The American girl on lockdown yelled out her good-bye and slipped a packet each of coffee, creamer, and sugar through the opening on the door for me. The Singaporean woman added another creamer to the pile of treats. The small packets of creamer and sugar were not enough to sweeten coffee the way I was used to, but the hot, flavorful liquid ignited my taste buds as if it were nectar from the gods.

The inmates watched me anxiously and smiled when I closed my eyes and exaggerated a moan of pleasure. The familiar aroma indeed reminded me of the morning coffee my family and I used to enjoy, swiftly taking me back to those weekend mornings when I used to make cups of extremely white, ultra-sweet coffee as special treats for Zu and Tyler. It wasn't the bitter coffee that suddenly clogged my throat; it was the tender memory of my family and the kindness I didn't expect to see in this place of misery.

When I knocked on their cell doors to say good-bye the next morning, they woke promptly to the tapping and smiled as they pressed their hands against the glass where mine was.

In these unlikely benefactors, I felt the hands of God. The kind deputies and caring inmates set the pace for my transition, a gentle introduction to prison life. No matter that my descent from honor to shame seemed like a free fall, the safeguards were there to cushion the fall. Such would be how I would make my way through purgatory.

Oklahoma Federal Transfer Center
April-May 2003

The plane ride from Harrisburg to Oklahoma made several stops in between to drop off and pick up prisoners. Marshals poured out of the plane at every stop to take charge of the movements. Several stood guard on the perimeter of the plane with shotguns on the ready in the crooks of their arms. If the reality were not so tragic, I would have smiled at the hilarity of the scene. The shotgun-toting marshals were, without exception, older, the white-haired grandmother and grandfather types, who would have made perfect castings for *The Golden Girls* and *Grumpy Old Men*. However, they looked serious and committed to the mission at hand, as I used to be, faithful cogs to a benevolent wheel.

In some aspects, this flight was not so dissimilar to the one that took me away from Vietnam decades ago. Here it was again, a burst to another lifetime. Why was it always this way for me? Changes were to be gradual, over months or years, not minutes.

The marshals were much older than the soldiers who serviced that desperate flight out of Vietnam, but still alike in their military bearing. The tearful woman by my side reminded me of those earlier passengers who wept for the loss of all they had held dear. The guns … the tears … I could see again Tan Son Nhat Airport in the grips of war.

Oklahoma was neither good nor bad and meant to be neither. It wasn't the beginning or the end, merely a way station. Time-wise it was of little import, for I spent just ten days there, in a large pod with one hundred-plus other women. Its consequence was in supplying what I needed to know for the journey.

First, a touch of obscenity to prepare me for what was to come: the strip search, the bend and the cough, the close examination of one's body orifices by complete strangers; second, the kindness that was an intrinsic part of life, that which could always be found regardless of where one was. A big, tough black girl who was obviously from the wrong side of the tracks in for drug peddling and involuntary manslaughter asked her equally rough-looking friends to form a close circle about me to keep me warm as we sat for hours in the frigid holding cell waiting to be processed. There was another, a young girl with the fresh, innocent look of a girl next door, my roommate for the first two nights, who saved a bagel from that morning's breakfast for a "bunkie" she knew would arrive in the late afternoon flight, too late for the last meal of the day.

Days passed in grief and pain, with periods of lucidity then numbness. These different emotions chased through me in quick succession at times, more slowly at others. Not thinking about my life was good, so I tried not to. When I was not lost in the business of writing, of perpetuating the illusion that I was there merely to chronicle, I produced just enough energy to take care of the most basic of needs. I got in line at chow when I heard the shouts and saw the queue forming, ate the food from my tray, showered on seeing an empty stall after dinner. I washed my underwear and hung it on the bed frame hidden behind my pillow and out of the guard's view, just as my cellmate had shown me, since the bed had to be made neatly and free from encumbrances for the daily walk-through inspection.

When the numbness faded, faces began to filter in—faces of my children, of Acey, of my parents. With images came memories and pain. There was no solace. Just fear, confusion, and despair, and a constant need for validation of a life just ended. Immersed in the quicksand of my tortured mind, I watched my memories unfold and ached for all that I could not change.

I also saw all the things I would not have changed for all the worlds and finally realized what it was that God had given me, the single quality that really defined who I was. It was compassion, that softening of the heart on seeing the misfortune of others, the tears I shed for their suffering, the wish to provide relief. For the first time, I recognized how important this was. It was so essential to my life's purpose that not only was it inherent in my makeup, it was obvious in those of my parents as well, who spent their entire lives showing me in the flesh how it was done, just in case I did not understand the concept. I did learn well, but my shallow mind limited that softening of the heart to the poor and their suffering, and even there, only when it was convenient. I was far from being my parents' daughter. I remained judgmental on others, among them most assuredly the "criminals," the misfits.

On our transport out of Oklahoma, I saw Acey for the first time since the nightmare had started. My spirit lifted at the sight of him. We smiled at each other through the tears. I mouthed the words "I love you. We will be okay" and saw tears come to his eyes. He smiled and kept watching out for me. As we shuffled in single file to the plane, similarly garbed in the tan prison uniform of the Federal Transfer Center, he glanced at the marshals then contrived to lag behind to get closer and closer to me, until he reached whispering distance. The clanging of chains receded, along with the pain. In their place was a rising euphoria from seeing him whole and real and seemingly high-spirited. I had not heard from him through Shen for over ten days and had feared the worst—that they had locked him up somewhere for some sort of interrogation.

I lifted my face to the sun as we shuffled onto the tarmac and silently thanked God that I, we, had survived. I was stronger now, stronger than I was two weeks previous, stronger even than I was the day before. Little did I know I would need to be for my next stop at Sacramento, California.

THIRTY-THREE

IN THE NEWS: ABUSES OF PRISONERS OF WAR IN IRAQ.

Sacramento County Jail
Sacramento, California
May 2003

The jail at Sacramento County sat at the bottom of hell. For the first time in my life, I saw how a human spirit could wither and die. The longer I stayed, the more baffled I became at the savagery of men toward other men. Surely I had seen enough obscenity in my journey through war-torn Vietnam. But it was different here. There was neither fear of death nor any real purpose to justify the barbarity. The jailers became inhumane simply because they could.

The jail was a travesty of justice, a hall of shame for a civilized people.

I had changed much from the days when

my blood used to run hot with conservative fervor, when my beliefs were guided by the principle of "survival of the fittest." On traveling the world and seeing my share of poverty and suffering, I had become more aware of human weaknesses and foibles and all the conditions that make that "will to succeed" an exceptional commodity rather than a simple willing of the mind.

Still, I had not seen enough, not the abject inhumanity of incarceration, the hopelessness of the dispossessed, nor the cruelty and corruption of power so prevalent in prisons. What I saw within those walls shocked me to the core and muddled my senses of values and civility. But even as my mind mired in confusion, I thought there was something familiar about the jailers' critical condemnation. Then I realized what it was—I used to be that biased and judgmental once.

From a humble beginning, I, like many others, had worked hard to achieve the American dream. To the weak of character came the irony. The pride that prompted us to excel became our downfall. The more august our success, the more prideful and less humble we became. Hand in hand, the tangible and intangible, both born of the ego. Some of us would be more arrogant than others. We would be harsh, measuring all others by the standards we had set for ourselves, giving no quarters to the weak of mind and worn of body. Now the self-made, the strong, the invincible, we would tolerate no parasites infringing on the fruits of our hard labor. We would be hypocritical, judging them by an even more rigorous standard than we did ourselves, for we could not bear to be reminded of our own fallibilities. Where we once knew kindness, now we would have none for others. What price had I paid for success...

I saw officers of the court corrupted by pride and prejudice, who measured their successes by convictions, by the lengths of sentences. I used to think of them as impartial, benevolent figures with wisdom like that of Solomon in whom we entrusted a system to punish, deter, and rehabilitate. I did not count on them being so fallible that they would let arrogance and ego, or that something as insignificant as allegiance to a godless and meaningless political ideology, reduce them to that lowly place of the morally impotent. To some of them, the criminals were no longer people, but only cases and numbers. They touted vengeance, justice for the victims—a laudable war cry to mask their own loss of humanity. They would be regularly affirmed and praised by their own kind with words like "total commitment," "devotion to the job," "justice is done," "selfless dedication."

I used to be one of them. I had stood there once upon a time and received similar accolades with a beatific smile on my face, proud of what I had become, believing with all my heart that what I did, what I had, really defined who I was.

Sacramento was a sad place, a place that was the antithesis of Christ, of God, a place of man's judgment and self-righteousness. It was a place where men judged and practiced vengeance and, at the end of the day, strutted home in their fine cloaks of mighty morals.

Not all jailers are blessed with an open mind or a kind heart to understand the dismal human conditions. Within the sullen walls, the corrupt give in to their darker, tyrannical impulses. Prisons must be one of the few places where the former schoolyard bullies could "be all they can be" with immunity. Impoverished in humanity, they grabbed a perfect opportunity to prey on the helpless.

Mercifully, even in cases of steel, time passed by rather quickly. We kept track of time by the meals served—breakfasts that began at 4:30 a.m., lunch at 10:30 a.m., dinner at 3:30 p.m., and head counts several times a day. The once-a-day dayroom slot was not reliable—sometimes occurring twice daily and other times not for several days, all depending on the whims of the deputies on duty. The sound of the overhead speaker spitting out "dayroom" lingered in my mind still and reminded me of how sweet that much-awaited word used to be.

Unfortunately, the mean-spirited guards also knew what dayroom meant to the inmates and so dispensed them in the manner one did valuable commodity—sparingly. Dayroom was the cherished hour during which calls to attorneys and families were made and also a time for the much-needed shower. It was held in the area that was the hollow of the horseshoe-shaped, thirty-two-two-person cell pod, sixteen cells on each tier. In addition to half a dozen stainless steel tables and chairs and a TV, there were four shower stalls, two of which were regularly infested by leeches that came through the drainage pipes, and a bank of five telephones. Depending on when the last dayroom was, inmates either filed out of their cells in orderly fashion or raced past one another toward one of the working telephones or the shower stalls.

The cells, the deputies, the rules were expertly designed to destroy the feeble of mind. I suppose the intimidation and humiliation could be likened to the military training methods of turning boys into soldiers, except for one thing: in addition to being stripped of their dignity, prisoners were treated as though they would never be anything again, quite unlike boot camp recruits, who could look on their hardships as a small price to pay for the pride and honor that would come at the end of training.

There was no part of me that remained unscathed. Physically, I was a body defeated, trying to survive hardships I had never known—an eight-by-eleven-foot jail cell, a hard plastic mattress four inches thick, a rolled-up towel that was my pillow, cellmates and companions from among the most debased, hopelessly lost people on earth. Emotionally, I fared little better. The failure to care for my children, the distance from them, the loss of control over my life and theirs, devastated me. Psychologically, I was a total wreck, having been denied of all I had, which, I thought mistakenly at the time, meant everything I was.

My mission, to keep myself centered amid the oppression and the vulgarity, the anger, the tension, and the despair was to withdraw within, detaching myself from my present physical reality as often as I needed to. The inhabitants of this new world were so strange and different that I sometimes questioned my sanity as well as our joint reality. As I listened to their hooting laughter when a new inmate was admitted to the cell and their contrived chant of "fresh meat, fresh meat" to scare the uninitiated, I had to shake my head, wondering anew where it was that I had arrived.

However, because my companions were faithful subscribers to the credo of "living for the moment," they managed to infuse spontaneous breaths of joy into the despairing madness. On the occasion of my first birthday in jail, one of the younger, long-term inmates, nineteen-year-old Tara with a beautiful voice, sang "Happy Birthday" to me as others added to the melody by creating riotous drum rolls from stainless steel tables in the dayroom area. I don't believe I had ever cried on my birthday before, but there and then I did, on being serenaded by women who were so condemned they should have had no heart left to celebrate anything.

Often, I tried to slip into the comfortable role of an observer, where I intended to feel no contempt and no disappointment, but merely photographing incidents with my mind's eye as if I were a historian keeping watch for a future people to let them know of a civilization's folly, of our inability to differentiate between the dangerous and the needy, and the harsh judgment brought to bear on the least among us. But try as I might, I could not remain objective writing about incidents as mere occurrences for I, too, felt the burden of subjugation, of debasement.

The tools for subjection were all around us. A daunting black chair, complete with arm and leg restraints, stood darkly under the stairs, waiting to discipline any who might foolishly think she still had "rights." A paper bag was sometimes added to the restraining apparatus, supposedly so that angry inmate could not spit in the face of the deputy. It didn't matter that the offender ended up sitting quite alone in an empty room during that "time out." Properly dehumanized and well restrained, she was supposed to be learning a lesson in respect and obedience. Not surprisingly, what she ended up learning was an increasing hatred for authority.

Periodically, we were marched out of the cells in the middle of the night so deputy sheriffs could rush in and toss the cells, looking for contrabands, things like hoarded fruits, extra socks, blankets, and books, or fishing lines ... yes, those fishing lines of the lovelorn.

A fishing line consisted of strips of sheets tied together into a long line. A letter or photo ID from the jail, protectively encased in a watertight plastic bag, would be tied to one end of the line. At a warning shout through the toilet, the sender flushed the encumbered end down the toilet, while holding on to the other end. Simultaneously, the intended recipient flushed his or her own empty line down. Somewhere in the bowel of the jail's sewer pipes, the two lines met and entangled. The recipient then reeled in his catch. The condition of the line often showed where it had been by look or smell, or both. This was made worse by the fact that there was no cleaning or disinfectant solution available, so inmates had to make do with what they had, which meant little bars of soap. Thus, one consequence of going fishing was a foul-smelling cell, and the reward, a friend of the opposite sex from another floor.

If caught, the offender would be subject to a period of solitary confinement or a change of cell. The punishment rarely deterred. On release from her sojourn, the offender would be at it again, emptying the toilet bowl of water after the guard had come through for cell check, then dipping her head into it and shouting her greetings to the cell immediately above or below, hoping to meet a new friend or to send a message to an old one.

For a time, I thought this was quite a bizarre way to behave and could not comprehend the attraction. Really, how desperate could one get? But as I ventured deeper into the wasteland of my tortured mind and saw the bleakness that threatened to consume my every thought, the view became clear. There they were, either cut off or alienated from their support systems, while facing intimidation and coercion from government prosecutors and oppression from jailers. In desperation, they clutched at anything to feel less alone and scared, even for a brief moment. Laden with self-doubt and fear, they sought to find understanding, affection, or simply a reprieve from their inner demons. From among their own kind, at least they could count on lavished empathy.

The affection, fleeting as it might have been, and the companionship, inadequate though it was, however provided the uplifting these men and women needed to continue for another day. Who was I to judge them? Who was I to presume that I even understood their circumstances or lots in life?

Many of my comrades turned into what some labeled jailhouse Christians, the negative connotation referred to the condemned's desperate reach for God in their despair only to forsake him upon gaining freedom from the cells.

However temporary the connection, I don't believe Christ minded. What mattered was that they did find him, and for a time turned to him absolutely and totally, learning for the first time how to leave everything in his hands, at last breaking free from the grip of the ego. Henceforth, in moments of despair, the erstwhile Christians would know where to find peace again, and at the right time in their lives would feel a stirring in their hearts, a call from their souls to connect to God and begin living a Christ-like life of love and compassion.

Raised a Buddhist, however, to me Buddhism was always a way of life rather than a doctrinal religion, a life without avarice, envy, or fear, one of love and compassion. I would get to know that such was what had also been termed a Christ-driven life, one that my parents exemplified and which I had never before fully understood.

That such a life meant oneness with God…

As my mind fled, my open heart found the Divine, and for many hours and many days there were only God and me. Slowly I came to realize the meaning of life and the purpose of mine. Even so, the transition was slow and painful as I struggled to overcome the torture of losing all that I'd understood was precious while keeping a tenuous hold on the truth of the message.

Often I asked, "Am I being fanciful, God? Could it be this simple, this easy to find you?" As my body collapsed, I wept and begged for salvation. He responded to my plea for deliverance faithfully—in my nightly dreams, in sending kindness my way.

His presence kept my hopes alive and my heart centered in this place of savagery. Three times a day, we filed out to the door of the pod to receive meal trays from inmate workers. During meals, the cops really showed their true colors. The bullies kept an eye on our procession lest any of us decide to give up some of the almost-inedible food to the more hungry and desperate among us. Our floor, the only women floor in the jail, was an easy mark for a few uninspired deputies and, of course, the bullies. There was a proud team of two who called themselves the "dream team."

On one occasion, they sat in the glass-enclosed control booth and watched an inmate bending over with stomach cramps, unable to make use of the one-hour dayroom time because she was overcome with the urge to defecate. She had made the mistake of asking to be allowed back in her cell to take care of that bodily function. Not only did the team deny that request, they extended the liberty hour to prolong her agony, while they laughed at her discomfiture. With like enthusiasm, the team found amusement in ridiculing the deaf, the old, and the mentally challenged.

Fortunately, not all were as passionate about their need to subjugate. For some, the inhumanity was in their indifference. And there were others who were extraordinarily kind, who tried to handle a difficult job as best they could. Because of them, I retained the faith that there was still humanity among men. For the others, I wished I could tell them about the lessons I was learning on compassion, and kindness, and on walking in someone else's shoes.

Most of the inmates in my pod came from a disadvantaged background. Many had never held a job. Most were in for drug-related crimes. Damaging as the crimes these non-violent offenders conspired to perpetrate, they had started out as victims—victims of abuse, of a culture of spiritual deprivation, of instant gratification, and runaway materialism.

It sickened me to see the ravages of drugs on faces of girls in their twenties—mouths with few teeth left and vacant, lifeless eyes. What the drug had started, the "justice" system would now finish through its process of dehumanization.

I was the more fortunate among them, for I'd had a lifetime of accomplishments to shield me from the system's corrosive assault. I had thoughts and ideas and knew about possibilities no matter the odds. Most of all, I had my faith in God. But this faith was new and fledging, and so I sometimes weakened and staggered under the darkness of incarceration—the isolation from all I knew, the separation from my beloved, the degradation and relentless efforts by the system to reduce all within its hold to worthless, hopeless creatures by telling them and treating them as such. What chance did these outcasts have?

They laughed and cried and rushed to call family and friends whenever we got an hour outside the cell to beg for money, to hear words of love, of promise, and to find validation of their worth. Many returned to their cells afterwards emptier than before, empty of hope. Defeated, they limped along in their misery, while the rest of the world rose and played under the warmth of the sun and danced and dreamed by the glow of the moon. When I looked at them and listened to their stories, I saw only chilling images of shadows and desolation.

God was there every time I faltered. Even so, the dark forces hovered near so that for many days, I hobbled along in the same gray landscape as other inmates, sometimes a nurturer, often a fellow sufferer. Slowly, from enlightenment came a simple truth. If there was a Divine purpose in my tribulation, there must have been so in theirs. But knowing so didn't make their lots look any better from where I stood; there was simply too much misery. Compared to some of the horrors of their journey, mine seemed a mere walk in the park.

THIRTY-FOUR

IN THE NEWS:
4/15/2006–CHERRY BLOSSOM
FESTIVAL IN SAN FRANCISCO

The Long Journey to Self
April 2006

Who would have ever thought anyone could feel elated arriving at a prison camp to serve out her sentence? But it is true. As I sit on my narrow bunk in the four-person room at this three hundred-plus women's camp, I reflect on those wretched days—twenty long months to be exact—awaiting plea and sentencing at the contemptible Sacramento County Jail, and remember anew my delight on arrival at the camp in Dublin, California.

Spring has arrived. The trees in front of our buildings have awakened from their winter repose and are presently sporting proud young leaves of that soft color green that always stirred me so. Innumerable varieties of birds dwell here, flitting through the leaves of the cottonwood from branch to branch, chirping noisily to celebrate the return of life. While squirrels peek from their nesting hollows and frolic among the grass, which is verdant still from the sweet rains of winter, the trees sway and bow their heads to the passing breeze as if paying homage to the perfection of nature. None of these creatures seems to know they are on prison ground. But perhaps they do, and their song and dance is both consolation and counsel, a balm and a reminder, to the inmates, that in spite of the high wall, the wires, and the hardships and privations, that the most precious things in life are still within our reach—things such as the liberty of our minds, the freedom in our hearts and the sights and sounds of life.

The days are becoming more sunny and bright. Plants shoot free of their earthy confines in wild abandon, vying with perennial blooms for a favored spot under the sun. Inmate landscape crews have done a thorough job on preparing the yard for spring's return. Where there used to be dirt and skeletons of last summer's blooms, now violet and blue flowers preen and flutter over lush green limbs that move sinuously to the silent rhythm of the wind.

I enjoy the scene with all my senses, as a child might, at her first awareness of nature. Alas, I also behold it with desperation, as a very old woman would, on her last breaths, knowing how quickly scenes as common as this could be taken away.

I still remember my first touch of a rose petal after the distance of almost two years. The velvety feel soothed my soul but wrenched my heart, for it had been far too long since I'd touched it last.

While my senses re-acclimate to life outside the cage, my emotions rise and dip in breathless wonders under the gentle ministrations of nature. My body rejoices in knowing again the warmth of the sun, the gentle touches of the wind, and the invigorating lashing of the rain—all the spectacular bounty of the earth I had once thought as belonging to all men, in all circumstances, for all times.

My first job upon arrival in December 2004 was with the Camp yard detail. Naturally, I could not simply focus on the task of raking leaves. In moments of self-pity, I would lift my head to show the familiar Mr. Sun of childhood my pale, pale face, to let him know what had happened to me. Day after day, placid rays reached down from the heavens in tender caress, as if to reassure me that all was well again. After a few short days, brown blotches animated across my face, from forehead to chin, ear to ear, making me look like a gypsy, a happy gypsy at that, or as Ma would have said, a dirty, endearing little savage.

Away from the netherworld of the jail, I can finally reflect without the prejudicial colors of pain. Perhaps the county jails of the world are necessary insofar as their systematic and total destruction of our worldly encumbrances produces a despair so sweeping it incapacitates the mind, thus forcing a man to retreat within and, at the right moment in his life, find the meaning of existence and the purpose of his life. Or he might just come away with a finer sense of what's important in life.

If conditions had not been so oppressive, if prisoners had been treated with human decency and not as animals captured and caged, if I had not been subject to bear the unbearable, I would not have sunk so deep inside my soul and there, in darkness and isolation, found my Self and God. But for this experience, I would never have known the simplicity of life and the complexity I'd made of mine.

The relative absence of cruelty at the Camp has restored reason to my once-insensible mind. I work hard at the teaching job I've gained following short stints with the yard, then the kitchen work details, obey the rules, write, and generally exult in the peace I've found, even though my immediate surroundings continue to roil with contentions, as befitting a microcosm of the turbulent world outside the fence. Anger and tension flare as the women rail against one another, the system, and their own lots.

From the serenity of my spiritual perch, I watch the fear being perpetuated—moving from the system to the inmates, from the inmates back to society, then from one inmate to another. The cycle of hate goes round and round, gaining strength with each new salvo of aggression and counter-aggression.

Inasmuch as love and compassion for our fellow men is the only answer for us, both individually and collectively, I wonder what it would take for us to banish judgment from our minds and hate from our hearts.

I think now of the war that took up the whole of my formative years. If the Buddhists had responded to Diem's oppression with good will and forbearance, if President Diem had bestowed on the people like compassion, it would have altered the course of the war. Aggressive and determined as some of the Communist bosses were in their conquest, they would not have been able to generate enough fear to launch and escalate the deadly conflict.

But perhaps all the cruelty and inhumanity is unavoidable. So long as we continue to perpetuate the hate and the fear, no matter how minute our individual sphere of influence, such shall remain the collective legacy we inherit. The karmic sequence is perfect; its brilliant cause and effect actually parallels Newton's Third Law of Motion, "for every action, there is an equal and opposite reaction." For a long time, I thought karma was direct and simple payback—punishment for trespasses or rewards for good deeds. Now I know differently. That experiencing what we have created in others, personally or collectively, is neither reward nor punishment but part of the Divine plan to spur us onward in our evolution to perfection, and that only by understanding and accepting the impermanence of, and reason for, all things could we hope to break the cycle of fear and hatred.

The bad, the good—what are they but opportunities for us to show our humanity and thereby softening the color of this blessed quest to accomplish the purposes of our souls.

The darkness on my path was there no longer. With peace and clarity, I could now let go of grievances of the past, condemnations for the present, and expectations for the future. On finishing the final leg of this incredible journey, I will be heading home.

On that December day when I left Sacramento, colors and light burst from the morning sky as if the heavens too rejoiced. When the call came to the cell, I jumped up from my bunk and rolled up the bedding as I had seen countless of my cellmates do before. I ran around the pod, glancing at the reflective mirror all the while, mouthing apology to the deputy in the control booth so I would not get reprimanded for talking to others outside of dayroom, the only allowed "social" hour. I tapped on doors around the horseshoe-shaped pod to say good-bye to the old-timers who had been through it all with me as tears streamed down my face, tears of joy, for leaving the saddest place I had ever been, while my heart bled, for the men and women I left behind, all fellow travelers on the darkest journey I had ever known.

There they were, in those awful, bright orange uniforms, aligning their faces on the narrow strips of glass on the solid steel doors so I could see their heartbreaking smiles. I heard their shouts through the doors, "Have a good life! Don't come back to this place," and felt my heart fracture.

I could not have done it without them. And as I now reflect, seventeen months from those final good-byes to the occupants of that county jail, I realize that for our collective suffering, for all the pain and the relentless assailing on the psyche, I had gained answers, answers to questions I'd never known to ask. From the darkness of despair, I found the illumination of God. From the most miserable of human conditions, I understood men and learned more about me. From the pitiless jail cell, I found the meaning of existence. Out of suffering, I discovered bliss.

In Dublin, whenever the inmates complain of the Camp as being less in comparison to the better-equipped camps, camps such as the exalted Camp Alderson in West Virginia, I thank God for his blessings, for I remember the dark days at Sacramento. I've since realized that the darkness itself was a benediction, for I would not have appreciated the grandeur of its opposite so well otherwise.

I have resolved never to forget what I saw and experienced. I know now what happiness is. It is being true to me and others and giving the people I love and the world the very best of me. I have learned that life is to be lived in all its glory and sorrow; that experiences of every nature are to be embraced; and that the paradoxes are gifts from God. I've also discovered that understanding the wisdom within every suffering is key to man's peace and happiness.

When the "Campers" complain of the long wait for the showers, I remember those times when we were locked down for several days at a time in our cells, where my cellmate and I made use of the little stainless steel sink to keep ourselves clean, giving each other a minuscule measure of privacy by taking turns facing the wall. When my fellow prisoners decry the tastelessness of the meat served, I remember the inmates in Alexandria and the scrawny chicken drumsticks that comprised the long-awaited feast. When there is a dinner of mystery meat, I remember my ma digging into the slop bucket for precious pieces of meat—any kind would do—and how my heart jumped with joy for every morsel she salvaged. When they bemoan the dismal condition of the cracked, uneven quarter-mile track where we walk round and round to drain sadness and sorrow, I remember looking out the slivers of window of my jail cell and watching spring and summer pass me by. Oh, how desperately I yearned then to feel the softness of grass under my feet, to breathe in the almost-forgotten freshness of spring, and to know again the mustiness of the soil after the sweet touch of a rain.

How fortunate was I to have been sent to this camp so as to be among the nature I had always loved but never appreciated. Now my heart weeps at a mere touch of the rough bark of a tree and stirs by the cool breath of a wind.

But I am not as content as I could be. I still feel intense longings for my children wherever my thoughts find them. Sometimes I cannot breathe for missing their touches. I remember the little bouquet of wildflowers that Tyler picked for me on our walks and the feel of Zu's frail, little body against mine. I remember her sorrowful whimpers when she needed water in the dark of night and couldn't make me understand.

Whenever the pains come, I would feel weary and tired. I would be tempted to withdraw from the world, to find a little corner of the earth where I could live my life out in simplicity and peace, to a place where I would no longer be bothered by this seemingly tiresome, capricious life.

But most of the times I know I am, and was, cherished by God, by life. What a good run I have had, what a journey! From the depth of poverty, that abysmal fringe of existence, I rose to the top of privilege and affluence then survived the descent to stand shoulder to shoulder with the dregs of society. From the horrors of war to the life of a jetsetter to the world of the downtrodden, I have been privileged enough to know the lowest of conditions and the highest of glory and, somewhere in the abyss of my shattered spirit, discovered the key to life and my role in it.

This tragic, cosmic journey turned my life upside down and yet has given me peace. I have much farther to go, but I am not afraid. I will neither seek success nor fear failure. I will neither indulge in complacency nor surrender to worldly ambitions. I will live every day as if that's all there is, commit all that I am to make the world a better place, and embrace the journey with a peaceful and lightened heart. The future beckons. I now approach it with a certainty, a sureness of knowing that whatever it holds, it is the best for me.

I know how to live now. There is no longer the wistfulness of "if only" but simply the total and glad acceptance of what is. From the soothing calm of autumn to the vibrant stirring of spring, there is a time to ponder and a time to grow. Spring was late in coming, but what matters is that it did come, in the wake of the most powerful storm of my lifetime. Magically, in withdrawing deep within to seek refuge, I discovered my mystical Self and found the path to that rapturous, illusive utopian state of being called bliss.

There's no sunset as stirring as the one I will be watching with my family, no walk on the beach as joyful as the one we will take together, and no road as tranquil as the one I now follow to eternity.

Like the most worthy of antagonists, adversity has brought out the best in me. I am ready for whatever come, ready to experience more of this amazing life, my celebrated journey.

It is true. Life is what we make of it, and more. To be more, it also has to be less, for what is Life but a continual unfolding of the Self, ridding itself of the superficial encumbrances, the fear, the greed, the ego, the pride … until only the virtuous heart of matter, the Divinity that is in all of us, remains. 龍